GOURMET

Getaways

GOURMET
Getaways

50 TOP SPOTS TO COOK AND LEARN

JOE DAVID

travel

Guilford, Connecticut

The prices and rates in this guidebook were confirmed at press time.
We recommend, however, that you call establishments
before traveling to obtain current information.

Portions of the text on pp. 77–82, 172–76, and 263–65 appeared in an article in
Incentive magazine in January 2009.

Text design by Sheryl P. Kober

Library of Congress Cataloging-in-Publication Data is available.

ISBN 978-0-7627-4684-2

Printed in the United States of America

10 9 8 7 6 5 4 3 2 1

CONTENTS

INTRODUCTION

My mother had many noble qualities, but cooking wasn't one of them. She was the only person I have ever known who, when in the "mood," could turn a perfectly fine roast into something even our cocker spaniel would reject. I often believed she did this deliberately to make a point to Dad.

If this was her purpose, it proved to be very effective. My father, you see, was an old-world gentleman who appreciated fine food and drink, and ruining his dinner was an excellent way to get his attention. But he was too wise to allow her culinary misconduct to become an issue; instead he used it as an excuse to introduce me to the flip side of the universe, where impoverished palates like mine could experience wondrous creations—*escalopes de veau, canard à l orange, crème brûlée,* and other such gastronomic delights. This angelic act of mercy, bestowed upon me at some of Chicago's trendy restaurants, made it possible for me to survive puberty without major trauma.

From him, and from my worldly sister (a longtime Pan American stewardess), I learned to appreciate *good* cuisine. At an age when many of my colleagues were following a sensible career path to glory and riches, I was traveling the world eating. Although I can't consider myself a cook of merit (nor do I ever care to become one), when I do cook for friends, few leave the dinner table unsatisfied. From my travels—and from the support of more talented cooks—I have learned to master a few of the basic skills of cooking fine food.

My interest in cooking school getaways began in the nineties, when I was searching for suitable subjects for magazine articles. Because of my food fetish, a result of my scarred childhood, I began to write about international cooking schools from time to time. When my publisher asked me to write a book about cooking-school getaways in the United States, I became very excited. I saw it as an opportunity to travel the United States and to devote some major time to a subject I love very much.

Many of the schools mentioned in this book are seasonal, and they only offer classes during certain times of the year. Some even have a very limited focus or a focus that contradicts popular points of view. To avoid disappointment, it is important that readers contact the schools and get acquainted with the program choices before making a commitment. I have included a mix of schools with enough information throughout the book to help readers decide what may work best for them. To help evaluate each school, I provide, whenever appropriate, the schools' and the chefs' mission or philosophy. This should give you some clue as to what direction the school is heading.

Remember: What I have to say about each school shouldn't be taken as the final word. Programs change and personnel leave, even suddenly. This is largely because for schools to succeed, they must adapt to new trends. A few of the schools are forever true to their commitment, and they become the standard by which others may be measured. But for the most part, even they, to keep pace with the times, must transition to new levels occasionally.

Questions to ask yourself before committing to any school: What do I expect from the school—a fun-filled getaway, serious learning, or a social experience? What will they teach me? What are the credentials and experiences of the staff? Do they have what it takes to deliver what they promise? And, most importantly, is the cost of the program within my budget?

With that said, you are now ready to make your escape to what will hopefully become a gourmet getaway to remember.

—*Joe David*
Warrenton, Virginia

NORTHEAST

Wheatleigh. PHOTO COURTESY OF WHEATLEIGH

NORTHEAST

CONNECTICUT

The Conscious Gourmet
Greenwich, Connecticut

*M*ost people make food choices based on what's tasty and available, without consideration of what's best for their body. As a result, they unconsciously create health issues for themselves, like weight gain, mood swings, food sensitivities, and even accelerated aging.

Thanks to nutritionists, researchers, doctors, the media, and the food industry, many Americans are beginning to improve their eating habits. They are finally reading the fine print on packages to learn exactly what's in their food and asking themselves, is this really good for me? Some are even beginning to understand that wholesome food is needed not only to sustain the body, but to heal it. This new awareness has led to a noticeable movement in America toward high-quality foods that contain more whole grains, vegetables, and fruits.

Diane Carlson, owner of the Conscious Gourmet, is one of the many who have been helping to develop this emerging interest in healthier eating. Students who take one of her three- or six-day retreats are introduced to a wide range of health-supportive foods and the techniques for preparing them. More importantly, students attending her classes learn to make food choices that will contribute to their health and well-being, and support their personal goals.

ABOUT THE INSTRUCTOR
Some time ago, Diane experienced a series of health issues including high blood pressure, a perforated ulcer, mood swings, and more. Through the assistance of holistic practitioners, she identified the underlying causes

Diane Carlson (center) oversees students at work. PHOTO COURTESY OF CONSCIOUS GOURMET

and changed her diet to a whole-food eating style. As a result, she was able to bring about a significant improvement in her life and health and move it in a new direction—from living to eat to eating to live.

Her first step in this new direction began in 1988 when she graduated from the Natural Gourmet Cookery School in New York City (currently known as Natural Gourmet Institute for Health & Culinary Arts). Shortly afterward, she founded her own business, Five Seasons Whole Foods Cookery and Education Center in Minneapolis. In 1993, after returning to New York, she became the copresident, director, and instructor at the Natural Gourmet Institute. She remained in this position for eleven years, until she resigned in 2003 to found the Conscious Gourmet.

PHILOSOPHY

Diane believes that when the body is no longer stimulated by chemicals, additives, and preservatives, and when foods devoid of nutrition are replaced with high-quality whole foods, people experience a change in how they feel—mentally, physically, and emotionally—and they start losing weight naturally. She doesn't call eliminating problem-causing foods dieting (because that implies taking something away); instead, she

Wild Rice and Chestnut Dressing

Compliments of Diane Carlson

This dressing makes an excellent addition to a meal as well as a delicious stuffing for poultry or for your favorite squash, such as acorn, sweet dumpling, or hubbard (a large blue- or orange-skinned sweet squash). Since it has a complement of grains and nuts, it offers a complete vegetarian protein source.

One of Diane's favorite tricks is to use a hubbard squash in the shape of a turkey. She cuts off the "neck," removes the seeds, and partially bakes both the squash and the neck. She then stuffs the squash with the wild rice and chestnut dressing, replaces the neck with toothpicks, and continues to bake the squash until soft to the touch. When served on a platter surrounded by greens or colorful vegetables, it looks just like a turkey.

Ingredients
- $1/2$ cup raisins brought to a boil with 1 cup water
- $1/2$ cup reserved raisin stock
- 1 tablespoon extra virgin olive oil
- 1 cup chopped Spanish onions
- 1 cup diced celery
- 1 cup shredded carrots
- 1 cup chopped mushrooms
- 1 large clove garlic, minced
- $1/2$ teaspoon dried thyme
- $1/2$ teaspoon dried sage
- $1/4$ teaspoon dried rosemary
- $1/4$ teaspoon celery seed (optional)
- $1/4$ teaspoon sea salt
- $1/8$ teaspoon black pepper

prefers to call it a new style of eating—or, to use her words, a way to become a conscious gourmet, someone aware of the effects of their food choices.

As a teacher, she is committed to providing students with solid information that is essential for their health and well-being—and for liberating their bodies from food cravings caused by nutrient deficiencies. To feel satisfied after a meal, free of such cravings, Diane rec-

- 4 cups cooked wild rice or 2 cups cooked wild rice and 2 cups cooked brown Basmati rice
- $1/2$ cup vacuum-packed, roughly chopped chestnuts
- $1/2$ cup roughly chopped roasted walnuts
- $1/2$ cup minced parsley
- $1/2$ cup finely sliced scallions
- 2 tablespoons tamari or shoyu*
- 2 tablespoons lemon juice
- Sea salt and freshly ground black pepper to taste
- Chopped fresh parsley (for garnish)

* Shoyu is a soy sauce consisting of water, soybeans, wheat, sea salt, and koji. Diane prefers the Eden brand. Wheat-free shoyu is often called tamari. It is found in any health food store.

1. In a pot, bring the raisins to a boil. Lower heat and simmer until raisins are plump. Drain and reserve $1/2$ cup of the raisin stock. Set aside raisins and reserved stock.
2. Heat oil in a 12-inch frying pan over medium heat. Add onions and sauté until soft and translucent. Add celery and sauté until crisp tender.
3. Add carrots, mushrooms, and garlic and sauté until mushrooms become limp.
4. Add herbs, celery seed, sea salt, and black pepper, and sauté an additional minute.
5. Add the rice to the sautéed mixture. Add the raisins and reserved raisin stock. Add the next six ingredients and combine well. Season with salt and pepper to taste. If the dressing is to be served as a side dish, place it in an oiled covered casserole and bake in a 350°F oven for 30 minutes. Serve garnished with chopped parsley.

Serves 8–10.

ommends choosing the highest quality foods available. Ideally, this includes whole, fresh, natural, seasonal, local, and organic foods that are sustainably produced. It is also important that the meal is delicious, balanced, and satisfying by consciously including a variety of colors, flavors, cooking methods, and textures. If any of these menu-planning principles are out of balance, it can lead to after-meal food cravings. For example, a meal with too much or too little fat will likely bring about a craving for sugar. A meal that is predominantly soft in texture will often send the diner looking for something dry and crunchy later. When the willpower breaks down, people often seek the very food they are trying to avoid, and they end up consuming excess calories to satisfy the craving caused by an imbalanced meal. Being consciously aware of these principles and planning meals accordingly will result in a meal that will leave diners feeling content. (See Diane's recipe for Wild Rice and Chestnut Dressing as an example of a food with all the right ingredients.)

ABOUT THE CLASSES

Although her mostly vegetarian retreats appeal to vegetarians and vegans, Diane also offers classes with fish and organic, grass-fed animal protein. Each retreat, intensive in nature, provides students with hands-on steps to preparing healthier meals.

The retreats are comprised of five cooking classes (one demo and four hands-on, a total of twenty hours), plus a two-hour knife skills class. There are also four two-hour lectures. The lecture portion focuses for the most part on references to both Eastern and Western nutritional models. The purpose is to illustrate how students can connect the dots between what they eat and their emotional and mental health. The knife skills class focuses on Japanese and French technique and basic cutting skills (like dicing, shredding, mincing, etc.). Diane also instructs on how to select high-quality foods that are natural, fresh, and whole, and what to look for in the vast majority of health-supportive foods (such as sea vegetables, oils, natural sweeteners, and more).

Special programs may be arranged to meet individual or group needs, such as ethnic cuisine, beyond-the-basics classes, adventure retreats, and even personal retreats for groups of four or more. All the retreats are hands-on, and many are set in relaxed, enjoyable destinations (like Santa Fe, Sedona, or West Palm Beach). Most retreats begin on a Sunday and end on a Friday, and they include yoga, hikes, and natural-food meals. Retreats vary in type, length, and content.

Class Costs: Approximately $1,400 per person, depending on length. Transportation and lodging are usually extra, depending on location. Discounts are available for early payment.

Class Frequency: An average of six retreats per year; special classes are offered at Diane's Greenwich, Connecticut, home.

Class Length: Cooking classes run four hours each day.

Class Type: Hands-on/demonstration.

Class Size: Groups of six to twelve students, depending on the size of the kitchen. For more information call Diane Carlson in Greenwich, Connecticut, at (203) 622-1189, or visit www.theconsciousgourmet.com.

Silo Cooking School
New Milford, Connecticut

*C*onnecticut brings to mind images of eighteenth-century colonial revival homes perched gracefully on rolling hills, painted white with black shutters and a three-foot-high rock wall at the entrance. Some are even set against laurel and pine-scented glades or rest near cool-flowing, serpentine lakes and streams.

Unlike these genuine historic properties, the Litchfield Inn is only a circa 1982 copy. But it is an attractive copy, designed to revive images of bygone days when people traveled by stagecoach or horse and sought such inns for cheer and rest.

The best time to visit the inn in the northwest Litchfield Hills is when the Silo Cooking School at Hunt Hill Farm is offering one of its celebrity cooking classes (which could be any time of the year). It is then that the inn offers a two-day, one-night culinary package in cooperation with the Silo Cooking School that will dazzle the taste buds of any aspiring gourmet. Although class days vary, they are usually on Friday, Saturday, and Sunday.

The Silo is only about fifteen minutes away from the inn by car, hidden in a remote hideaway. Some consider it to be a local epicenter for gourmet cooking, which certainly may be true for even the most discriminating. This is because some of the hottest names in the food business have shown off their cooking skills here since the school flung open its barn doors to recreational cooks in 1975. Headliners like Jacques Pépin, Martha Stewart, Julia Child, and Rachael Ray have all made their way to this out-of-the-way spot to perform miracles with pots and pans.

ABOUT THE STAFF
Responsible for the school's conspicuous success are Skitch and Ruth Henderson, the founders. Skitch's background as a bandleader for Hollywood greats (Judy Garland, Mickey Rooney, Frank Sinatra, Bing Crosby,

and many more), and his and Ruth's successes in the sixties and seventies with their restaurants (The Wooden Horse Inn, St. Thomas; The Bird & Bottle, Garrison, New York; and Daly's Dandelion and Daffodil, New York City) provided them with the friendships and know-how to attract names to their farm.

Provolone Salad with Red-Basil Vinaigrette

From *Ruth and Skitch Henderson's Seasons in the Country,* Viking Studio Book, 1990. Compliments of the Silo Cooking School.

Nothing is as pleasant as a salad in the summer, especially if the vegetables and herbs are from your own garden. Below is a pleasant-tasting salad that can be enjoyed alone or with a main meal. Ruth Henderson recommends that you always use the freshest ingredients and the best available oil.

Ingredients
- 1 head red oak-leaf lettuce, separated into leaves
- 1 head green leaf lettuce, separated into leaves
- $1/2$ cup chopped scallions
- $1/4$ cup whole or chopped olives (optional)
- $1/4$ pound provolone cheese, cut into 2-inch strips $1/4$-inch thick
- 3 sprigs fresh marjoram, chopped, or 1 tablespoon dried
- $1/4$ teaspoon Dijon-style mustard
- 2 tablespoons red-basil vinegar
- Salt and freshly ground white pepper to taste
- $1/2$ cup Greek olive oil

1. Wash the lettuce leaves and pat dry. Line a salad bowl with the red leaves, and arrange the green leaves in the center. Place the scallions, olives, and cheese around the center of the green leaves. Sprinkle with the marjoram.
2. To make the vinaigrette, combine the mustard, vinegar, and salt and pepper in a small bowl. Whisk in the oil. Toss the salad with the dressing just before serving.

Serves 6.

PHILOSOPHY

Although Skitch passed away a few years ago, the school's mission has not changed. Ruth has made certain of that by making sure that the school still attracts the top chefs in the business and that the program still offers students more than just a few recipes and techniques. Her goal is to share with Silo students healthy ways to prepare tasty foods that will nourish the body.

This dedication to sensible eating was born out of Skitch's and Ruth's

A chef and her assistant prepare a dish.
PHOTO COURTESY OF HUNTS HILL TRUST, INC.

experiences in the restaurant business. Hardworking achievers with refined palates, they have always been drawn to the restaurant world; for them, the challenges of succeeding in the kitchen meant they had to prepare quality meals *daily* to meet the highest standards of their demanding customers. Silo teachers share this dedication to quality and show it by offering students the latest techniques and recipes that will help them meet high nutritional standards at home.

ABOUT THE CLASSES

All classes have a primary focus, and each chef brings to his lesson his special style. As a result, there is no fixed format. Classes can be hands-on or demonstration, run for only three hours or for a succession of days, with the class size varying, depending on the approach. Examples of what have been taught in the past include preparing spring rolls with familiar and not so familiar ingredients (demonstration), mating chocolate

Touring the Hills of Connecticut

The historic village of Litchfield. *Only minutes away from the Litchfield Inn and the Silo Cooking School, this small but charming community overflows with old homes, churches, and a famous old law school.*

Aer Blarney Balloons, a nondirect "airline service." *You drift along an unchartered course high above the Litchfield Hills and enjoy unforgettable vistas (www.aerblarney.com).*

Musical plays performed by the Goshen Players. *For nearly sixty years they have been singing and dancing off Broadway the hottest show tunes ever created on Broadway. For more information visit www.goshenplayers.org.*

Local food stops. *At their Rustling Winds Creamery and Stables in Falls Village (www.rustlingwind.com), mother and daughter Joan and Terri Lamothe milk their cows and goats daily to produce their trademark English-style Cheshire cheese and Canaan Mountain goat milk cheese. For lightly smoked meats, fish, and cheese, there is Nodine's Smokehouse (www.nodinesmoke house.com) in Goshen, a family-operated business that supplies foods to Dean & DeLuca, Zabar's, and Citarella. And for organic, hormone-free meats—and a choice of interesting classes in healthy living—there is the New Morning Store in Woodbury (www.newmorn.com).*

with other flavors for sweetness and richness (demonstration), removing the mystery from preparing French pastries (hands-on), and creating a five-course meal that includes a fillet of beef with Courvoisier sauce and white truffle potatoes (hands-on).

From time to time the Silo also offers practical mini cooking classes, which run about two hours (on topics such as ways to use the Cuisinart and ways to prepare sauces in the hollandaise family). Upon request, customized classes for groups of twelve to forty-five (demonstrations or hands-on or both) are offered. These classes may include such themes, for example, as preparing hors d'oeuvres, wedding cakes, or elegant desserts.

On weekdays, special team-building classes may be arranged for company employees. And during select seasons, the Silo hosts its popular hands-on classes for children, designed to acquaint them with food preparation and make it enjoyable. Favorites include the cooking camp with different holiday themes, from Chinese New Year to the Fourth of July (about $200 per student), and a five-day cooking/music camp that explores global food and music (about $250 per student).

The culinary package offered by the Litchfield Inn in concert with the Silo Cooking School is for two people, and it includes one class at the Silo, dinner at the acclaimed eighteenth-century restaurant Woodbury House (located in Bethlehem, Connecticut), and a standard room for one night at the inn with continental breakfast.

Class Costs: About $85 per class for adult programs, and about $200 for the children's classes. Team-building classes run $150 per person; the special two-day getaway package for two at the Litchfield Inn runs from $463 to $547.

Class Frequency: Held from March to December.

Class Length: Varies from a three-hour, one-day class to a several-day series of classes.

Class Type: Hands-on or demonstration.

Class Size: Hands-on classes for adults have a maximum of sixteen people, with one instructor and four or five assistants. Hands-on classes for children are smaller, about twelve students per class. Demonstration classes may include up to thirty students.

Lodging: Each of the inn's thirty-two guest rooms has its own pleasant personality (some with fireplaces, four-posters, and canopied beds).

Amenities: All the usual first-class amenities expected in a small inn.

For information about lodging contact the Litchfield Inn, 432 Bantam Road (Connecticut Highway 202), Litchfield, CT 06759; (860) 567-4503; www.litchfieldinnct.com.

For information about the cooking school, contact the Silo Cooking School, 44 Upland Road, New Milford, CT 06776; (860) 355-0300; www.hunthillfarmtrust.org.

Sally Maraventano addresses a class on Italian cuisine.
PHOTO COURTESY OF CUCINA CASALINGA

Cucina Casalinga
Wilton, Connecticut

*F*rom the moment Catherine and later Maria de Medici landed in France and took up housekeeping in their respective palaces as queens, the culinary world has never been the same. These two social-climbing heiresses from Florence brought with them the culinary wonders of Italy, using them to dazzle the kings and courts of France. Eventually, chefs from around the world began to look to Italy and its culinary savoir faire for ways to refine the taste buds of the globe.

In Wilton, Connecticut, another gal with strong Italian roots, Sally Maraventano, has also been working at refining taste buds. A former high school language teacher, Sally serves up her Italian culinary legacy, inherited from her mother, to her cooking school students with panache, as she re-creates happy childhood memories of times spent around the dinner table with family and friends.

ABOUT THE INSTRUCTOR

Sally began to show promise in cooking as a youngster, assisting her mother in preparing family meals for thirty or forty people. She majored in Italian and minored in French at Georgetown University and the University of Florence, and she taught junior high French and Italian. After

---

Torta di Bietole

(Swiss Chard Torte)

From Sally Maraventano's book *Festa del Giardino*

This is a flaky, buttery pastry with the exotic flavors of raisins, pine nuts, and Swiss chard. If Swiss chard is not available, fresh spinach can be substituted, although the chard has a sweeter flavor.

Special tips for perfect results:
- Let the ricotta sit in a sieve to drain for 15 to 20 minutes. This will remove unneeded liquid from the puff pastry.
- Golden raisins make this dish more authentically Sicilian and have a much sweeter taste than dark raisins.
- If time is an issue, omit step 2 in the directions.

Ingredients
- 2 pounds Swiss chard, leaves and upper stalks cut into 3-inch pieces
- 4 tablespoons extra-virgin olive oil
- 2 cloves garlic, finely minced
- $1/4$ cup sultana raisins (golden)
- 1 15-ounce container ricotta cheese
- 3 eggs, beaten
- $2/3$ cup freshly grated Parmesan cheese
- $1/4$ cup pine nuts
- Salt and freshly ground pepper
- 1 tablespoon butter
- 1 sheet frozen puff-pastry dough, thawed for 30 minutes
- 1 egg plus 1 tablespoon water, lightly beaten (for egg wash)

1. Cook the Swiss chard in 4 cups of lightly salted boiling water until tender. Drain and squeeze to remove as much water as possible. Chop coarsely and set aside.

she had her first child, she opened the doors to her home-based cooking program in 1981, bringing together two of her favorite things: teaching and cooking.

Her success as a teacher has led to television appearances, which have included some of her family recipes being featured on such programs as

2. In a large skillet, sauté the olive oil and garlic gently for 3 minutes. Add the Swiss chard and cook for 5 minutes to let the flavors blend. Turn off the heat and add the raisins.

3. Preheat the oven to 400°F.

4. Transfer the Swiss chard and raisins to a mixing bowl and stir in the ricotta, the eggs, the Parmesan cheese, and the pine nuts. Add salt and pepper to taste.

5. Lightly grease a pie pan or a 9-inch springform pan with butter. Roll out the pastry to line the pan, leaving 2½ inches overhanging all around.

6. Fill the pastry-lined pan with the Swiss chard mixture. Fold in the pastry to cover the filling. (The center of the torte may not be totally covered with pastry and may open somewhat during baking.)

Torta di Bietolie (Swiss Chard Torte)
PHOTO COURTESY OF CUCINA CASALINGA

7. Brush all exposed pastry with egg wash.

8. Bake for about 40 minutes, until puffed and golden. Remove the torte from the oven and let it rest for 10 minutes. Remove the sides of the springform pan. Place the torte on a platter and serve it warm or at room temperature.

Serves 6.

In Food Today on the Food Network and NBC's *Weekend Today* show, and regular appearances on *The Exchange* on Connecticut Cable Television. She has taught at the Institute of Culinary Education and the Italian Culinary Institute and authored the cookbook *Festa del Giardino,* a collection of 125 Italian vegetable recipes that are prepared without animal fat and arranged in menu order.

ABOUT THE CLASS

Weekly hands-on/demonstration classes, held in Sally's state-of-the-art kitchen, unravel the secrets of Italian regional cooking and the joys of growing up Italian. Classes can be as simple as making a multicheese pizza in her outdoor, wood-burning brick pizza oven or as complicated as creating a manicotti that her Grandma Lo Cascio might have prepared.

Students learn how to prepare, plate, and serve "knock-'em-dead" foods such as *brodo di pollo con tortelloni* (chicken soup with tortelloni filled with chicken and prosciutto), *frittata alle erbe* (Italian omelet baked with fresh herbs), and anything else Sally can dream up to prepare on her six-burner Thermador stove.

Four types of culinary experiences are offered, three in her home and the fourth in Italy. The latter is a choice of either a conducted tour to Italy in which leading Italian chefs provide an intensive cooking program or an upscale culture tour with some cooking, fine dining, and shopping.

The classes conducted in her home include one for children, one for adults, and one for corporate team building. The first, the Kids Cook Italian series, is for young chefs between the ages of eleven and sixteen. These classes run for three days and introduce children to the art of preparing fine food. Sally loves working with children and has discovered that they can prepare almost anything an adult can, from gnocchi to homemade pasta. Since both parents in many households work, she feels teaching children to be independent in the kitchen is a real value to them and the family.

One of Sally's favorite classes is the one for adults, which some use as a getaway and pair with an overnight at the historic Inn at National Hall in nearby Westport. Students traveling to Wilton from Boston or New York can package their cooking classes with some off-time shopping in the antiques shops and boutiques in the area. A list of a few noteworthy restaurants will be provided upon request. These classes are usually offered on weekdays, although she occasionally offers weekend workshop classes. Since none of her classes are back-to-back, she only offers one adult class each week. Foods are prepared from scratch, but usually her meals appeal to adults who want to prepare tasty yet quick meals that they can easily serve to family and friends, so she provides tips on how to prepare foods in advance.

In all of her classes, Sally introduces students to a large selection of herbs, which she grows on her property. Since table setting is part of the allure of the meal, she gives serious attention to the arrangement of the food and table decorations. Each meal is served with fine china and silver, just as it would be at home for company.

Class Costs: The weeklong or ten-day tour of Italy runs about $3,800 to $4,400 for land costs, including cooking lessons, wine tasting, excursions, food, and lodging. Airfare is extra. Corporate class prices vary depending on the menu, from $145 to $160 per person, plus a 20 percent gratuity. The three-day Kids Cook Italian series runs about $300 per child. The adult classes are $135 per student.

Class Frequency: Frequency varies; some weeks as many as three classes are offered, while others as few as one are offered.

Class Length: Classes are usually held from 10:00 a.m. to 2:00 p.m. or from 6:30 to 9:30 p.m.

Class Type: All classes are strictly hands-on.

Class Size: Italy tours may include twelve to sixteen participants; corporate classes ten to twenty; children's classes eight to twelve; adult classes six to twelve.

Lodging: The Inn at National Hall in Westport, Connecticut, is a charming nineteenth-century inn overlooking the Saugatuck River. Many consider the area the Beverly Hills of the East because of the many prominent stage and screen stars that live here. The inn, a Relais & Châteaux property, is intimate, elegant, and stunning. Each room has its own personality, with four-posters and unique names that invoke romantic images, such as the India, the Turkistan, and the Equestrian. Some have crystal chandeliers and staircases to second-level quarters. For more information contact: Inn at National Hall, 2 Post Road West, Westport, CT 06880; (203) 221-1351; www.innatnationalhall.com.

For more information about cooking classes, contact: Cucina Casalinga, 171 Drum Hill Road, Wilton, CT 06897; (203) 762-0768; www.cucinacasalinga.com.

MAINE

Hartstone Inn Cooking School
Camden, Maine

*A*uguste Escoffier pointed out decades ago that fine cooking begins with creating the most important basic ingredient in food preparation: the stock! To prepare it successfully, the finest foods available must be used. When the stock is good, what follows will also be good. This classic attitude of faultless attention to a singular ingredient may seem foreign to many fast-order cooks who pull together a variety of meals at instant notice, but to prize-winning chefs, such attention to detail is the cornerstone to their success.

Chef Michael Salmon shares this attitude. Schooled in fine cooking, he has been trained to build a meal carefully. As the chef at his own small inn, which serves only twenty dinner guests each night, he has the freedom to do exactly what he wants in the kitchen. In his case, this means preparing one fixed-price, five-course meal for everyone.

Concentrating exclusively on just one specialty each night, uninterrupted by a multitude of different tasks, allows gifted chefs to refine what they prepare before serving it, something fast-order chefs haven't the time to do. At the Hartstone Inn, Chef Michael does this seven nights a week in the summer (six nights in the winter) for a filled dining room.

Some Americans may find a fixed menu with no substitutes unacceptable, but at the Hartstone, this is a nonissue. Everything the chef prepares is done so well with such a complete focus on the food's freshness and seasonality that no one complains. They just eat and smile. Chef Michael's success can be attributed to two things: his responsiveness to diners' requests and his complete focus on providing a well-prepared meal with classic finesse.

Recreational cooks, serious about improving their skills, may want to take a few lessons from the chef. His food, not his impeccably furnished properties, is his draw.

ABOUT THE CHEF

Since 1998, Chef Michael and his wife, Mary Jo, have been operating the twenty-one-room Hartstone Inn. Both have bachelor's degrees in hospitality, and Michael received his early training at the Culinary Institute of America in New York, refining it by working in many four- and five-star hotels throughout the United States. While employed by the Sonesta Beach Resort Hotel and Casino in Aruba, he became fond of the flavors of the Caribbean, which he fuses with some of his classic dishes. For his achievements during his years in Aruba, he was named Caribbean Chef of the Year in 1996.

PHILOSOPHY

Chef Michael's goal is to be responsive to the needs of his students and provide them the professional training they desire, either one on one or as a group.

ABOUT THE CLASSES

The inn offers three types of cooking programs—Chef for the Day, private cooking classes, and a weekend package—which vary based on season and theme. In fall, for example, the meals are hearty and may include the chef's famous Roasted Sweet Potato, Rutabaga, and Green Apple Soup; during the holidays the focus is on hors d'oeuvres with seasonal toppings, like Baked Brie with Hazelnuts and Frangelico. Other themes may include Caribbean cuisine, dim sum, or Maine seafood. Some memorable dishes prepared in the past include Red Curry of Maine Lobster with Shrimp and Pineapple, and the chef's famous dessert soufflés (see recipe). In each class, he strives to be both informative

Chef Michael Salmon's Signature Soufflé

Tips and recipes are from Chef Michael Salmon's book, *In the Kitchen with Michael Salmon: Recipes of Distinction from the Hartstone Inn*. Used with permission.

Soufflés have become Chef Michael's signature dessert, and guests are always asking him for the recipe or a cooking class on soufflés. Making them can be tricky, so it's important that you follow the instructions carefully. Timing is the key to successful soufflé service, as they wait for no one: When they are ready to be served, they must be hastily escorted to the table and consumed immediately, or they will become, as his wife, Mary Jo, says, "flat tires."

Michael has about thirty-five different flavor combinations that he uses for his soufflés. While the following recipe has berries and Chambord (raspberry liqueur), you can simply substitute these ingredients with one of the following alternatives to create your favorite flavor:

Chef Michael Salmon's
Signature Soufflé
PHOTO COURTESY OF THE HARTSTONE INN

* Grand Marnier: ¹/₄ cup Grand Marnier
* Chocolate-amaretto: ¹/₄ cup cocoa powder, ¹/₄ cup amaretto liqueur, and 2 tablespoons finely ground almonds
* Pumpkin: ¹/₂ cup fresh canned pumpkin puree and 1 teaspoon pumpkin pie spice
* Cappuccino: 2 tablespoons strong coffee or espresso and ¹/₄ cup Kahlúa
* Blueberry-hazelnut: ¹/₂ cup fresh or frozen blueberries, ¹/₄ cup Frangelico (hazelnut liqueur), and 2 tablespoons finely ground hazelnuts
* Pistachio: ¹/₄ cup finely ground pistachios and 2 tablespoons amaretto liqueur

Fresh Berry Soufflé with a Chambord Crème Anglaise

Ingredients

- 1 cup whole milk
- 2 oz unsalted butter ($^1/_2$ stick)
- $^1/_2$ cup flour
- $^1/_2$ cup granulated sugar
- 5 large eggs, separated
- 1 tablespoon unsalted butter, softened
- 2 tablespoons granulated sugar
- $^1/_2$ cup fresh berries (raspberries, blackberries, and sliced strawberries; reserve some for garnish)
- 2 tablespoons Chambord
- $^1/_4$ teaspoon cream of tartar
- Powdered sugar (for garnish)
- Chambord Crème Anglaise (recipe follows)

1. In a 2-quart saucepan, heat the milk over medium heat. In another 2-quart saucepan, melt the butter over medium heat. When the butter is melted, stir in the flour and mix until combined well. Reduce heat to low and stir frequently.
2. When the milk comes to a simmer, stir in the sugar. Continue to stir, dissolving the sugar for 2 minutes. Pour the milk mixture into the butter mixture and stir with a whisk to combine, cooking over medium heat until a ball forms and the mixture releases from the sides of the pan.
3. Immediately place the mixture in a mixing bowl and stir with an electric mixer (using the flat paddle) on medium-low speed for 10 minutes.
4. One by one, stir in the egg yolks, allowing each to be completely incorporated before adding the next. When all of the egg yolks are incorporated, set the mixture (the soufflé base) aside and allow it to cool. This base will keep refrigerated for up to one week.
5. Generously butter four 1$^1/_2$-cup soufflé dishes, covering the entire surface area on the inside of the cups, including the rim. Coat the buttered cups with granulated sugar, rotating the cups to coat them evenly. Tap out any excess sugar. Set the prepared cups aside.
6. Place the soufflé base in a mixing bowl and stir in half the berries. Add the Chambord, mixing well.
7. Preheat the oven to 350°F.
8. In an electric mixer fitted with a whisk, whip the egg whites and cream of tartar until stiff peaks form. With a large rubber spatula, gently fold half of the egg whites into the soufflé base. Continue to fold in the remaining egg

whites. Gently pour the batter into the prepared soufflé dishes, filling them four-fifths of the way full. Be careful not to drip the batter on the rims, or the soufflés may not rise evenly.

9. Bake in the center the oven for 35 minutes, or until lightly browned on top. Remove from the oven, place on a small serving plate, and top with a small mound of the reserved fresh berries. Dust with powdered sugar and hurry the soufflés to the table. Serve with a side of Chambord Crème Anglaise, pouring it into a hole poked into the top of the soufflé at the table. Eat immediately.

Makes 4 soufflés.

Chambord Crème Anglaise

Ingredients
- 2 cups whole milk
- 3 large eggs
- 2 egg yolks
- $^1/_2$ cup granulated sugar
- $^1/_2$ cup fresh raspberries
- 1 tablespoon Chambord

1. In a 2-quart saucepan over medium-high heat, bring the milk to a simmer.
2. In a medium-size mixing bowl, whisk together the eggs, egg yolks, and sugar. Have ready a large bowl half full of ice water (with plenty of ice) and a medium-size bowl that will fit inside the ice bath. Also have on hand a fine mesh strainer, a wooden spoon, and an instant-read thermometer.
3. When the milk reaches a simmer, slowly pour about $^1/_2$ cup of the hot milk into the egg mixture, whisking constantly. (This is called tempering.) Add another $^1/_2$ cup of hot milk, whisking constantly. Now whisk the tempered egg mixture back into the saucepan with the milk, whisking constantly. Set the whisk aside and stir this mixture with the wooden spoon constantly over medium heat until the mixture reaches a temperature of 175°F on the instant-read thermometer, or until the mixture just coats the back of the spoon. Remove from the heat and immediately pour the mixture through the fine mesh strainer into the medium bowl. Immediately set this bowl in the ice bath to stop the cooking. Stir the mixture, occasionally, until it cools. Stir in the raspberries and Chambord.
4. Refrigerate in a covered container until needed, for up to one week.

Serves 5–6.

and entertaining, exciting palates with pleasant renditions of familiar flavors.

In the Chef for the Day program, a student has the opportunity to work alongside Chef Michael for four hours, helping him prepare the evening meal for guests and gaining an understanding of what it takes to cook for a large group. (Students with recipe preferences may make arrangements in advance with the chef; these meals often appear on the dinner menu.) After a tour of the kitchen and general orientation, class begins with a review of the dinner menu and the assignment of duties. That evening, the class ends, if the student chooses, with everyone enjoying what the student created. The dinner, which is extra, costs $45 per person.

During private cooking classes, the student selects from twenty-five different foods that Chef Michael has put together or from the hundreds of recipes that appear in his cookbook.

The weekend package includes a cooking class for one person that could be focused on any one of a broad range of foods (ethnic, regional, or international), as well as some irresistible extras: two nights of lodging, breakfast, afternoon tea and cookies, and a gourmet candlelight dinner for two.

Class Costs: Chef for a Day: $325 for first person and $50 for one additional person; private classes: $350 for the first six students, $45 for each additional student; weekend package: $305 to $485 (depending on living quarters) for two, $45 extra for the second person taking a cooking class.

Class Frequency: Chef for a Day: one class on Wednesday through Sunday throughout the year; private classes: available by appointment throughout the year; weekend package: once a month, November through May.

Class Length: Chef for a Day: four hours; private classes: two hours per day; weekend package: two hours on Saturday or Sunday.

Class Type: Primarily hands-on; some demonstration.

Class Size: Chef for a Day: one or two persons per class; private classes: minimum of six persons, maximum of twelve; weekend package: twelve-person maximum.

Lodging: The inn is an 1835 Victorian house elegantly decorated with French and Victorian furnishings. Each room has its own personality, tastefully decorated with the guests' comfort in mind. This includes high-thread-count sheets, handpainted Quimper Faience plate service, original artwork, decorator duvets, Jacuzzi tubs, special soaps, and truffles each night on your pillow.

Amenities: All the expected first-class amenities are available, and guests may make special arrangements in advance (for an extra fee) to have chocolate-dipped strawberries and Mumm's champagne, a wine and cheese platter, and much more delivered to their room. The inn also has spa treatments (sea salt scrub, massage, and hot stone therapy).

Activities: The inn can arrange a choice of pleasant food-related outings (extra fee; prices vary). They may include a tour of Appleton Creamery, where guests taste local cheeses and learn about cheesemaking; a tour of Sweet Sensations Pastry Shop, where certified pastry chef Steven Watts teaches the tricks of the trade; and a wine-tasting tour of Cellardoor Winery, which overlooks Camden Hills State Park. As a special extra, the inn offers a backpack gourmet picnic for two with a bottle of Cellardoor wine to enjoy at the winery or wherever you desire. Other activities include a sugarhouse tour (for maple syrup lovers); lobster lunch aboard a sailing boat, with a brief ride to see the seals and eagles; and a list of favorite places to visit, like chocolate shops, farmers' markets, orchards, and cooking stores.

For more information contact Hartstone Inn, 41 Elm Street, Camden, ME 04843; (207) 236-4259; www.hartstoneinn.com.

The Inns at Blackberry Common
Camden, Maine

*M*ost people face midlife career change squarely. If they have been in touch with themselves most of their lives, they know exactly what they want to do when they are no longer accountants, secretaries, or lawyers. Their private dreams, which they have only shared with friends and loved ones, are pulled from the attic of their mind, dusted off, and pursued.

This is what Jim Ostrowski, a retired nuclear engineer from Delaware, has done: made his midlife change by living his passion. In Jim's case, this has meant becoming an innkeeper. While other successful retirees sail around the world or pound golf balls, he has put on an apron and prepares and serves food, and he even teaches cooking classes to his inn guests (when he isn't making general repairs on the inn property).

When he and his wife, Cyndi, decided to run an inn in New England, Jim enrolled in the Restaurant School at Walnut Hill College in Philadelphia to prepare for their new life. He took a two-year program that was carefully designed to provide him with the culinary and hotel management skills he needed to run a bed-and-breakfast. Before heading to Maine, he did his externship at the five-star Hotel Dupont in Wilmington, Delaware, where he worked as a chef in the Green Room dining room.

When the Ostrowskis opened their inn, they had no intention of including a culinary program for guests. The idea for that came about several years ago when guests, impressed with Jim's breakfasts, started requesting recipes—and even cooking classes. What began as an experiment has in the past couple of years evolved into a full-blown weekend-getaway program.

PHILOSOPHY

Jim's philosophy is to create healthy meals prepared with seasonal, locally grown, and sugarless ingredients. The foods prepared are neither vegan nor vegetarian, but instead are the best of what is available in the marketplace, including (but not limited to) organic ingredients. His goal is

Blackberry Sage Sauce

Compliments of Jim Ostrowski, the Inns at Blackberry Common

This sauce can be used over French toast, pancakes, or waffles. Garnish with a chiffonade of sage leaves and a bit of lemon zest, and finish with a sprinkle of cinnamon and ground anise powder. (Chiffonade is made by rolling several sage leaves tightly together and slicing them thinly at a forty-five-degree angle.) The sauce will last for several days in the refrigerator or up to one month in the freezer.

Ingredients

Blackberry Sage Sauce over French toast
PHOTO COURTESY OF THE INNS AT BLACKBERRY COMMON

- 2 cups fresh or frozen blackberries
- ³/₄ cup sugar
- ¹/₄ cup honey
- ¹/₄ teaspoon ground cinnamon
- ¹/₈ teaspoon ground anise
- 2 tablespoons lemon juice
- ¹/₂ cup blackberry liquor or blackberry brandy
- 2 sprigs fresh sage
- 2 tablespoons cornstarch mixed with 4 tablespoons cold water (optional)

1. Combine blackberries, sugar, honey, cinnamon, anise, lemon juice, the liquor, and the sage sprigs in a medium saucepan. Heat at medium temperature and bring to a simmer.
2. Simmer gently for 5 minutes. Do not allow to boil.
3. Check sauce for desired thickness by dipping a tablespoon into it to see if it coats the back of the spoon.
4. If too thin, add 2 tablespoons of cornstarch dissolved in 4 tablespoons of water.
5. Continue to simmer another 2 minutes until desired thickness. Remove sage sprigs.

Serves 6.

The Inns at Blackberry Common are only a few blocks from the harbor.
PHOTO COURTESY OF JOE DAVID

to encourage students to buy local products directly from their primary sources (farmers and producers).

ABOUT THE CLASSES

The culinary weekends begin on a Friday with a welcome reception of hors d'oeuvres, a hearty stew, and wine. Although the classes generally don't have a theme, ones held on certain holidays like Valentine's Day, for example, do. The hands-on class is held on Saturday afternoon, which either Jim or another chef (sometimes from the immediate area, other times from Portland) conducts.

The class routine is standard. About fifteen minutes are spent showing students how certain primary skills are performed (especially knife skills), and the remaining time is spent working on recipes, which may even include preparing mother sauces (some made with berries). During

 Activities in Camden

*A*bout twenty thousand years ago during the Ice Age, huge glaciers covered Maine's coastal plains and formed, during the meltdown, what are now Maine's rocky shores, islands, and deepwater coastal harbors. For travelers along the Maine coast today, the islands and harbors have become a string of picturesque fishing villages with boats, grand hotels, and "cottages" to enjoy.

Of the many villages along the coast, the one that remains most popular (next to Kennebunkport and Bar Harbor) is Camden. To many Americans, Camden is best remembered as the setting for the movie Peyton Place, a steamy love story about small-town New England's sins. Although Camden doesn't steam these days—at least not any more than other New England towns—one noteworthy thing about it is its annual Maine Fare, a weekend food festival that celebrates the state's food bounty. Food writers, chefs, farmers, producers, and artisans all descend on Camden for a weekend each September to enjoy professional cooking classes, lectures, book signings, cooking demonstrations, tips on preparing and selecting seafood, and more. It's a foodie's holiday with a delicious mix of tasty treats and entertainment. For more information visit www.mainefare.com.

During the first weekend in December, Camden has its annual Christmas by the Sea celebration. It begins with a Friday-night parade, some car-

each class, Jim only uses seasonal Maine products, and he keeps the meal preparation basic (for example, wild mushroom risotto, Maine crab cakes, or seafood "chowdah"). Students enjoy a four-course gourmet dinner on Saturday evening, which includes some of the savory dishes made in class. On Sunday, after a bountiful breakfast, the weekend getaway ends with a wrap-up of what's been taught.

oling on the square, and the lighting of the village tree at the harbor. All of this takes place beneath a fifty-foot star on top of Mount Battie (which is lit on Thanksgiving Day). On Saturday, Santa arrives by lobster boat, and the weekend ends on Sunday with a tea and a tour of the inns in the area. For more information visit www.visitcamden.com.

Other activities include:

- *Hiking, camping, skiing, and picnicking at 5,700-acre Camden Hills State Park, one of Camden's major attractions*
- *Gazing at and photographing the lighthouses, eagles, and harbor seals from the deck of a Maine schooner sailing from Camden harbor*
- *Visiting museums such as the renowned Farnsworth Museum for the paintings of the Wyeth family and the Owl's Head Transportation Museum for a priceless exhibit of antique autos and planes*
- *Attending the renovated, 500-seat Victorian Opera House with its head-line entertainment (in season)*
- *Shopping for name-brand goods at the discount stores in Freeport (between Portland and Camden)*

For a few food-related activities beyond the two recreational cooking programs in the village, see what the Hartstone Inn has to offer.

Class Costs: From $385 per couple, including two nights of lodging, class, break-fasts, and Saturday-night dinner (for two).

Class Frequency: About six times a year during the three-day weekend holidays.

Class Length: Classes last about two and a half hours on Saturday, and the wrap-up on Sunday lasts about thirty to forty-five minutes.

Class Type: Some demonstration; mostly hands-on.

Class Size: Maximum twelve students, minimum four.

Lodging: The setting for this gourmet getaway is the restored 1849 Victorian Black-berry Inn and the 1806 colonial homestead the Elms. Both properties have period furnishings and have been remodeled to preserve their historic character. The Blackberry Inn's spacious parlor and dining room, for example, still have the original tin ceilings and plaster moldings. Some rooms have fireplaces and whirlpool or claw-foot tubs; others have decks or private entrances or secret gardens. Accord-ing to Jim, one of the second-floor bedrooms of the Blackberry Inn is where actress Bette Davis slept while partying with the cast of *Peyton Place*. Both inns are only a few blocks from the harbor, where guests can shop at the unique boutiques and galleries or gaze at the windjammers and schooners that cruise the coast.

For more information contact: The Inns at Blackberry Common, 82 and 84 Elm Street, Camden, ME 04843; (800) 388-6000; www.innsatblackberrycommon.com.

L'École des Chefs Relais Gourmand at the White Barn Inn
Kennebunk Beach, Maine

*I*t is often difficult to distinguish one fine inn from another. Although they each may have unique settings, which at first glance set them apart from the others, they all share similar qualities. Every fine inn understands what the French mean by l'art de vivre (the art of living), so visiting one is like visiting another. The service, the amenities, and the cuisine are all world-class—and expected by the discerning traveler.

The unpretentiously named White Barn Inn isn't an exception. Set in picturesque Kennebunkport, a fashionable seaside Maine resort town, the property came to life in the 1860s (as the Forest Hill House) and hosted some of Boston's and Portsmouth's most elite families seeking escape from the summer heat. Since 1973, the property has been known as the White Barn Inn (currently a Relais & Châteaux property). Like the other eighteenth- and nineteenth-century, colonial- and Federal-style homes nearby, the inn fits snugly in the neighborhood, where it discreetly entertains prominent guests from around the world seeking relaxation and privacy.

Leading magazines like Condé Nast Traveler, Bon Appetit, Travel + Leisure, Departures, and Food & Wine have all generously acknowledged the inn's smoothness of service and handsome accommodations. If there is perhaps one thing that pushes it to the top among the great inns and keeps it there, it is the inn's complete respect for food. In what has become America's golden age of culinary discovery, the White Barn Inn has demonstrated that its culinary refinement is right up there with the best.

Their complementary mating of ingredients—like the seared scallops garnished with caviar, fresh asparagus, and champagne sauce, or a crumbly shortcake biscuit with ripe strawberries peeking through a cloud of vanilla-flavored whipped cream—keeps the fashionable returning and asking for more. Like so many world-class restaurants around the world, the inn prepares each meal with a delicate balance of ingredients and presents it with a stunning flare for simplicity.

This combination of fine food, luxurious accommodations, and service may seem like enough to keep the guests happy and returning. But like all really special properties, striving to stand out against the tough competition, the White Barn is always searching for new ways to please its guests. One way is to offer cooking lessons. At the White Barn that isn't just a lesson teaching recipes and techniques, but a lesson introducing guests to the graceful art of entertaining.

ABOUT THE CHEF

Overseeing the program is Executive Chef Jonathan M. Cartwright. A native of London, Chef Cartwright began cooking at the age of fifteen. His culinary mastery has led to his employment at some of the finest hotels in the world, including the Relais & Châteaux member properties Blantyre (Lenox, Massachusetts), the Horned Dorset Primavera (Rincon, Puerto Rico), and the Hotel Bareiss (Baiersbronn-Mitteltal, Germany). His early training was at the Savoy Hotel, London, under the supervision of Anton Edelmann, the hotel's respected maître chef des cuisines.

PHILOSOPHY

Chef Cartwright's goal is make food preparation enjoyable by reducing last-minute pressure. He does this by introducing students to professional kitchen tricks that they can use to improve and hasten the cooking process at home.

ABOUT THE CLASSES

On television or during gourmet store food demonstrations, viewers are often overloaded with recipes and little else. At the five-star White Barn Inn, this isn't the case. For those who seek the ultimate culinary experience, they will find the hands-on/demonstration classes to be well-planned to achieve lasting learning.

Chef Jonathan Cartwright (second from left) began cooking in London at age fifteen.
PHOTO COURTESY OF THE WHITE BARN INN

Students work alongside key members of the kitchen staff, where they slice, dice, baste, and grill together. They prepare turkey, cold-water lobsters, hand-picked scallops, as well as other local and seasonal foods. During the cooking lesson, the secrets of a great kitchen are revealed to them as they create flavorful regional food with a focus on eye appeal.

The lessons are simple. Everything is made from scratch, using only top-quality products, which will be prepared with care and served with finesse. But the lesson doesn't end with preparing and designing an attractive meal. It expands to include training in the golden rule of entertaining: the art of making your guests feel special.

The weekend begins on a Friday night with a typical English tea (finger sandwiches, sweets, scones, and a choice of fine teas and coffee) from 3:30 to 4:30 p.m. Tea is followed by a cocktail party from 6:00 to 7:30 p.m., during which canapés are served. Chef Cartwright and the guest chef use this informal social gathering to introduce themselves and give

Brighten Your Meal like a Professional

Chef Cartwright shares some of his expertise by making four important recommendations to hosts planning a dinner party:

- **Eye appeal.** *A meal begins the moment it is seen; therefore, its presentation is very important. Chef Cartwright recommends that you make the food as engaging as possible, with a variety of colors, shapes, and textures. One way to do this is to pay attention to the garnish. A fresh sprig of rosemary, some chopped chives, or freshly ground pepper can add irresistible eye appeal to a meal.*

- **Advance preparation.** *Several days in advance, you should plan your meal and purchase all the basic ingredients (such as butter, saffron, champagne, and root vegetables, for example). On the day of the dinner, you should buy the ingredients that need to be fresh, such as seafood and herbs.*

- **Practice ahead of time.** *You should practice preparing your entree, exactly as you will serve it for the big dinner, at least a week in advance. This will allow you to test the recipe and decide what needs to be done to make it work perfectly. You will also be able to discover where to shop for the best and freshest ingredients.*

- **Ingredient resources.** *It is always wise to talk to the workers at your local market and ask them questions. How often do they get shipments of salmon? Is the fish farm raised? The more questions you ask, the easier it is to decide what you should buy that particular day.*

the students an opportunity to get acquainted. During the reception, the chef will explain the concept of preparing for a theme dinner party—what should be done before and after the guests arrive.

The next day, after a full continental breakfast, the students meet at 10:00 a.m. at the local village store, Keys to the Kitchen, for their cooking class. The class is broken into two parts: what's to be done before and what's to be done after the guests arrive. During the morning class, students learn relevant techniques for cooking what needs to be prepared the day before the party.

At noon, students take a break to enjoy lunch at any of the fine restaurants in the village. After the break, students return to the kitchen, where they perform the last-minute work needed to be done before the guests arrive. No attempt is made to prepare an entire four-course meal during this short lesson, only the main course. The purpose of the class is to teach students to plan their time so that they are free of cooking chores when it is time to receive guests. After class, students may take afternoon tea at the inn. At the Saturday-evening dinner, students are offered a choice of foods to try, which will include selections from the demonstration class.

The weekend getaway ends on Sunday morning with a continental breakfast.

Meals that have been prepared in the past by students include Grilled Tenderloin of Midwestern Bison on a Horseradish and Cipollini Onion Marmalade with Spring Vegetables, Shiraz Sauce, and Sun Choke Tower; and Ragout of Maine Salmon with Local Seafood Medley and Saffron Champagne Sauce (see recipe).

Class Costs: About $550 per person, which includes classes, lodging (with late checkout), Friday-afternoon English tea, cocktail reception, and full continental breakfasts; $150 per person for nonguests, which includes cooking demonstration and kitchen tour.

Class Frequency: Six to ten classes are scheduled each year in February, March, and November.

Class Length: About four hours on Saturday.

Class Type: Hands-on/demonstration.

Class Size: Two to fourteen students; sometimes up to twenty with back-to-back classes.

Lodging: The twenty-nine-room White Barn Inn, like other Relais & Châteaux member properties, has as its mission to be an ambassador for France's *l'art de vivre*. It achieves this by maintaining a commitment to excellence and a loyal support to the five Cs: courtesy, charm, character, calm, and cuisine.

Ragout of Maine Salmon with Local Seafood Medley and Saffron Champagne Sauce

From *The White Barn Inn Cookbook: A Collection of Recipes* by Jonathan Cartwright

To go with the salmon, Chef Cartwright recommends a mushroom salad (preferably one from his cookbook). Select salad ingredients based on what's fresh and in season. A chardonnay would be his choice for the wine, preferably one with an oak flavor. It would complement both the salad and the main course. Another option would be a fruity and light sauvignon blanc from New Zealand. For dessert he recommends a citrus-flavored sorbet such as blood orange and pink grapefruit.

Ingredients
- 1 cup fruity white wine, such as riesling
- 8 mahogany clams or other medium clams in the shell, scrubbed
- 12 mussels in the shell, scrubbed and debearded if necessary
- 1$1/2$ tablespoons unsalted butter
- 1 shallot, diced
- 1 clove garlic, minced
- Pinch saffron (about 20 threads)
- 1 cup heavy cream
- 1 cup champagne
- Salt and freshly ground pepper
- 1 large celery root, peeled
- 1 large carrot, peeled
- 1 large Yukon Gold potato, peeled
- 1 large beet, peeled
- 1 pound skinless salmon fillet, cut into 1-inch cubes
- 4 diver-harvested scallops

About forty-five minutes away from the port city of Portland and an hour and a half from Boston, it is close enough to important travel hubs to attract guests from all over the world. To make guests feel comfortable, all accommodations have luxurious appointments, which in some rooms include Oriental rugs and antiques.

Amenities: Continental breakfast, newspaper, afternoon tea, port and brandy, lending library, touring bicycles, Molton Brown toiletries, fruit basket, and much more.

1. In a large skillet with a heavy bottom, bring the wine to a boil over medium-high heat. Add the clams and mussels and cover. Cook, shaking the pan occasionally, until the shells open. Discard any clams or mussels with unopened shells. Strain the pan juices through a fine sieve lined with cheesecloth to remove any sand, and reserve.

2. Heat 1 tablespoon of the butter in a medium skillet over low heat and add the shallot, garlic, and saffron. Sauté for 3 minutes, until the shallot is translucent but not browned. Add 1 cup of the reserved pan juices, increase the heat to high, and boil, uncovered, until the mixture is reduced by half. Add the cream and ½ cup of the champagne. Reduce the heat to medium and simmer until the sauce thickens enough to coat the back of a spoon. Add salt and pepper to taste and strain through a fine sieve.

3. Using a mandoline or an Asian vegetable slicer, cut the celery root, carrot, potato, and beet into ribbons 1 inch wide. Heat the remaining butter in a medium sauté pan over medium heat. Add the celery root, carrot, and potato, and cook, turning gently, for 1 or 2 minutes, until tender. Add the beet ribbons and cook for 1 to 2 minutes, turning gently, also until tender. Remove from heat.

4. Season the salmon and scallops with salt and pepper. In a deep skillet or casserole set over medium heat, combine the salmon and scallops with the remaining ½ cup of champagne. Bring to a boil, then reduce the heat to medium and cook for 2 to 3 minutes, until the salmon and scallops are tender, with rare centers.

5. Add the cooked mussels and clams, reserved sauce, and vegetable ribbons to the skillet, stirring gently to combine without breaking up the salmon. Serve immediately in large, warmed soup bowls.

Serves 4.

Extras include luxury spa services, swimming pool, waterfront cottages, and convenient access to the trendy restaurants and shops in the village, a short walk away.
Activities: The inn has a yacht, the *True Blue,* that is available to guests for luncheon cruises, champagne receptions, and private cruises along the coast from late April through October. Other activities available in the area include whale-watching, sailing, walkingin wildlife preserves, touring a Franciscan monastery, shopping, horseback riding, and deep-sea fishing.

 ## Down East Foods

Down-Easters know how to tease the palate with their tasty home cooking. How can they miss? They have fertile lands; oceanfront exposure; in many cases, organic and pristine food products; and, on top of that, cooks who are willing to be boldly creative in the preparation of local foods.

Everyone knows about Maine lobster—from the no-frills lobster dipped in butter to a dressed-up-gourmet dinner with sauces. But how many realize that lobster has even been added to ice cream? Maine-lobster lovers will go to any lengths in order to enjoy their favorite crustacean.

Blueberries are another local product. Nearly 99 percent of the wild blueberries enjoyed in America are produced in Maine. Those wonderful-tasting little berries loaded with healthy antioxidants that are supposed to have the power to fight aging, cancer, and heart disease pop up in different foods, from pies to sauces. Blueberries and other wild berries have become a big business in Maine due to demand. Some health-food devotees eat blueberries daily for their nutritional value.

A Maine delicacy harvested in spring is the fiddlehead (young sprout of an ostrich fern). It is used in pasta dishes, salads, quiches, and more. When lightly salted, boiled for ten minutes, and served with melted butter,

Annually in late winter, the inn hosts the International Guest Chef Series, in which renowned chefs from around the world offer special cooking demonstrations. Each chef also creates a special menu for multiple evenings at the White Barn Inn Restaurant.

For more information contact: The White Barn Inn, 37 Beach Avenue, Kennebunk Beach, ME 04043; (207) 967-2321; www.whitebarninn.com.

fiddleheads have a delicate flavor almost resembling asparagus. Considered a good source of vitamins A and C, this gourmet treasure has one drawback. According to the Centers for Disease Control, a number of food-borne illnesses have been linked to fiddleheads when they're not boiled long enough. Make certain it's been properly cooked before you eat it.

Many people have heard about Whoopie Pie (a chocolate cookie with a gooey center), but how many have tried it? Oprah and Bobby Flay have introduced it to millions of television viewers. Is it good? You'll just have to try it and decide for yourself. They're sold everywhere Down East.

If you have only associated cheese with Wisconsin, you will be happy to learn that it has made its debut Down East. Over seventeen producers have been brought together to form the Maine Cheese Guild, some winning national awards for their artisanal wheels. For information about where local cheese is sold, visit www.mainecheeseguild.org.

Is there more ahead for foodies in Maine? Yes, indeed, there is a cornucopia of meats and vegetables to enjoy, but the most favorite food of all that has put Maine on the map comes from the chilly waters. What makes seafood taste better here than anywhere else is that it's fresh from the ocean—and it's served, garnished with fresh, local ingredients, in one of the most beautiful settings in America: Maine.

MASSACHUSETTS

Kushi Institute
Becket, Massachusetts

*M*an is what he eats, and macrobiotics (a Greek word for "long life") attempts to prove this by focusing on the yin and the yang of healthy dieting and lifestyle. To put it more clearly, macrobiotics is a way of life, a belief that the proper balance of food and activity is the key to a healthy existence.

If not enough vegetables and whole grains (yin) and too much meat and eggs (yang) are eaten, it can cause a dietary imbalance that can change the personality and affect health. But when key body-building foods are properly prepared to preserve their natural nutrients and are regularly consumed, these foods will strengthen the immune system.

Although many healthy people may be traumatized by the thought of considering a macrobiotic diet, others feel just the opposite and embrace it hopefully. The idea of using food as an alternative medicine to strengthen the immune system and fight diseases seems like a miracle solution worth considering to those with an infirmity. Despite the resistance of healthy people who don't want to change their dietary routine, macrobiotics is still gaining a following and slowly winning worldwide credibility.

The primary reason for this is because it is beginning to receive some important public attention. Researchers from Harvard, for example, discovered some years ago in the groups it studied that the cholesterol level in the macrobiotic group was lower than in the group following standard American dietary practices. To add to the credibility of macrobiotics, startling stories have appeared in the media about the healing effects of macrobiotics among patients with degenerative diseases. As a result, major governments (such as the United States and Japan) and organizations from around the

Lectures at Kushi Institute run one-and-a-half hours. PHOTO COURTESY OF KUSHI INSTITUTE

world have given Michio Kushi, founder of the Kushi Institute, awards for his remarkable holistic health-care program. Major publications like the Sunday Globe Magazine, Life Magazine, Paris-Match, *and more have published profiles about him.*

ABOUT THE FACULTY

Influenced by his Japanese mentor, educator George Ohsawa, Michio Kushi (and his late wife, Aveline) became interested in macrobiotics at an early age. Although his graduate education was in international law, he never pursued it as a career and instead founded (with Aveline's assistance) the Kushi Institute in 1978, where he began to train potential leaders with worldwide affiliations to spread macrobiotic education. Over the years, his work has brought him world attention. For the past fifty years, he has dedicated his life to advocating balanced eating, a simple lifestyle, and a positive world outlook as his remedy to contemporary health issues. His writings, which have included several dozen published books on macrobiotics, have advanced this position.

To join the staff, all Kushi Institute faculty members (representing all walks of life) have had to go through a rigorous training program in macrobiotic philosophy and practice, and be personally selected by Michio Kushi to teach at the institute.

PHILOSOPHY

Japanese educator George Ohsawa was the father of the macrobiotic approach to health. In his lifetime, he taught that food was the way to good health, and good health was the way to peace. His thinking was that if a man returned to a whole foods diet, he would enjoy a physical and mental balance, which would in turn lead to a more peaceful personality. This philosophy is behind the Kushi Institute's way to better health. The goal of the program is to teach students the health impact of various types of foods, and how to create satisfying meals that have healing properties that will contribute to improving health, vitality, and well-being.

ABOUT THE CLASSES

For students eager to learn about macrobiotics, the school has a variety of classes in food and exercise. One of its main seminars, offered twice a month, is the Way to Health program, which focuses on the fundamentals of macrobiotic living and eating. This intensive, weeklong program introduces students to food choices that are right for their bodies' needs, techniques and activities that improve and monitor their health, and hands-on cooking classes that focus on the preparation of satisfying and healthy meals.

Weekend workshops, which begin on Friday and end on Sunday, have included ways to build strong immunity by using foods to cleanse and strengthen important organs; the Kushi Institute secrets to preparing eye-appealing, palate-satisfying foods that are right for the body and soul; and learning to make fermented pickles that provide needed enzymes and beneficial microorganisms. Other classes have included topics such as health and healing, breath control, shiatsu chair massages, ginger compresses, and much more.

Class routine is standard. The day begins with gentle stretching exercises, followed by breakfast. A two-and-a-half-hour hands-on/demonstration cooking class is held either in the morning or afternoon, as well as a lecture, which either follows or precedes the cooking class each day. These lectures (including the four in the evening throughout the week) cover such subjects as the benefits of a balanced diet, how to eliminate negative foods from your diet, and ways to become attentive to your own body. Since each teacher is trained to observe individual proclivities (i.e., recognize inner health issues revealed by their outer appearances), students will be taught to identify key signs to serious health concerns.

Class Costs: Classes begin at $220 per person for a weekend class, not including lodging, and can climb to $1,950 per person for the weeklong Way to Health program. (There is a 10 percent program fee discount when paid in full two weeks prior to the start date.) Way to Health includes three meals a day; lodging is additional.

Class Frequency: Classes meet daily, depending on the program.

Class Length: Each cooking class runs two and a half hours; there are usually two per day, depending on the subject. (Each lecture runs one-and-a-half hours.)

Class Type: Some hands-on, mostly demonstration.

Class Size: Up to twenty students per class.

Lodging: The Kushi Institute sits on six hundred scenic acres overlooking the town of North Becket, in the heart of the Berkshire Mountains. The rustic Main House, once the home of Boston banker George E. Armstrong, was built in 1901. The dark-paneled, interior-oak woodwork from northern Belgium lends to the house a country-manor appearance. Way to Health participants normally stay in the unpretentious but comfortable Main House, which is perfect for a rustic getaway. Most rooms have single beds; two have a double.

To support a peaceful and relaxing environment, there are no telephones or TVs in the bedrooms, and cell phones should only vibrate when inside the building.

Amenities: Rooms are reduced to only essential extras.

For more information contact: The Kushi Institute, P.O. Box 7, 198 Leland Road, Becket, MA 01223-0007; (800) 975-8744; www.kushiinstitute.org.

 Miso Soup

This high-protein, all-purpose soup has been an important part of the Japanese diet for centuries. It is usually made with a combination of fermented soybeans, cultured grain, and sea salt that is often used for pickling, sauces, spreads, and salt in addition to soup.

What makes it especially healthy is that it contains enzymes and living microorganisms that help digestion and provide a balance of nutrients (vitamins and some carbohydrates and essential oils). In 1981 the Japanese National Cancer Center documented reports that people who ate miso soup daily had a lower rate of cancer and heart disease than those who didn't.

The most popular types of miso are mugi miso, which is made from barley; hatcho miso, which is made from 100 percent soybean and used for pickling, making condiments, and soup; and genmai miso, which is made from light brown rice and served frequently during the summer months.

When purchasing miso soup from your local store, you should be certain that it is organic and contains no chemicals or additives. It is important that it also hasn't been pasteurized, because this can reduce the enzymes and bacteria that are helpful at aiding digestion.

Miso soup PHOTO COURTESY OF KUSHI INSTITUTE

Miso Soup

Compliments of the Kushi Institute

This simple miso soup recipe takes about fifteen minutes to prepare. Although the soup can be used as a base for other foods, you will probably prefer to use it as prepared. All the ingredients may be purchased at your local health food store.

Ingredients
- 4-inch strip dried wakame sea vegetable
- 3 cups high-quality water
- 1 small onion, peeled
- $^1/_4$ block extra-firm tofu, cut into 8 cubes
- 2 to 3 teaspoons unpasteurized, naturally fermented barley miso paste
- 1-inch piece scallion greens, sliced thinly on the diagonal

1. Place the wakame in a small bowl and cover with $^1/_2$ cup of cold water to soften. Set aside.
2. Bring the remaining $2^1/_2$ cups of water to a boil in a pot. While waiting for the water to boil, slice the onion in half lengthwise; cut each half lengthwise into very thin half-moons. The thinner they are sliced, the faster they cook.
3. When the water is boiling, put the onions into the pot and boil uncovered for 3 minutes over a high heat.
4. Remove the wakame from the water and slice into $^1/_2$-inch strips. (Do not discard the water.) Add the wakame, the water it was soaked in, and the tofu to the pot. When the water returns to a boil, continue to cook for 2 more minutes over a high heat.
5. Turn the heat down to the lowest setting, bringing the soup to a low simmer. (If necessary to get a simmer, place a flame diffuser under the pot.)
6. Put 2 teaspoons of miso paste in the wakame soaking bowl and dilute by slowly adding simmering soup broth a little at a time, mixing and stirring until the paste liquefies. After the paste has liquefied, pour the mix back into the pot and stir.
7. Taste and add more miso if you like. The soup should not have a strong or salty miso flavor. Let the soup simmer for 2 more minutes.
8. Put 4 cubes of tofu into each serving bowl and ladle in soup. Top with scallion garnish and serve.

Serves 2.

Captain Freeman Inn
Brewster, Massachusetts

A cooking class at Captain Freeman Inn is like sailing on the Mediterranean Sea. At each port of call, your pots and pans will be filled with the distinctive foods and spices of the area, which you will turn into memorable culinary dishes. There will be assorted appetizers (Serrano ham and manchego cheese in tapas from Spain), stews (the seductive blend of meat and spices in tagines *from Morocco), casseroles (layered meat, spices, and roasted eggplant in moussakas from Greece), and desserts (pears poached in brandy from Italy or the creamy Black Cherry Clafoutis cake from France). For one day, depending on which program you book, you will find yourself docked on the culinary shores of one of these sunny, romantic Mediterranean countries—without ever leaving the States.*

Captain Freeman Inn is located in the historic village of Brewster, Cape Cod, in an 1866 sea captain's house—a burly Victorian mansion, immaculately maintained—a short stroll from Cape Cod Bay. Furnished with four-poster beds and antiques and some of Captain Freeman's nineteenth-century personal possessions, it has all the right touches of yesterday to make it a pleasant culinary escape from the worries of today.

ABOUT THE INSTRUCTOR

The hands-on cooking classes at Captain Freeman Inn are taught by Norma Jean Anderson, who has been running her own Cape Cod catering business, On-Site Catering, for more than a decade. To each of her meals, whether as a caterer or a teacher, she brings the fresh and uncomplicated ethnic flavors that she loves dearly—especially those from eastern Mediterranean countries. It was under the supervision of the former chef-owner of the Captain Freeman that Norma Jean learned the art of teaching cooking.

The Captain Freeman Inn is a short stroll from Cape Cod Bay.
PHOTO COURTESY OF THE CAPTAIN FREEMAN INN

ABOUT THE CLASSES

Small groups of students work together to prepare a preplanned menu with a specific theme. Before beginning work in the kitchen, students will discuss the flavors, ingredients, and history of the food that they will be preparing. Each student has the choice of observing or participating in the cooking. Midway through preparation there is a brief tea break, then more meal prepping and finally a regional wine tasting before the evening meal. A weekend package includes two nights of lodging, breakfasts, class, and a four-course, student-prepared dinner. It's open to local residents and guests alike.

Class Costs: Weekend package rate is $600 to $700 per couple, depending on room; single occupancy $485 to $585. Nonguest price is $130 for Saturday class and dinner.
Class Frequency: Six classes are scheduled from January through May.
Class Length: Classes run seven hours, beginning at 2:00 p.m.
Class Type: Demonstration/hands-on.
Class Size: Maximum eighteen students per class; minimum four.
For more information contact: Captain Freeman Inn, 15 Breakwater Road, Brewster (Cape Cod), MA 02631; (508) 896-7481; www.captainfreemaninn.com.

Wheatleigh
Lenox, Massachusetts

uilt in 1893 by New York financier Henry H. Cook for his daughter, the then-soon-to-become wife of Spanish count, Carlos de Heredia, Wheatleigh is one of those gilded palaces that was created for the occasional pleasure of the mighty and rich. Today it is a handsome nineteen-room boutique hotel that has an ambience and style suited to such a magnificent heritage "cottage." Visitors to this replica of a sixteenth-century Florentine palazzo are received like members of America's elite. From the moment they step foot on the twenty-two-acre property, they will experience twenty-first-century luxury in a nineteenth-century setting.

Food at Wheatleigh is as pleasing to the palate as the property is to the eye. Each dish is light and made without excessive cream and butter; it is fresh food prepared simply, without any attempt made to disguise the main ingredient. This is to-the-point cuisine, with emphasis on quality and taste, and a strong classic French influence, modernized with hints of the European and American to give it a new dimension, like the roasted turbot cassoulet or the chef's ever-popular Cipollini Onion Soup (see recipe).

Students eager to learn to prepare cuisine in the Wheatleigh style may want to sign up for one of Chef Jeffrey Thompson's cooking classes during their visit and turn their vacation into a gourmet getaway.

ABOUT THE CHEF

Chef Jeffrey began cooking in the kitchen of a family friend at the age of sixteen. What began as a casual interest turned into a passion, triggered by his determination to become good at what he prepared. His struggle to learn was slow, first as an apprentice at the Broadmoor Hotel (Colorado) and later as sous chef at the Sun Mountain Lodge (Washington), where he was allowed to test his ideas freely. His two years at the Sun Mountain Lodge were followed by one year as sous chef at the Williams-

This suite at Wheatleigh offers a view of the Berkshire Mountains.
PHOTO COURTESY OF JOE DAVID

burg Inn (Virginia). There he met Chef J. Bryce Whittlesey. Together the two men moved on to Wheatleigh in 2002, where today Chef Jeffrey runs the kitchen. Chef Jeffrey's successful progression from job to job and up the ladder to recognition at Wheatleigh is the result of hard work and a driving obsession to devise new twists on classic creations.

PHILOSOPHY

Chef Jeffrey's goal is to teach students techniques that they can use at home to create spectacular meals at a reasonable cost. More importantly, he wants to bring joy into the kitchen and show students how to make uncomplicated foods that are tasty and appealing to the eye.

Cipollini Onion Soup

Courtesy of Wheatleigh

This is Chef Jeffrey Thompson's signature recipe, a modern version of the classic French onion soup. To give it elegance and a more rounded taste and texture, he uses cipollini onions, which have a mild, pleasantly sweet flavor. For the base, he prefers a chicken stock instead of beef, which doesn't overwhelm the flavor of the onions. In lieu of cream, he prefers to use fat-free milk, which makes the soup lighter and easier to froth with a hand blender. Lastly, the lemon juice introduces a touch of acidity, which gives the soup a pleasant balance of flavors.

This soup can be prepared and served in the fall, winter, or early spring as a starter, as part of a meal, or as a primary dish for lunch. A good accompaniment would be a spinach salad with haricots verts, duck confit, and mustard vinaigrette.

Ingredients
- $^1/_4$ cup canola oil
- 8 medium-size cipollini onions, peeled and sliced
- Salt and white pepper
- 2 sprigs thyme
- 2 bay leaves
- $1^1/_2$ ounces white wine
- 1 quart chicken stock
- 1 cup fat-free milk
- Lemon juice (optional)

1. In a heavy-bottomed pan (like a rondeau) over medium heat, caramelize the onions in canola oil. Season with salt and pepper and cook until golden brown.
2. Add thyme and bay leaves; deglaze with white wine and reduce to *au sec* (until it is dry).
3. Add stock and simmer for 10 to 15 minutes.
4. Add milk and puree with a hand blender. Season with salt and pepper to taste. If the soup needs a little acidity, add some lemon juice.
5. Garnish the soup with slices of baguette that have been covered with Gruyère, lightly sprinkled with cayenne pepper, and toasted.

Serves 4–6.

ABOUT THE CLASSES

Two types of classes are offered: a fixed lesson made up of foods that Chef Jeffrey is particularly interested in teaching, and a private class that includes recipes the students want to learn. In each class, Chef Jeffrey and the students work together to prepare each recipe from start to finish. The best in-season ingredients that produce the best taste are used (which may not necessarily include organic foods).

Classes are offered during the fall, winter, and spring, and all fixed programs have themes (such as creating homemade pasta, entertaining for brunch, or planning hearty fall/winter meals). In a seasonal salad class, for example, the chef will teach students to use innovative combinations and techniques, including flavored oils and vinegars, and hot or cold ingredients, for starters or meals. In a cheese class, students will learn how to use cheese as the main ingredient of a meal.

In the private classes, the students determine what they want to learn—Tuscan, French stews, whatever. The chef will then prepare a proposal and work out the details with the students. All such private classes will need at least fourteen days' advance notification. A gourmet getaway package may be created around the private classes, either during the week (arrival on Tuesday, class on Wednesday, and departure on Thursday) or on the weekend (arrival on Friday, class on Saturday, and departure on Sunday).

Other classes, offered upon request, include wine and champagne classes, in which Wheatleigh's sommelier will take students on an around-the-world voyage that will highlight some popular wines and champagnes, and classes for children (between the ages of six and fourteen), primarily in making pastries like croissants or cinnamon Danish.

Class Costs: $125 per student, which includes a French breakfast, lunch, and non-alcoholic beverage; personalized chef jacket is extra ($45). Wine and champagne classes are $125; children's classes are $25 (personalized chef jacket is $45). The package rate for two people, including two nights of lodging, runs $1,760 to $4,000.

Timeless Good Taste

*L*ike so many great houses in the Berkshires, Wheatleigh came to life during the Gilded Age of American excess, when industrialists, financiers, and railroad tycoons created European-style palaces, amusingly called "cottages," to use briefly during the summer season to entertain. It was an era of conspicuous consumption, first-generation wealth burned ceremoniously at the altar of vanity.

Although income tax has wreaked havoc on the vast financial empires of the nineteenth century that made this extravagance possible, time hasn't changed the Berkshires. Many of the great properties still linger in or near Lenox to remind visitors of its grand past—like the Mount Estate and Gardens (www.edithwharton.org), for example, built by novelist Edith Wharton, or Ventford Hall (www.gildedage.org), built by Sarah and George Morgan. (Both are open to visitors.)

Beyond touring the "cottages," Lenox offers a broad choice of activities year-round, including fine dining, art shows, health spas, outdoor concerts, snow sports, ballooning, hiking, boating, antiques shopping, and more. A few special places to visit are:

The Norman Rockwell Museum, Stockbridge; www.nrm.org. This museum houses the largest selection of original Rockwell art, especially some of the most memorable from Saturday Evening Post covers.

Tanglewood, a few minutes by foot from Wheatleigh; www.tanglewood.org. This is the summer home of the Boston Symphony Orchestra, and classical, popular, and jazz concerts are performed here regularly during the season.

Shakespeare & Company, www.shakespeare.org. For many decades they have performed Shakespearean plays and provocative new works by leading or new talents.

Class Frequency: Two fixed classes are held during the weekdays during off-season; private weekend or weekday classes are arranged to fit the chef's schedule.

Class Length: Classes begin at 9:00 a.m. and end at 2:00 p.m.; wine and champagne classes are from 4:00 to 6:00 p.m.; children's classes are from 2:00 to 4:00 p.m. during the week.

Class Type: Hands-on.

Class Size: Maximum class size is six; minimum is two.

Lodging: The rooms have all the contemporary touches needed to make guests comfortable (Bang & Olufsen televisions, blackout curtains, huge English bathtubs), plus extra amenities like chocolate chip cookies, fresh flowers, and twenty-four-hour room service.

Amenities: Wireless Internet, fitness center, helicopter access, swimming pool, and more.

For more information contact: Wheatleigh, Hawthorn Road, Lenox, MA 01240; (413) 637-0610; www.wheatleigh.com.

New Hampshire

The Balsams Grand Resort Hotel
Dixville Notch, New Hampshire

Surrounded by the rugged White Mountains of New Hampshire, the Balsams rests on an expanse of land almost equal to the size of Manhattan. In this peaceful setting, accessible only through a narrow gorge, the well-manicured 202-room resort, with its columned porches, dormers, and four-story turret, sits alone, comfortably dominating the valley.

Many visitors think of this alpinelike hideaway, which is only a few miles from Canada, as the Greenbrier (see the Southeast section) of New England, a lingering remnant of old-world hospitality. But what ties the two resorts together is more noteworthy than gracious old-world style. Like the Greenbrier, this four-star resort also offers a professional culinary program for aspiring cooks. In 2007 its food, ranked among the best in the world, received a perfect rating from Condé Nast Traveler *magazine.*

Aspiring cooks interested in refining their cooking skills will have the opportunity to acquaint themselves with some of the special cooking techniques and recipes that make such fine dining possible. Each year resort guests may select from four different types of culinary programs and unravel the mysteries of preparing fine food. Heading the recreational and professional programs at the Balsams is Chef Steve Learned.

ABOUT THE CHEF

A second-generation Balsams employee who grew up in the hotel's kitchen, Chef Learned graduated from the Culinary Institute of America and received a bachelors degree in hospitality management from Florida National University. He was executive chef at the Park Terrace Hotel

(Washington, D.C.), the Doubletree Hotel (Tyson's Corner, Virginia), and the Gibson's American Grill (Indianapolis, Indiana) before returning to the Balsams in 1998. Currently he is the resort's chef de cuisine and president of the culinary school.

PHILOSOPHY

The recipes in each class are chosen to highlight important culinary techniques that will be helpful to home cooks. Each class is designed to provide a solid grasp of some important culinary fundamentals (creating sauces, sautéing, braising, ways to simplify cooking, shortcuts without sacrificing quality, organizational skills needed for quick food preparation, and more). It is the belief that once these basics are mastered, students can apply this knowledge not only to solving unexpected cooking problems, but also to creating new flavors, hopefully as tasty and as innovative as those at the Balsams.

The Balsams are surrounded by mountains in a small valley, accessible only through a narrow gorge. PHOTO COURTESY OF JOE DAVID

ABOUT THE CLASSES

There are four programs available to recreational cooks throughout the year.

For about six or seven weekends per year from October through November, the resort has a visiting chef series. The subject and presen-

---

Pan Seared Duck Breast with Cherry Jus Lie

Compliments of Chef Steve Learned, the Balsams Grand Resort Hotel

The following recipe may be served with sautéed spinach and baby carrots, and paired with a Beaujolais Villages or a light Rhône Valley red.

Tip: The duck should be as cold as possible before you attempt to score it. The chef recommends placing it in the freezer for fifteen to twenty minutes if necessary. This will firm the fat and make it and the breast easier to score. This tip also works well when trying to cut anything fatty, such as bacon or salt pork

Ingredients
- 4 6-ounce boneless duck breasts with skin
- Kosher salt, fresh ground black pepper, and ground clove to taste

1. Preheat the oven to 350°F. Place a heavy-bottomed oven-proof skillet over medium-high heat until hot.
2. Score the skin of the duck in a diamond pattern. Cut through the skin and fat without cutting the flesh. This requires a very sharp boning or paring knife and some practice. Scoring the skin allows the fat to render more easily.
3. Season both sides of the duck with salt, pepper, and ground clove. Lay skin side down in the heated skillet and reduce the heat to medium.
4. Cook the duck until most of the fat has been released. This may mean adjusting the heat, depending on your stove, so most of the fat melts away. Do not allow the skin to become too dark.
5. Turn the duck over and immediately place the pan in the oven. Roast to an internal temperature of 145°F.
6. Remove the duck from the pan and let it rest on a cutting board for at least five minutes before slicing. (This allows the natural juices to stay in the duck and not run all over the cutting board.) Slice and top each breast with Cherry Jus Lie.

Serves 4.

---

tation of the classes are usually determined by the visiting chef. Chefs selected for participation in the series are often shining culinary stars, established in his or her particular community, or on-the-rise culinary alumni of the Balsams's three-year professional cooking program. Students taking these weekend classes receive two nights of lodging, all meals,

Cherry Jus Lie

Ingredients
- 1/4 teaspoon vegetable oil
- 2 tablespoons chopped celery (medium chop)
- 2 tablespoons chopped carrot (medium chop)
- 2 tablespoons chopped onion (medium chop)
- 1 garlic clove, minced
- 2 tablespoons balsamic vinegar
- 2 tablespoons maple syrup
- 2 cups chicken broth
- 1/4 cup roughly chopped dried cherries
- Salt and black pepper to taste (optional)
- Cornstarch (optional)
- 1 tablespoon softened butter

1. In a hot pan, add oil. When the oil is heated, add the mirepoix (celery, carrot, and onion) and caramelize. .
2. Add garlic and cook briefly. Deglaze with the vinegar, then add the maple syrup and broth. Bring to a simmer and cook for 10 minutes.
3. Strain the sauce, then add the cherries and return to heat. Simmer until proper flavor is reached. Season with salt and black pepper, if desired. If necessary, thicken with a little cornstarch dissolved in water.
4. Whisk in the butter, making sure not to boil the sauce once the butter is whisked in. Serve immediately over the sliced duck breasts.

and a morning and afternoon demonstration class with some hands-on experience. Topics that have been taught in the past include modern New England cuisine, regional Italian, and Polynesian. The structure for the getaway package is basic: wine and cheese reception on Friday, two demonstrations on Saturday, and a brunch on Sunday before departing. Free time is spent enjoying the resort's many activities.

On the last Wednesday in January, the resort has a culinary symposium in which four or five prominent chefs provide a series of cooking demonstrations and lectures (8:30 a.m. to 5:00 p.m.; lunch is included). This intensive culinary demonstration usually appeals to advanced home cooks. Some of the subjects covered include modern interpretations of classic French cuisine, traditional New England seafood dishes, current trends in plated desserts, and Italian extra virgin olive oil tastings. These symposiums are popular and have attracted crowds of up to two hundred people. The getaway package for the symposium is similar to the visiting chef series, except it is offered midweek.

During the first week of February and March, the resort offers an intensive Taste of the Balsams cooking program for guests. The program begins on Tuesday with a wine-and-cheese reception, where students are introduced to their instructors and classmates. It is followed by classes on both Wednesday and Thursday. At the end of each class, participants dine on the food they have prepared, paired with wine chosen by the sommelier. Each guest is encouraged to invite a friend for lunch. After the classes, participants are free to enjoy everything the resort has to offer.

Finally, during the summer season, two demonstration culinary classes are conducted each week. Each demonstration is offered in a public room at the resort, and they run about an hour and a half. Past demonstrations have included cake decorating, hot and cold hors d'oeuvres, and classic French sauces. How they are conducted or what is taught is left to the discretion of each chef.

Class Cost: Visiting chef series: $139 per night per person (includes wine-and-cheese reception with visiting chef, lodging, cooking demonstration, five-course dinner, jazz breakfast, and access to all resort activities); culinary symposium: $45 per person (includes lunch and demonstrations; lodging is additional); Taste of the Balsams: $350 per person (includes wine-and-cheese reception, classes, and two lunches; lodging is additional); demonstration classes: complimentary with hotel stay (rates vary).

Class Frequency: Visiting chef series: six or seven weekends per year; culinary symposium: the last Wednesday in January; Taste of the Balsams: the first week of February and March; demonstration classes: two demonstrations per week in July and August.

Class Length: Visiting chef series: about five hours; culinary symposium: eight hours; Taste of the Balsams: about five hours each day for two days; demonstration classes: one-and-a-half hours.

Class Type: Demonstration/hands-on.

Class Size: Visiting chef series: no limitation; culinary symposium: no limitation; Taste of the Balsams: eight maximum and four minimum students; demonstration classes: no limitation.

Lodging: The hotel is listed on the National Register of Historic Places. The oldest section, what was once the twenty-five-room Dix House, was opened in 1866 as an inn, and a more recent addition, the Hampshire House, was opened in 1918. The hotel has many public rooms for guests to enjoy, including a scenic lobby, sunroom, captain's study, and the Ballot Room. All of the spacious rooms and suites have a mountain or lakeside view, and all are decorated with period furniture.

Activities: The Balsams offers winter sports (Nordic and alpine skiing, snowshoeing, ice skating, horse-drawn sleigh rides) and, in the summer, swimming, golfing, hiking, tennis, mountain biking, fly fishing, and more. There are also staff-supervised children's activities. Golfers enjoy the eighteen-hole panorama championship golf course designed by Donald Ross, challenging with its deceptively wide fairways and tiny greens.

For more information contact: The Balsams Grand Resort Hotel, 1000 Cold Springs Road, Dixville Notch, NH 03576; (603) 255-3400; www.thebalsams.com.

A Taste of the Mountains
Cooking School at Bernerhof Inn
Glen, New Hampshire

From the outside, the Bernerhof is an overbuilt, three-level Bavarian inn with too many fussy touches—gables, dormers, turrets, and a wraparound porch. But inside, it is as welcoming and cozy as an alpine chalet during a blizzard.

Constructed in the 1880s in the shadow of Mount Washington, the inn has been broken into comfortable-size rooms decorated with sensible old-world furnishings. In this setting, usually twice a year, but sometimes more frequently, classes are held for students eager to learn some German-Swiss recipes.

ABOUT THE CHEFS

The two chefs who oversee the cooking classes are Gary Bunnel (who prepares the savory dishes) and Steve James (who prepares the pastries). Although Chef Gary hasn't had any formal culinary training, most of what he knows he learned on the job, working in respected kitchens in the Mount Washington Valley area (as sous chef for both the Christmas Farm Inn and Spa in Jackson and Bellini's Ristorante Italiano in North Conway) for a total of fifteen years. At the Bernerhof, where he has been the head chef since 2005, he prepares all the popular old-world specialties (like fondue, Wiener schnitzel, delice de Gruyère, and raclette) and his personal favorites (like veal Oscar, roast duck, and confit). One of Chef Gary's strengths, mastered when he was a line chef at the Lobster Pot in Florida, is his stock, which he gives special attention, sometimes taking as long as four days to prepare it.

Chef Steve, a graduate of Johnson & Wales College of Culinary Arts, has been the guest chef for the cooking school for almost twenty years. He was the executive pastry chef at the Balsams, in Dixville Notch, New Hampshire, for twenty years, and during that time he received numerous

At the Bernerhof Inn students learn how to prepare German-Swiss recipes.
PHOTO COURTESY OF JOE DAVID

awards and gold medals for his pastries and pastry displays. Chef Steve is presently executive chef for the Galley Hatch family of restaurants and the managing partner of Popovers on the Square in historic downtown Portsmouth.

PHILOSOPHY

The cooking program primarily strives to provide students with an enjoyable weekend preparing German-Swiss foods and mastering the tricks and shortcuts to cooking. But most importantly, students will learn to experiment and approach cooking with creativity by knowing when to improvise and adjust a recipe to their personal tastes.

ABOUT THE CLASSES

Cooking classes have been offered at the Bernerhof Inn since 1985, when barbecue king and author Steven Raichlen first launched A Taste of the Mountains Cooking School while executive chef at the inn. With a few tweaks here and there, George and June Phillips, the current inn owners, have made the program more adaptable to their needs without essentially changing it.

 Enjoying Fondue

It is widely believed that cheese fondue originated in Switzerland, and beef fondue (fondue bourguignonne) in France. In the case of the former, making fondue was a practical way to use hardened cheeses and dried breads in the winter months when fresh foods were depleted. The origin of fondue bourguignonne, on the other hand, is more vague. It is believed that it originated in France as an efficient way to provide field workers with a quick meal (beef dipped in hot oils) while harvesting the crops.

For a few decades, beginning in the fifties, fondue parties were quite the rage in the United States. But like all trends, it peaked and faded. In recent years it has once again come into vogue as a pleasant and practical way to entertain. Because it requires the use of a communal pot, certain courtesies are expected around the dinner table. Here are a few tips on eating and preparing fondue courtesy of the Bernerhof Inn.

Cheese Fondue Tips

- *Don't allow your mouth to touch the fork that goes into the communal bowl.*
- *Whenever you dip bread or vegetables into a fondue pot, stir in a figure eight. This keeps the cheese smoothly blended and evenly heated.*
- *Before removing dipped bread from the pot, allow the excess cheese to drip back into the pot.*

Classes are offered twice a year, in November and May, and occasionally four times a year if demand warrants it. The class begins on a Friday at about 6:00 p.m. with welcoming cocktails. A hearty four-course fondue dinner with wine tasting and food demonstrations follows. The first course is a cheese fondue (see recipe), followed by a tableside Caesar salad, a surf-and-turf fondue, and a chocolate sauce fondue with fresh fruit.

- *The crust formed at the base of the pot should be peeled off carefully and shared with others at the end of the meal. This is considered a delicacy.*
- *If anyone loses bread (or a vegetable) in the pot, they must be punished. Tradition is that the man must buy drinks or another pot of fondue, and the woman must kiss the man nearest her. The host/hostess may make up any punishment he/she chooses to suit party plans; whatever it is, though, the guests should be told in advance.*
- *For best results, melt the fondue on the stove and transfer it afterward to a communal fondue pot, where it should be kept warm at a low temperature. You don't want the cheese to become rubbery.*
- *If you want to be creative, only mix cheeses of the same family. For example, Parmesan and Romano, or Camembert, Brie, Muenster, and Bel Paese.*
- *If the fondue becomes too thick, add more wine; if it becomes too thin, add more cheese.*

Beef Fondue Tips

- *The fork should completely penetrate the bite-size cuts of meat. Its tips should protrude through the meat. This will prevent the meat from sticking while it rests in the pot, boiling in the oil.*
- *Before you eat the meat, take it off the fondue fork so you can cut it up on your plate. Enjoy it with sauces such as chutney, horseradish, and mustard.*
- *To reduce fat, you may cook the beef in boiling broth instead of oil.*

Bernerhof Cheese Fondue

Compliments of the Bernerhof Inn

Ingredients
- Garlic-infused oil
- 4 ounces Gruyère cheese, shredded
- 4 ounces Emmental cheese, shredded
- $1/4$ teaspoon nutmeg
- 2 tablespoons flour
- 1 cup white wine (preferably a good sauvignon blanc, Riesling, or fendant)
- 1 tablespoon kirsch brandy
- Salt and pepper

1. Rub pot with oil and melt cheese. Add remaining ingredients. Stir until warm and smooth. Don't allow to bubble or boil.
2. Serve with baked French bread cut into bite-size chunks for dipping. Extras for dipping may include apples, and blanched vegetables like broccoli, baby carrots, and red pepper chunks.

Serves 4.

The hands-on portion of the class is from 9:00 a.m. to noon on Saturday, starting after a light breakfast. First students are introduced to basic safety tips and cooking techniques, and then they break into groups to prepare a four-course meal under the guidance of Chef Gary. From 2:00 to 6:00 p.m., the students have a break and may visit North Conway (about seven miles away) or just walk off a few calories in the sleepy community of Glen. At 6:00, Chef Steve takes over and introduces students to pastry making, which may include anything from stretching strudel dough to baking German bread. The weekend ends with students preparing an elegant brunch on Sunday.

The working kitchen, where classes are taught, isn't particularly large, but the chefs manage to make it work. The key to this is in the preplanning, but also important are the chefs' creative spontaneity and lack of rigidity. Students working with chefs Gary and Steve will acquaint themselves with their looseness of style, which hopefully will encourage them to expand their culinary personality and overcome any hesitation to be creative in the kitchen.

Class Costs: From $299 to $459 per person, including classes, two nights' lodging, meals, welcoming cocktail party, and wine pairing.

Class Frequency: Twice a year in November and May.

Class Length: Three days of hands-on cooking and demonstrations, with the average class running about two to three hours.

Class Type: Hands-on and demonstration.

Class Size: Minimum eight students, maximum twelve.

Lodging: The inn offers nine guest rooms, varying in size from a standard bedroom to two-room suites. All have private baths and king or queen beds; some even have two-person Jacuzzi spa tubs. Each room has its own personality and is furnished with period furniture, including brass, four-poster, or canopy beds, and fireplaces. The inn's sister property, the Red Apple Inn, which is connected to the main inn by a wooded path, is not as expensive as the main house, and it offers seventeen rooms and traditional motel-style furnishings.

Amenities: All rooms have color cable TVs, telephone with free local dialing, and more.

For more information contact: The Bernerhof Inn, P.O. Box 240, New Hampshire Highway 302, Glen, NH 03838; (603) 383-9132; www.bernerhofinn.com.

White Mountain Cooking School at the Snowvillage Inn

Snowville, New Hampshire

Snowvillage Inn sits humbly in a mountain clearing, a mix of New England and Swiss good taste, surrounded by nature in all its raw beauty. In this glorious sanctuary of sky, trees, and mountains, the rolling White Mountains stretch ahead unendingly. It is easy to experience the sheer majesty and strength of nature here——and feel insignificant in its presence.

At this serene hideaway, frazzled nerves and exhausted bodies rejuvenate, and weary expressions lift into easy smiles. Modern conveniences like BlackBerrys and laptops are set aside, forgotten, in the face of the surrounding beauty.

Amid this natural splendor, Snowvillage offers a weekend getaway cooking program designed for lovers of fine cuisine. The classes are all conducted by the inn's executive chef, Matthew Mitchell. Tasty examples of his subtle and simple cooking style are his Grilled Shark with Melon Barbecue Sauce (see recipe) and pan-seared chicken breast stuffed with cranberries and apples, two of his favorite recipes. He insists on using the freshest foods, which he brings to life with a gentle mix of seasoning. His meals are then slowly cooked, allowing the ingredients' flavor to expand .

 ## New Hampshire Pleasures

East-central New Hampshire has something for everyone. For theater lovers, for example, there's the oldest professional summer theater in the United States, the Barnstormers Theatre in Tamworth (www.barnstormers theatre.org).

Children or children at heart will love the Story Land Park in Glen (www.storylandnh.com). The thirty-five-acre fantasy theme park offers about twenty-one rides (such as a pirate ship and a pumpkin coach) and a choice of live shows for children to participate in (such as launching a rocket to the moon or growing their own garden), as well as many other activities.

The Attitash alpine slide in Bartlett (www.attitash.com/alpineslide .html), a mile-long mountain slide, provides sleigh riders spectacular thrills and vistas as they travel at controlled speeds down the mountain. Other activities in Attitash include horseback riding, mountain biking, golfing, hiking, and skiing. (For more information visit www.attitash.com.)

Train rides are another favorite pastime, and area visitors have a choice of three types. One is aboard the oldest mountain-climbing, smoke-puffing

ABOUT THE CHEF

A graduate of the Culinary Institute of America in New York, Chef Matt has worked in several of America's prominent hotel restaurants, where he has prepared meals for Presidents George H. W. Bush and George W. Bush, as well as for celebrities like Julia Child, Denzel Washington, Bruce Willis, and Demi Moore. In 2006, at the age of twenty-eight, he became the third-youngest certified executive chef in the United States, a title that is bestowed only on candidates with appropriate culinary education, several years of management experience, and an acceptable American Culinary Federation–approved professional examination score.

cog train (an engine with a center cogwheel) in the world, which can be boarded in Mount Washington. Built in 1866, the train took its maiden voyage to the peak of Mount Washington in 1869. Today it travels to the top from April to October on some of the steepest railway tracks anywhere to a 6,288-foot-high summit. On a clear day, you can see the ocean, Quebec, and four states. (For more information visit www.thecog.com.)

The second train ride, Notch Train Service (www.conwayscenic.com) also has vintage cars, which are pulled by diesel or steam-engine locomotives. It travels past cascading streams, magnificent mountain vistas, and steep ravines on a five-hour round-trip from North Conway to Crawford Depot or a five-and-a-half-hour round-trip to Fabyan Station, which is located in Bretton Wood.

Lastly, the Valley Train service (www.conaysscenic.com) offers a fifty-five-minute round-trip past woodlands and fields from North Conway to Conway, or a nearly two-hour round-trip to Bartlett. A vintage 1898 Gertrude Emma observation car (restored to its original first-class look with shiny mahogany woodwork) is attached to all Valley Trains, and meal reservations can be made for the climate-controlled dining car Chocorua.

Grilled Shark with Melon Barbecue Sauce

Compliments of Executive Chef Matthew Mitchell

This tasty barbecue shark entree goes well with an udon noodle cake or wild rice and fresh spring vegetables, and it pairs well with Rock Rabbit Sauvignon Blanc.

Chef Matt recommends that you always use a variety of ripe melons for the best flavor, that you grill the shark slowly over medium heat, and that you don't allow the flame to be too high when preparing the barbecue sauce (the sugars in the melon will caramelize).

Grilled Shark

Ingredients
- 4 pieces black tip shark, seasoned to taste with kosher salt and white pepper

  Grill over a medium open flame until thoroughly cooked. Serve with Melon Barbecue Sauce.

ABOUT THE COOKING PROGRAM

The program is designed to be a relaxing and informative experience that will put fun into cooking. It appeals to people who enjoy working with food and who want to spend a vacation in the kitchen. No attempt is made to turn anyone into a great cook. Chef Matt only wants students to learn to prepare foods tastefully and simply, and to serve them attractively, using newly acquired skills and techniques.

Classes are offered monthly from September to June; sometimes a few extra classes are held during the year. The weekend program begins around 5:00 p.m. on Friday with a wine-and-cheese reception/orientation class. During the orientation, guests swap funny stories about "mistakes" in the kitchen after the innkeepers provide a brief history of Snowville, the inn, and some of the well-known guests (such as Teddy Roosevelt and Helen Keller) who stayed in the house before it became an inn in 1948.

Melon Barbecue Sauce

Ingredients
- 3 assorted melons (cantaloupe, honeydew, papaya)
- $^{1}/_{2}$ cup chicken stock
- 4 tablespoons cornstarch
- 2 tablespoons oyster sauce
- 1 tablespoon molasses

1. Peel and seed melons, and cut them into quarters. Place in a medium-size pot with chicken stock and boil for 30 minutes.
2. Strain the melons, reserving the liquid. In a blender, blend the melons together. Mix a little of the reserved liquid with the cornstarch to form a paste. Mix the paste with the remaining liquid and heat until thick and bubbly. Add the blended melons.
3. Add oyster sauce and molasses. Cool and set aside.

Serves 4.

Saturday and Sunday classes begin after breakfast, at 10:00 a.m., and end with lunch, at about 1:00 p.m. Each of the weekend classes gives students hands-on experience and provides them with important cooking techniques relevant to what they are preparing. All classes are small, and students get individual attention. Included in the price for the weekend are lodging, two breakfasts, two luncheons, and one four-course dinner. All classes have themes (such as Tuscan, Caribbean, vegetarian cooking, and more).

For candy lovers there is a special class in December, in which students will exclusively prepare cookies, candies, and other tasty sweets. During the three-night program, students will enjoy a cookie and candy tour and visit sixteen nearby country inns, decorated for the holidays.

Class Costs: Weekend package begins at $446 per person, double occupancy, and $586 per person for single occupancy. Nonparticipating companions start at $346 per person. Prices include the wine and cheese reception, cooking classes, meals, and lodging.

Class Frequency: One weekend each month, sometimes several more, from September to June.

Class Length: About three hours each day.

Class Type: Primarily hands-on, with some demonstration.

Class Size: Maximum usually eight students per class; minimum four.

Lodging: The eighteen-room inn, a cozy turn-of-the-twentieth-century house with updated facilities, is within easy reach of Boston and New York. Two additional buildings, which belong to the inn, circle the driveway only footsteps away from the main house. Each room, decorated in soothing matching colors and period furniture with fluffy comforters and quilts, has a private bathroom, and some have fireplaces and magnificent views of the mountains.

For more information contact: Snowvillage Inn, 136 Stewart Road, Snowville, NH (physical address); P.O. Box 180, North Conway, NH 03860 (mailing address); (603) 447-2818; www.snowvillageinn.com.

NEW YORK

❧

Culinary Institute of America
Hyde Park, New York

Traditionally, to reach the top in the culinary world, a chef would have to spend years learning as an apprentice, sweating in kitchens where, if lucky, he or she would develop a refreshingly unique or elegantly traditional food style. In recent years, that has changed. Aspiring chefs can now hasten professional development by seeking divine intervention—which for many is the Culinary Institute of America (affectionately called the CIA).

Considered one of the top culinary schools in the country, the CIA has been turning out talented chefs for over a half century. What began as a small school with fifty students in New Haven, Connecticut, in 1946 has turned into one of the largest culinary schools in America, enrolling over 2,400 students each year from the United States and overseas. Today the school has over 37,000 successful alumni from around the world—like Sara Moulton (executive chef, Gourmet magazine), Thaddeus DuBois (executive pastry chef, the White House), and Cat Cora (media personality, Food Network)—who attribute their culinary success to the training they received at the CIA.

ABOUT THE INSTRUCTORS

All CIA teachers have two things in common: a passion for food and years of professional experience. Many have had to make personal sacrifices to improve their skills and achieve their goals. For a lucky number this has paid off. Along the way, they have so successfully distinguished themselves that they have won Culinary World Cups or Gold Medals or published books that have been excerpted in leading magazines and

Chef John Ash (center) talks to students.
PHOTO COURTESY OF JOHN T. ASH, CHEF, AUTHOR INSTRUCTOR, CIA GREYSTONE

newspapers. (For example, CIA president Tim Ryan was trained at the school and went on to lead the United States team to a gold medal in the Culinary Olympics.)

ABOUT THE CLASSES

Contrary to popular belief, the CIA doesn't limit itself to just a professional program. Noncredit classes for food enthusiasts are also offered. They include boot camps, which are intense culinary immersion courses that may run from one to five days. In the past, the boot camps have included such practical subjects as Gourmet Meals in Five Minutes, Techniques of Healthy Cooking, Skill Development, and many more.

A five-day, hands-on basic skill training boot camp might, for example, include lessons in knife skills, dry-heat cooking (i.e., roasting, grilling, sautéing, pan-frying, and stir-frying), moist-heat cooking (i.e., braising, shallow poaching, deep poaching, and steam), pairing food and wine, and wine tasting. In these classes, students learn more than just a few basics like mirepoix (dicing carrots, onion, and celery with herbs) or mille-feuilles (creating several layers of puff pastry with alternating fillings like a Napoleon). They learn to think while they cook and make quick, wise decisions on the spot.

THE HYDE PARK PROGRAM

To appeal to a variety of students, a broad choice of five-hour, intensive one-day classes in specific subjects (like preparing sauces, fish, soups, etc.) are offered at the CIA facility in Hyde Park. Although the recreational classes are intended for the casual, nonprofessional cook, each class is taught seriously by a competent and knowledgeable staff member. The same standard of excellence that is the hallmark of the credentialed program is applied to the recreational program. Students learn to grill, prepare fresh fish, cook with herbs, and create ethnic meals like a professional.

Class Costs: $325 for the one-day boot camp to $2,095 for the five-day program, which includes meals, specific kitchen materials, and course guide.
Class Frequency: Daily from one to five days, depending on program.
Class Length: From nine to fourteen hours of intensive learning each day, depending on class.
Class Type: Hands-on/demonstration.
Class Size: Sixteen students maximum.
Team-building classes are also available at the Hyde Park location for companies, and special weekend and weeknight food-enthusiast classes are now being offered at the CIA's new Astor Center facility in Manhattan. Fees range from $95 to $225 per class.

THE GREYSTONE PROGRAM

The CIA also offers classes at its Greystone campus in St. Helena, California (see sidebar on pages 260–61). The Sophisticated Palate program, aimed at food lovers eager to expand their culinary experiences, runs from one to four days. The day is divided into two parts: The morning program focuses on teaching culinary flavors and hands-on food preparation techniques, and the afternoon is spent visiting a variety of local sites, ranging from olive groves to wineries for tastings. Such subjects as A Taste of Northern California, Foods and Flavors from the California Harvest, and Cooking for the Next Half of Your Life are offered.

Class Costs: One- to four--day program costs up to $3,995 per person.
Class Frequency: Four or more times per year, depending on class.
Class Length: Five hours per day with an additional four hours of field trips, and three meals each day.
Class Type: Hands on/demonstration.
Class Size: Twelve students.
Lodging: Since there isn't any on-campus lodging for recreational cooks, the CIA provides students with a list of hotels and motels nearby.
In Hyde Park, they recommend:
Courtyard by Marriott, 2641 South Road/New York Highway 9, Poughkeepsie, NY

 The Pot Counts

What you cook your food in matters. Using the wrong pot or pan can ruin a meal. With the numerous choices of pots and pans available on the market, which ones do the experts at CIA think work best for you?

Bargain-basement pots and pans made of tin, for example, are totally inadequate for conducting heat evenly. Cast iron ones, on the other hand, are exceptionally heavy and impractical, even though they do cook food evenly. Aluminum and copper ones are lighter than cast iron, but unfortunately they react with some foods. What's the solution? According to the CIA pros, aluminum and copper bonded pans with nonreactive stainless-steel interiors will give you the best results for your money.

Most importantly, when buying such pots and pans, the CIA recommends that you buy only those that can transition well from your stovetop to the center of your oven. So always avoid anything that has parts that won't tolerate heat.

Bistecca Alla Fiorentina

(grilled T-bone steak, Tuscan style)

From *Grilling* by The Culinary Institute of America (John Wiley & Sons, 2006). Used with permission.

The best way to prepare a thick cut of meat (like the recommended one-and-a-half-inch T-bone) is over direct and indirect heat. Direct heat should be used to char the outside with grill marks, and indirect heat should be used to finish the cooking without scorching the meat. The steak pairs nicely with an herbed polenta (recipe follows).

Ingredients
- 4 1^1/$_2$-inch-thick T-bone steaks
- ^{1}/$_4$ cup extra virgin olive oil
- ^{1}/$_4$ cup minced garlic
- 4 teaspoons salt
- 2 teaspoons ground black pepper
- 2 teaspoons minced rosemary leaves
- 3 tablespoons lemon juice

1. Preheat a gas grill to high; leave one burner off. If you are using a charcoal grill, build a fire and let it burn down until the coals are glowing red with a light coating of white ash. Spread the coals in an even bed on one side of the grill. Clean the cooking grate.
2. Brush the steaks with a bit of the oil and season generously with garlic, salt, pepper, and rosemary.
3. Grill the steaks over direct heat until marked, about 2 minutes on each side. Move the steaks to the cooler part of the grill and continue to grill over indirect medium heat until desired doneness—6 to 7 minutes per side for medium (cook slightly less for rare, slightly more for medium-well).
4. Transfer the meat to a cutting board or a large platter. Drizzle each of the steaks with 2 teaspoons of the olive oil, and finish by sprinkling the steaks with lemon juice.
5. Let the steaks rest for about 10 to 15 minutes before carving into slices. To carve the steaks, cut the meat from the bone with the tip of a knife; it will separate easily and cleanly from the bone if you use short strokes and keep the blade as close to the bone as possible. Once the meat is cut free, carve it into slices. Serve on a heated platter or plates.

Serves 8.

12601 (6 miles from campus); (800) 321-2211; www.marriott.com/hotels/travel/
pouch-courtyard-poughkeepsie. This is a typical, comfortable Marriott property.
The Poughkeepsie Grand Hotel, 40 Civic Center Plaza, Poughkeepsie, NY 12601,
(845) 485-5300; www.pokgrand.com. This is another typical first-class property.
La Petit Chateau Inn, 39 West Dorsey Lane, Hyde Park, NY 12538; (845) 437-4688;
www.lepetitchateauinn. This bed-and-breakfast has fireplaces and luxurious bathrooms in most rooms. Very close to CIA.

In Napa Valley (Greystone), they recommend:

Auberge du Soleil, 180 Rutherford Hill Road, Rutherford, CA 94573; (707) 963-
1211; www.aubergedusoleil.com. This very elegant Relais & Châteaux inn is about
ten minutes away from the CIA. The rooms have Mediterranean-inspired decor
and a contemporary feel.

Harvest Inn, 1 Main Street, St. Helena, CA 94574; (707) 963-9463; www.harvestinn
.com. The inn offers country-estate cottages and luxurious suites.

Hilton Garden Inn Napa, 3585 Solano Avenue, Napa, CA 94558; (707) 252-0444;

Herbed Polenta

From *Grilling* by The Culinary Institute of America (John Wiley & Sons, 2006). Used with permission.

Ingredients
- 4 cups chicken broth
- 1 teaspoon salt, or to taste
- $1/4$ teaspoon ground black pepper, or to taste
- 1 cup yellow cornmeal
- $2/3$ cup grated Parmesan cheese
- 2 tablespoons butter
- 2 teaspoons chopped rosemary
- $1^{1}/4$ teaspoons chopped thyme

1. Bring the chicken broth to a boil and season with salt and pepper. Add the cornmeal in a stream, stirring constantly until it has all been added.
2. Simmer, stirring often, until the polenta has thickened and starts to pull away lightly from the sides of the pot, 10 to 25 minutes depending on the coarse-ness of the meal.
3. Remove from the heat and blend in the cheese, butter, rosemary, and thyme. Adjust seasoning with salt and pepper, if desired.

Serves 8.

www.hiltongardeninn.com/en/gi/hotels/index.jhtml?ctyhocn=APCNHGI. This is a typically attractive Hilton Inn with the expected comforts.

Activities: Both schools are located in two of America's prime locations. The Hyde Park campus is in the Hudson Valley area, known for its Gilded Age "cottages" (the Vanderbilt Estate, Eleanor Roosevelt's Val-Kill, and Franklin D. Roosevelt's Springwood). The Greystone campus is located in Napa Valley, the wine capital of America (Beringer, Domaine Chandon, Robert Mondavi, and many, many more), only forty-five minutes away by car from San Francisco.

For more information contact: The Culinary Institute of America, Admissions Department, 1946 Campus Drive, Hyde Park, NY 12538-1499; (800) 888-7850; www.ciachef.edu.

The Institute of Culinary Education
New York, New York

*P*eter Kump, a former speed-reading instructor with a passion for sumptuous dining and spicy double entendres, made a career change in 1975 that ultimately resulted in revolutionizing the way the culinary arts are taught. What began humbly in his Upper West Side apartment grew within five years to become a successful cooking school with a firm commitment to culinary excellence, Peter Kump's New York Cooking School.

In an interview with Bon Appétit magazine before his untimely death in 1995, Kump attributed his success to his commitment to providing students with more than "spectacular recipes to repeat step-by-step ad infinitum." He offered them basic principles that would free them to express their taste, unencumbered by recipes. To guarantee their success, he had some of the most important names in food—like James Beard, Simone Beck, Sara Moulton, and Marcella Hazan—guide them.

Perhaps his most lasting contribution to the food industry—and his strongest statement of love for culinary perfection—was achieved when he founded and organized the James Beard Foundation in 1985 with Julia

Child. This nonprofit foundation has earned an international reputation, not only for preserving and nurturing culinary excellence by giving support to talented chefs of all ages, but also for its prestigious James Beard Foundation Awards, popularly regarded as the Oscars of the food industry.

In 1995 Peter Kump's New York Cooking School was acquired by Elm View Culinary Enterprises and renamed the Institute of Culinary Education (ICE). Rick Smilow, an entrepreneur with a strong interest in culinary education, took over the school and became the founder and principal owner.

Under Smilow's strong leadership, the school has grown significantly. Over the years, his school and its alumni have won all types of awards for their achievements, including the prestigious James Beard Foundation Award. Their success is attributed to Smilow's tenacious determination to remain true to Kump's goal. Although the school teaches over 26,000 stu-

Cooking with the Stars

*F*or three decades the De Gustibus Cooking School has brought together some of the most important chefs in the country to demonstrate their skills at Macy's New York City flagship store in Herald Square. A large selection of informative demonstrations and hands-on classes are regularly scheduled, with irresistible names like Stylish & Kosher, Mediterranean Miracles, and Definitely New York. Some classes are even held on location at trendy New York City restaurants. At each class, you will taste the cuisine, sip the wines, and receive a printed recipe of what you enjoyed to re-create at home. Class series aren't always offered on successive days; therefore, tourists may find it difficult to attend more than one class during their New York visit. Classes run about $90 each. For a schedule and more information, contact: De Gustibus at Macy's, 151 West 43rd Street, Eighth Floor, New York, NY 10001; (212) 239-1652; www.degustibusinc.com.

dents each year, making it one of the largest recreational cooking schools in the world, Smilow wants it to remain a big school with an intimate learning program.

So far he has been very successful. Today ICE is considered one of the oldest and most prestigious culinary training schools in the United States, and its reputation has spread worldwide, largely because of its famous staff of highly skilled chefs (such as Anna Teresa Callen; see the write-up for her cooking school later on in this section) and its numerous students who, after graduation, have established themselves in prominent positions. Although the school has been renamed ICE, many old-timers still affectionately remember it as Peter Kump's.

PHILOSOPHY

The school's mission is to provide outstanding culinary education and inspiration to a diverse range of students, from aspiring chefs and food professionals to recreational cooking, baking, and wine enthusiasts.

ABOUT THE COOKING PROGRAM

At ICE, three primary types of programs are offered: recreational classes, special events, and, of course, the professional cooking program. Students who want to take a few recreational classes and package them with a New York getaway may choose from about 1,700 cooking classes. Many of these are offered around the clock, seven days a week. They range from basic technique to some very specialized and esoteric lessons. Here are some of the most popular:

BASIC TECHNIQUE COURSES

The backbone of the school's recreational program are its classes in the techniques of fine cooking. Especially important for beginners, these basic courses do not focus on particular recipes, but instead on techniques that may be applied to any task, from fish to fruit. During each

Where Health and Taste Meet

*T*he Natural Gourmet Institute in New York has been a major contributor to the international interest in healthy eating. In 1977, noted lecturer and wellness consultant Dr. Annemarie Colbin founded the Natural Gourmet Cookery School (now the Natural Gourmet Institute for Health & Culinary Arts) in order to alert the world to the strong connection between diet and health. Since its founding, the institute has guided the public about and trained health professionals in better eating.

For the benefit of the public, the institute provides a crammed curriculum of eclectic classes that provide a sensible and comprehensive approach to preparing delicious, nutritious foods. Classes focus on various types of foods, including ethnic foods from around the world and familiar foods with a healthy twist.

Visitors to New York who are interested in attending the school can easily pack a few classes together during their trip. Many are single-session classes that can be lined up together on successive days. The institute also has a chef training program aimed at preparing students for a career in the culinary arts.

Class Costs: From $45 to $100 per person, per class.
Class Frequency: Daily.
Class Length: Classes average about three and a half hours.
Class Type: Hands on/demonstration.
Class Size: Maximum of sixteen students.
For more information contact the Natural Gourmet Institute for Food & Health, 48 West 21st Street, New York, NY 10010; 212/627-2665; www.naturalgourmet school.com.

class, students are introduced to important concepts that will always serve them well in the kitchen (such as why things go wrong and what can be done about it when it happens). Major cooking methods like grilling and sautéing are taught, as well as lessons that will give students a firm grasp of ingredients and equipment. More focused technique classes—such as techniques of Italian cooking, healthful cooking, Asian cooking, and more—are also offered throughout the year.

Class Costs: From $315 to $575 per person per program.
Class Frequency: Three to five consecutive days per week.
Class Length: About five hours per day.
Class Type: Demonstration/hands-on.
Class Size: Ten to sixteen students per class.

SPECIALTY CLASSES

The school has offered some intriguing specialty classes, such as Middle Eastern Street Food, the Art of Pastry Dough, and the Arthur Avenue Walking Tour, as well as the Essential Cuisines series, which is composed of numerous different one-day class categories (e.g., Tuscan, Cantonese, Greek, and more). Other options include cooking-for-couples classes, classes for kids and teens, and market classes. Students can combine a few one-day classes to make a two- or three-day New York Culinary Getaway. Since there are so many classes to choose from, it is often easy to find a class to suit your needs. Students are well supervised by prominent chefs.

Class Costs: About $100 per person per class.
Class Frequency: Varies by class.
Class Length: About four hours.
Class Type: Demonstration/hands-on.
Class Size: About ten to sixteen students per class.
Lodging: The school doesn't offer overnight accommodations, but there is a large choice of hotels in New York, from the affordable to the outrageous. ICE recommends the following hotels, which are near the school:

SoHo Grand, 310 West Broadway, New York, NY 10013; (212) 965-3000; www
.sohogrand.com. Hip, modern, and upscale.
TriBeCa Grand, 2 Avenue of the Americas, New York, NY 10013; (212) 519-6600;
www.tribecagrand.com. Sleek, minimalist, and comfortable.
Washington Square Hotel, 103 Waverly Street, New York, NY 10011; (212) 777-
9515; www.wshotel.com. A reproduction of a 1930s art deco Paris hotel, the
Washington Square is a haven for writers and artists.
Amenities: All three hotels provide maximum comfort and service, from wireless
Internet connection to concierge services.
For more information contact: Institute of Culinary Education, 50 West 23rd
Street, New York, NY 10010; (800) 543-8834; www.iceculinary.com.

Anna Teresa Callen
Italian Cooking School
New York, New York

*I*talians love their food, and for good reason: Layers and layers of culinary
tradition and history are packed into every mouthful. Since the Renaissance, when Italian cuisine began to be refined to glorious perfection, Italians have been creating miracles in the kitchen, drawing on the influences
of the different cultures that played a role in shaping the country's history.
What has emerged is a unique cuisine that is both complex and delicate.

In recent years, many Americans have discovered refined Italian cuisine,
moving beyond the popular red-sauce-and-meat "Italian" dinner. Teachers
like Anna Teresa Callen can be thanked for this. As a longtime protector of
Italy's culinary legacy, she has been quick to point out inaccuracies in print
or in conversation about Italian food, at times even launching into a veri-
table lecture on the history of true Italian cooking.

ABOUT THE INSTRUCTOR

Educated in Italian literature and the history of art at the University of Rome, Callen entered the cooking profession by accident. She left college with the dream of someday becoming an archaeologist, but instead she unexpectedly embarked on a different career after she left her home in Italy to settle in America. This decision was based on emotional reasons—in her case, "out of spite"—when she read an erroneous statement in an article in the *New York Times*. It claimed that Marco Polo brought spaghetti to Italy from China. "Nothing can be further from the truth," she said firmly. "The Etruscans were enjoying macaroni long before Marco Polo ever existed."

Perhaps the biggest horror she faced as a young, educated gourmand coming to America in 1961 was to discover that Americans (and even many Italian Americans) thought that all Italian "spaghetti" (i.e., macaroni) was made only with red sauce. In the past forty or more years, she has strived to set the record straight, writing six books and teaching thousands of students, including Armandino Batali, father of TV host and restaurateur Mario Batali. She began her teaching career at Peter Kump's New York Cooking School, which is now the Institute of Culinary Education.

ABOUT THE COOKING PROGRAM

Besides teaching at the Institute of Culinary Education, Callen also teaches at her own school, the Anna Teresa Callen Italian Cooking School. For those who may think of Italian food as either northern or southern, she will gladly set the record straight by letting you know that the regions aren't so broad.

Foods from smaller regions of Italy—Sicily, Campania, Veneto, or Emilia Romagna, for example—are featured in each class, where students will work together to make a memorable meal paired with an appropriate wine. Some students come simply to observe, others to work, so each class can be whatever the students want it to be—demonstration or hands-on.

The menu for each class is discussed with the students in advance. Included in the lesson are lectures on the history of food, with some relevant information about the culture. Students who take the class will learn to cook Italian—not Italian American or some new wave spinoff.

 *Pasta*

*W*hat makes pasta so wonderful is that it mixes well with different sauces. Almost every sauce imaginable has been added to pasta—pasta e fagioli *(beans)*, alla vongole veraci *(clams)*, and rigatoni con le zucchine *(zucchini)*. For the best results, however, you must start with the highest-quality pasta possible.

Anna Teresa Callen believes the best pastas are from Abruzzo, because the pasta factories there use the excellent water of the river Verde to make their pasta. Her favorite pastas are the Fara San Martino, De Cecco, and Del Verde brands. One pasta she particularly likes, because the sauce clings well to it, is a wheatflavored variety from the Giuseppe Cocco Factory.

In her book Food and Memories of Abruzzo *(Wiley Publishing Company, 1998)*, Callen provides the following tips on preparing pasta:

· *Pasta should cooked in a large pot with enough salted water to allow the pasta to swim freely. Cover the pot so that the water will boil quickly.*

· *When the water is boiling, add the salt (kosher, if possible) and then the pasta. Stir and quickly cover.*

· *When the water returns to a boil, stir the pasta; keep the lid on the pot as much as possible to minimize water evaporation. Pasta should be cooked in constantly boiling water according to instructions on the package, which is usually for 20 minutes. Test the pasta to be certain it is al dente.*

· *As soon as the pasta is ready, add a cup of cold water to stop the cooking. Drain, but reserve one cup of the cooking water to add to the sauce in case it is too dense.*

Pasta Dell'Estate (Summer Pasta)

Callen doesn't like cold pasta and pasta salads ("it's an abomination"), but she believes when pasta is served at room temperature and is dressed correctly, it is good. She says, "The sauce for cold pastas should be herbivorous, with uncooked or just blanched vegetables and a few tablespoons of good, fragrant extra virgin olive oil." She adds, "And don't forget the garlic. If cheese is used, it should be fresh like ricotta, cubed mozzarella, robbiola, stracchino. Grated cheese is a mistake because it makes the pasta gooey. If one wants to use Parmesan cheese, it should be in shards or slivers."

She recommends that when you prepare a recipe, new or familiar, you should always read, read, and read the recipe. No matter how well you know it, you are still likely to omit something if you don't keep the recipe in front of you.

This simple, tasty summer pasta recipe pairs well with Fiano di Avellino wine.

Pesto Ingredients
- 2 cups loosely packed fresh basil leaves
- ¼ cup extra virgin olive oil
- 2 garlic cloves, peeled
- 1 parsley sprig
- ¼ cup pine nuts or walnuts

Pasta Ingredients
- 1 cup pesto
- 1 pound short pasta (penne, ziti, fusilli, cartwheels, or bow tie)
- ¼ cup sun-dried tomatoes in oil, chopped
- ¼ cup olivata (olive paste) or ½ cup pitted, sweet California olives, sliced in the round
- 20 small cherry tomatoes
- Basil leaves for garnish
- 1 pound fresh mozzarella, cubed

1. In a food processor, place all the ingredients for the pesto except the nuts. Process until creamy. If using walnuts, chop coarsely by hand. Add the nuts to the other ingredients. Mix well and set aside.
2. Cook the pasta according to the instructions on the package. Drain the pasta, but reserve 1 cup of the cooking liquid. Toss the pasta with the pesto. Add all the remaining ingredients except the mozzarella, which should be added just before serving. Do not refrigerate, even if you want to serve the dish at room temperature.

Serves 6 to 8.

Class Costs: About $850 per person for five classes.
Class Frequency: Eight times a year.
Class Length: About four hours per day.
Class Type: Demonstration/hands-on.
Class Size: No more than six students per class.
For more information contact: Anna Teresa Callen Italian Cooking School, 59 West 12th Street, New York, NY 10011; (212) 929-5640.

Alice Ross Hearth Studios
Smithtown, New York

*H*istory must come alive to be fully understood. The thread that con- nects the present to its complicated past must be identified to bring understanding to existence. Some people are able to achieve this connection by merely visiting historic sights like those in Philadelphia and Williams- burg, the plantations along the Mississippi, and the gold-mining towns of Northern California. Others, on the other hand, need more. They need to relive history through direct involvement. At the Alice Ross Hearth Studios, students will have this opportunity during a hands-on culinary program.

After years of collecting antique cooking equipment, Dr. Alice Ross has turned her Smithtown, New York, studio into an authentic, working fac- simile of an early American kitchen. In this fully functional museum, she shares with her students everything needed to bring life to America's culi- nary past: a smokehouse, a Victorian woodstove, a hand pump, a replica of an eighteenth-century 10-foot indoor fireplace, and, most importantly, a library of authenticated early American recipes.

ABOUT THE INSTRUCTOR
Dr. Ross has over twenty years of researching and cooking experience and a Ph.D. from SUNY at Stony Brook. Although her doctorate dissertation

on turn-of-the-twentieth-century women, work, and cookery didn't win her world fame, it certainly prepared her well for her career direction. She is an adjunct professor at Hofstra and New York universities, and she was a senior editor and contributor to the *Oxford Encyclopedia of Food and Drink in America.* Like many of her classes, her cookbook, *The Taste of Brookhaven: 400 Years of History in the Kitchen,* integrates her research on cuisine with local history era by era.

Dr. Alice Ross's early American kitchen includes this hand water pump.
PHOTO COURTESY OF JOE DAVID

A student pokes the fire in an open hearth. PHOTO COURTESY OF ALICE ROSS

Over the years she has been a consultant in historical food for such respected museums as Virginia's Colonial Williamsburg and the Lowell National Historical Park in Massachusetts. Peggy Katalinich, food editor for the New York and Long Island *Newsday,* summed up her respect for Dr. Ross by simply saying, "Alice Ross is the first person I call when tracking down a question of food history."

Dr. Ross believes the best way to teach early American cooking is to use the same cooking devices, especially the hearth, that the people once used to prepare their food. "Nothing," she says, "is like a shared hearth for bringing people together. Hearth cooking creates a visceral empathy with the past, a gorgeous culinary connection with our forefathers."

ABOUT THE COOKING PROGRAM

In her class, her students will grow up fast, Dr. Ross often tells her students. They will learn different ways to make a fire and to determine when it has reached the right temperature for cooking. Like their forefathers, they will learn to do everything by relying on their senses. They will measure by approximation and know when the food is ready by how it feels, looks, and smells. During each lesson, she will share tips that will enable students to make independent and wise judgments about cooking that will always be useful—in either a vintage or modern kitchen.

Each class offers something significant for all types of serious cooks—teachers, museum people, historians, or anyone else eager to learn about early American food preparation. By working in an early American kitchen with authenticated recipes to guide them, students will discover that preparing food over searing coals with iron pots suspended over a temperamental fire is more than just an exercise in technique. For those lucky enough to take her class, it is a three-dimensional time capsule into the past, where they become tactual players at re-creating history—while mastering the nuances of controlling an open flame to prepare food properly.

For many, this can be a shockingly sobering experience, especially if they are only familiar with modern kitchen gadgetry and electric appli-

The vintage classroom, where students work, brings life to America's culinary past.
PHOTO COURTESY OF ALICE ROSS

Dutch Oven Corn Bread

An original recipe of Phoebe Underhill, Syosset, Long Island, 1834, modernized by Dr. Alice Ross

The success of this corn bread depends on quick mixing and immediate baking. It is a quick bread, and you can achieve its moistness and tenderness by having all the ingredients set out before you begin. Like muffins and biscuits, you must not over-beat, but rather leave the batter a bit lumpy. The batter should be thick, wet, and "ploppy"—not stiff. You can make adjustments, if necessary, by adding more corn-meal or buttermilk.

If you want to prepare this dish in your fireplace, place two shovelfuls of glowing embers on the hearth in front of the fire. Set the Dutch oven over the embers, cover, then place three shovelfuls of embers over the lid. This creates a portable oven. If you are a stickler for authenticity, measure in approximations and adjust the cornmeal or buttermilk to achieve the proper consistency.

Serve and eat the corn bread when it's hot. It loses some of its wonderful flavor and texture when it cools down.

Ingredients
- 3–4 tablespoons butter
- 2 cups cornmeal
- 1 teaspoon salt
- 1 teaspoon baking soda
- 2 eggs
- 1 tablespoon molasses
- 2 cups buttermilk

1. In a 375°F oven, preheat an 8-inch Dutch oven, both lid and pan, with half the butter inside.
2. In a large bowl, mix cornmeal, salt, and baking soda, rubbing the mixture between your hands until well combined.
3. Over the cornmeal mixture, drop the eggs and the molasses. Do *not* stir yet.
4. When the Dutch oven is hot, add the buttermilk and the remaining butter to the cornmeal. Stir all the wet ingredients in briskly and *briefly*. Adjust corn-meal or buttermilk if necessary to achieve a consistency of heavy cream.
5. Pour the batter into the heated Dutch oven. Cover with heated lid. Return to the oven and bake for 20 minutes, or until the corn bread begins to pull away from the sides and is golden brown on top.
6. Remove from oven and eat immediately.

Serves 6–8.

ances. To prevent this from becoming an obstacle to learning, Dr. Ross demystifies the challenges with her encyclopedic knowledge of food and culture and turns it into a painless journey into America's culinary past.

To appeal to diverse interests, Dr. Ross offers a large choice of subjects, such as hearth cooking, early American cookery, preserving seasonal foods, and the historical origins of ethnic foods. A passionate cook, she provides each student with well-researched information in a way that will accelerate absorption.

Students attending one of her classes receive an intensive introduction to the specific subject of their choice. They learn how to prepare such foods as planked shad, chicken and oyster pie, spicy gingerbread, spit-roasted venison, and baked Dutch Oven Corn Bread (see recipe) the old-fashioned way. For the serious students she has an impressive library of old recipes, collected over the years, that they may review and use to prepare a meal with her antique pots and utensils.

Classes are small and run about seven hours. Some are a series, such as her four-day class on American food history or her two-day class on baking. Many others are one-day, comprehensive classes that focus on specific subjects, from French cooking to the Passover table in history. The format is standard: an hour-and-a-half lecture, some historical background, a tour of the property, and a review of the menu and recipes. She divides students into pairs, with each pair receiving one long and one short recipe. After an ample lunch of what the students prepare, she ends the class with a summary of what they were taught.

Class Costs: Classes with three or more students cost $150 per person per class; classes with only two students run $200 per person.
Class Frequency: Classes are held regularly throughout the year.
Class Length: Some classes are a series that run for four consecutive days. Each class is about seven hours long.
Class Type: Hands on/demonstration.
Class Size: Minimum two students; maximum six.

Lodging: Dr. Ross doesn't offer sleeping quarters at her studio, but she will recommend several nearby inns in a manageable price range. Among those in the area, here are two to consider:

Three Village Inn, 150 Main Street, Stony Brook, NY 11790; (631) 751-0555. A restored inn with cozy, fussy country-style rooms, it is located on Long Island Sound near shopping, antiques shops, wineries, and more. It is about a ten- to fifteen-minute drive to the studio.

Towne House Motor Inn, 880 West Jericho Turnpike, Smithtown, NY 11787; (631) 543-4040. This clean and comfortable but undistinguished motor inn is located off the road in the woods near a pond. The studio is only about five minutes away by car.

Amenities: Business center and full breakfast at Three Village Inn; Towne House Motor Inn offers no special amenities. It is a typical motor inn.

For more information contact: Alice Ross Hearth Studios, 15 Prospect Street, Smithtown, NY 11787; (631) 265-9335; www.aliceross.com.

PENNSYLVANIA

Torte Knox
Hawley, Pennsylvania

*H*awley, Pennsylvania, is two hours from New York City and three hours from Philadelphia, far enough from the big time to be ignored. Yet thanks to Sheelah Kaye-Stepkin, that isn't happening.

The once-gray, working-class community, home to glassblowers and glass cutters, is peeling off its old facade and attracting visitors who come to

Sheelah Kaye-Stepkin shows off her southern biscuits. PHOTO COURTESY OF TORTE KNOX

clean their lungs of carbon monoxide and sample Sheelah's tasty cooking at her little touch of culinary heaven, Torte Knox.

Located prominently on Main Street, Torte Knox has set the standard for change in the community. What was once a stuffy, early-nineteenth-century bank has been reincarnated as an elegant cooking school and bistro. At first glance, little appears to have changed. Its blue stone face has been cleaned up, its brass trimmings polished, its windows shaded with blue awnings, and its exterior light fixtures replaced with turn-of-the-twentieth-century reproductions. Inside, though, the transformation is complete. While some nostalgic touches remain, the refurbished and retrofitted old bank has taken on an entirely different look. Pots and pans, ovens and burners occupy the space once used by bank tellers and officers. Mixed with the state-of-art Viking appliances is an eclectic collection of pre–Civil War antiques and old bank fixtures. The cooking center is a huge, dramatic space in the main room with mahogany cabinets and a large work area.

Within this space, those who would like to recharge their spirit in the kitchen before returning to the big city can experience a little food and fun. Since the school's opening in 2003, Sheelah has collected generous accolades for her savvy skills at teaching recreational cooks. Occasionally she will bring in a support staff of leading chefs and TV personalities to provide another dimension to her classes, but usually it's just Sheelah, her effortless smile, and her students.

ABOUT THE INSTRUCTOR

Sheelah runs the school with the skill of a Broadway headliner—she captures your attention immediately and holds it. Her years on the stage, her time spent before the camera (on NBC's *Cooking with Class—Just for the Health of It*), and her years promoting Gimbel's Department Store on television and radio all come together in one big, knock-'em-dead smile.

It all began when Sheelah was a child, standing on a Coca-Cola crate in the kitchen to watch her mother create culinary masterpieces. When her father died unexpectedly when she was thirteen, forcing her mother to return to full-time work, Sheelah was handed a *Betty Crocker's Cook-*

Torte Knox is housed in a historic bank turned restaurant and school.
PHOTO COURTESY OF JOE DAVID

book and asked to prepare the meals. Armed with only this cookbook, she made her first leap toward what would one day become a lifetime calling. Although she has had limited formal training beyond attending the Wilton School in Chicago (see the Midwest section) for a few weeks, she has extensive knowledge, mostly taught to her by her mother and learned on her own through trial and error.

Lah-shee-lah's Southern Fried Chicken and Biscuits

Compliments of Torte Knox

Learning to judge the moment of perfect doneness of fried chicken requires a little experiment-ing. After removing the chicken from the oil, peek inside the chicken with a small paring knife in order to avoid damaging the crust. The juices should run clear. If there is the slightest pink, you can finish the chicken off in a warm oven for a few minutes, or you can continue to deep fry it. Be careful when returning the chicken to the fryer after piercing it, because the released juices can make the oil splatter.

In true Southern fashion, you can pour honey over your warm chicken before eating it. Sheelah prefers to omit the honey and just pick up the chicken and have her way with it. A perfect meal for her is fried chicken with mashed potatoes and biscuits, slathered in butter and honey, and some "down and dirty" Southern coleslaw (with a vinegar base, not mayonnaise; a little cay-enne; sugar; and, of course, black pepper). To complete the meal, she adds a Southern touch: collard greens with Spanish onions and ham hocks.

Southern Fried Chicken

Ingredients
- 10 pounds chicken legs, breasts, and thighs (skin on)
- 1 gallon cold water or ice
- 1 cup kosher salt
- 5 whole eggs, well beaten
- 1 quart buttermilk
- Vegetable frying oil
- $\frac{1}{2}$ cup lard (optional)
- 4 cups all-purpose flour
- $\frac{1}{3}$ cup cornflake crumbs
- 2 generous tablespoons paprika
- 1 teaspoon cumin
- $\frac{1}{2}$–1 teaspoon cayenne pepper
- 1 tablespoon coarse ground pepper
- 1 tablespoon salt

1. Clean the chicken in cold running water. Place chicken in a container, cover with water or ice, and add salt. Keep the chicken in the refrigerator and allow to brine for a minimum of two hours.
2. Triple rinse the chicken in ice cold water to ensure that all the salt is removed. Dry chicken with paper towels.
3. Beat the eggs with the buttermilk, and add chicken. At this stage you can hold the com-bined chicken and buttermilk up to twenty-four hours in the refrigerator.
4. Preheat the oven to 180°F. In a deep fryer or a cast-iron skillet with high sides, preheat oil to 325°F. If you are using a skillet, you will want approximately 2 inches of oil to fry

the chicken. You can add lard to the frying oil. This is purely optional, although Sheelah wouldn't fry her chicken without it.

5. Mix together the remaining ingredients in a container or a ziplock bag. Sheelah prefers a large plastic container with a lid (her favorite is a large Maxwell House Coffee can).

6. Remove several pieces of chicken from the buttermilk mixture and drop it into the container of seasoned flour. Shake it up really well to coat the chicken. Carefully remove the chicken from the container so as to not rub off the coating, and gently place it in the fryer or skillet. If you are frying in a skillet, be sure not to crowd the pieces. They should float independently. Otherwise they will steam, and the coating will not fry evenly or be attractive. For skillet frying, carefully turn pieces every 5 minutes so that they will crust evenly.

7. Remove the pieces after approximately 10 to 15 minutes and drain on a paper towel. (Note that white meat will be done sooner than dark meat.) Place the chicken in the warm oven to hold as you continue to fry the remaining chicken in batches. Do not put chicken pieces on top of one another or let them touch, as they will steam each other. They will continue to stay crisp in the oven.

Serves 4–6.

Biscuits

Sheelah has been making these biscuits since she was a little girl. She prefers to use a food processor rather than hand mix the ingredients since it's more efficient. If you use a food processor, she recommends that you use frozen butter bits.

For a delicious biscuit topping, whip up ice cold butter in the mixer, adding honey to taste, until the combination is fluffy and light. If it becomes too soft, simply add more cold butter until you reach desired consistency. Place in a small covered container and refrigerate.

Ingredients
- 2$\frac{1}{2}$ cups flour
- 3 tablespoons sugar
- 2$\frac{1}{2}$ teaspoons baking powder
- 1 teaspoon baking soda
- 1 teaspoon salt
- $\frac{1}{2}$ cup butter
- $\frac{3}{4}$ cup buttermilk

1. Place all dry ingredients in the food processor. Pulse and add butter. When crumbly, add buttermilk until the mixture forms a ball. Let it rotate a couple times to knead the dough. If it becomes soft and falls out of a ball, add a little flour until it regains its ball shape.

2. Place the dough on a floured surface and roll it to $\frac{1}{2}$-inch thickness. Cut the biscuits and bake at 400°F degrees for 15 minutes.

Yields 12 biscuits.

She is now sought out by the rich and famous. Twelve of her turn-of-the-twentieth-century collection of toys, all made of sugar and exclusively for the White House, became so popular that they went from private display to become a *Larry King Live* feature. In past years she has appeared in *Bon Appétit,* and on NBC and *Good Morning America*.

What unites her with other gifted chefs is her love of food. She is always striving to perfect her skills, using different international techniques to give new and purer flavor to what she prepares. This willingness to experiment, which she shares with her students, is designed to encourage them to develop their own cooking style and tastes.

ABOUT THE CLASSES

Classes are held from July 1 through New Year's Eve. Most adult classes are offered in the evening, which leaves students free time during the day to mix their getaway with some Poconos fun. The choice of classes includes baking, regional cooking, ethnic, special-occasion classes, international flavors, and more. Private-party or special-events cooking classes are offered by reservation only during the winter.

In the summer months, Sheelah usually connects with camps nearby and arranges for them to deliver busloads of children to Torte Knox for cooking lessons. Classes are arranged by age and are aimed at developing age-appropriate cooking skills. She also has children's cooking classes throughout the season.

Class Costs: About $65 to $100 per person for a regular class; $125 to $150 per person for private-party and team-building classes, depending on ingredients; $50 per person for children's classes.

Class Frequency: Two or more classes on successive days can be arranged; private-party and special-events classes are held in the winter; children's classes are in the summer months.

Class Length: Three to four hours; two hours for children's classes.

Class Type: Hands-on; hands-on/demonstration for children's classes.

Class Size: Six to twelve students per regular class; ten to sixteen students per team-building class, broken into four groups; twelve to twenty-two students per children's class.

Lodging: The school doesn't offer lodging, but here are three recommended choices. The first two are within walking distance of Torte Knox.

The Settlers Inn, 4 Main Avenue, Hawley, PA 18428; (800) 833-8527; www.the settlersinn.com. Highly recommended is the rustic and comfortable Settler's Inn, a few blocks from Torte Knox. Amenities include full access to the Woodloch Springs Health Club. Massages, flowers, cheese platters, and more are available upon request.

Falls Port Inn and Steakhouse, 330 Main Street, Hawley, PA 18428; (570) 226-2600; www.fallsportinnandsteakhouse.com. The restored Victorian property has been renovated into a charming early American hotel. Smoking is allowed in the bar and certain restricted areas. The owners are a couple who formerly lived in New York's Greenwich Village.

Woodloch Pines Resort, RR 1, Box 280, Hawley, PA 18428; (800) 966-3562; www .woodloch.com. About fifteen minutes away from Torte Knox by car is the full-service Woodloch Pines Resort, which is considered one of America's better family resorts. It is especially appealing to those who love to golf. The selection of activities is broad, with something for everyone, from arts and crafts classes for children to a health spa for adults. Contact American plan service (breakfast and dinner).

Amenities: Settlers Inn: full-service hotel facilities with some nice extras upon request; Falls Port Inn: no room telephones, room service upon request, TV with cable; Woodloch: full family resort with a large choice of children's and adult activities.

Activities: The Poconos, the camping center of Pennsylvania, is life outside the pressure cooker. Tucked away from all the excesses of the city, Hawley may not be the Aspen of the East, but the area around it still draws its share of visitors. The choice of activities in season is impressive—hiking, swimming, boating, hunting, golfing, fishing, skiing, and skating, just to mention a few. For information about the area, visit www.poconosbest.com.

For more information contact Torte Knox, 301 Main Avenue, Hawley, PA 18428; (570) 226-8200; www.torteknox.com.

Tasty Edibles from Around the World

*C*harlotte Ann Albertson has been offering hands-on/demonstration classes in Florida and Pennsylvania since 1973. Headquartered in Philadelphia, the Albertson's Cooking School provides visitors to the City of Brotherly Love with a little sisterly love—classes in fine cooking served up elegantly by teachers well qualified in their specific disciplines.

With true culinary passion, she and her staff teach students how to prepare tasty dishes at her small, family-operated cooking school. Each one of her many classes reflects a commitment to preserve her passion for the culinary arts, whether taught by her, her daughters, or a well-known Philadelphia chef.

Charlotte Ann holds a master's degree in teaching from the University of Pennsylvania and culinary certificates from La Varenne and Le Cordon Bleu in Paris. Her daughter Ann-Michelle Albertson followed in her mother's footsteps and received her culinary training at La Varenne, and took classes at some prominent American schools.

Some of the classes that have been taught include Eat Your Way through the Italian Market (a visit to Philly's famous Ninth Street outdoor ethnic market), Hands-On: Fooling with Filo (the secrets to handling paper-thin dough), and Soups to Warm the Soul (preparing robust soups flavored with butternut squash, fennel, oven-dried tomato, white beans, and more). There are also team-building classes and culinary trips abroad. Prices for the two-and-a-half-hour classes run from $45 to $90, and they are mostly offered in the Philadelphia area. Each class is designed to be an informative, pleasant escape from routine, especially appealing for students who don't have time for a several-day program.

For more information contact: Albertson's Cooking School, P.O. Box 27, Wynnewood, PA 19096; (610) 649-9290; www.albertsoncookingschool .com.

Julian Krinsky Cooking School
King of Prussia, Pennsylvania

It is often difficult for teenagers, distracted by peer pressure and raging hormones, to think beyond the moment. To help broaden their focus, it often requires the assistance of savvy adults. At Julian Krinsky Camps and Programs, students between the ages of ten and seventeen receive such assistance each summer, in the form of an assortment of programs intended to excite their interest in a culinary arts career.

Since the program is intended to provide a real value to the students, it isn't just limited to cooking. To give them a broad understanding of the industry, students are taken into the marketplace, taught to shop smartly and read labels to decipher what they are buying and eating. They visit respected Philadelphia-area restaurants and hotel kitchens, where they talk to leading chefs and merchants about the business. And at the end of the three-week session, they are left free to plan and prepare the awards banquet for all the students at the program to enjoy.

ABOUT THE INSTRUCTORS

Tina Krinsky, Julian's wife, directs the cooking school program. A gourmet cook and a member of Les Dames d'Escoffier, she has learned what she knows about cooking by working with numerous well-established chefs like Gary Coyle (Tavern on the Green, New York City) and by studying at the Rhodes School of Cuisine in Lucca, Italy. Her purpose for creating the program was to introduce students to sophisticated flavors and dishes, and in the process develop their critical appreciation for food.

Each one of the eleven chefs who teach classes at the culinary program has been selected because of their personal accomplishments. They are made up of college- or high-school-level culinary arts teachers, restaurant chefs, cookbook authors, and other credentialed professionals.

A student demonstrates her newly acquired cooking skill.
PHOTO COURTESY OF THE JULIAN KRINSKY GROUP

All are equipped to provide students with a wealth of knowledge that will maximize their learning without watering down the program content.

ABOUT THE COOKING PROGRAM

In each summer session, a broad range of topics, from safety tips to creating eye-appealing foods, are taught. All are supported with practical lessons and activities that help teach students to cook to their taste rather than to the recipes. Underlining all lessons is a fundamental point: You

Orange Peel Chicken with Stone Fruit Salsa

Compliments of the Julian Krinsky Cooking School at Canyon Ranch Teen

This recipe makes a perfect meal any time of the year, especially when paired with a light summer salad of arugula with crisp Parmigiana Reggiano croutons, and a passion fruit sorbet with almond tuile for dessert.

Stone Fruit Salsa Ingredients
- 2 cups diced peaches
- $1/2$ cup diced red onions
- $1/4$ cup diced dried apricots
- 1 tablespoon chopped cilantro
- 1 tablespoon fresh lime juice
- 1 tablespoon balsamic vinegar
- 1 tablespoon white grape juice
- 1 jalapeño pepper, cleaned, seeded, and minced

Marinade Ingredients
- 2 teaspoons sesame oil
- $1/4$ teaspoon black pepper
- $1/2$ teaspoon salt
- 1 cup orange juice
- 2 tablespoons grated orange peel
- 2 tablespoons chopped scallions
- 1 teaspoon red chile flakes
- 1 teaspoon minced garlic
- $1/2$ cup chicken stock (use a natural or organic variety)
- 1 tablespoon Worcestershire sauce
- 4 skinless chicken breast halves, boned and defatted

1. Combine all ingredients for the stone fruit salsa and mix well. Refrigerate until ready to serve.
2. Combine the first 10 ingredients for the marinade in a glass bowl or baking pan. Add chicken and marinate for 2 hours.
3. Preheat oven to 400°F.
4. Heat a large sauté pan over medium-high heat. Sear the chicken for 1 minute on each side. Transfer to a baking pan and pour the marinade over the chicken. Bake for 15 to 20 minutes or until cooked through. Serve with stone fruit salsa.

Serves 4.

must always strive to buy and eat nutritious foods that are fresh and in season. By turning the students on to food, the staff is paving the way for developing a reality-based interest in the food industry without over-sweetening it with hyperbole.

The program is structured professionally, as it is, for example, at schools like the Culinary Institute of America. During the session, students are taught the important basics—the proper way to hold and use knives, prepare mother sauces, set up a *mise en place,* plan a main course, and create exciting desserts. Each class usually begins with a demonstration, which is followed by practical hands-on lessons to allow students a chance to apply their newly learned skills. Parents have reported that students who have completed the program are attentive to what they eat. Many have even taken on the responsibility of restocking the family pantry after discarding any unhealthy foods they find there.

Class Costs: Three sessions are offered each summer and cost $1,300 per person per week. Included in the price is room and board on a Main Line college campus; day camp options are available for $550 per person per week.

Class Frequency: The three-week summer camp program is scheduled three times each summer, at ivy-covered Philadelphia college campuses—Haverford College for the high school students, Cabrini College for middle school students, and Bryn Mawr for anyone interested in the healthy food program.

Class Length: About three to five hours per day. For the remainder of the day, students are offered a choice of activities to enjoy.

Class Type: Demonstration/hands-on.

Class Size: Fifteen students per class.

For more information contact: Tina Krinsky, Julian Krinsky Cooking School, 610 South Henderson Road, King of Prussia, PA 19406; (610) 265-9401; www.jkcp.com.

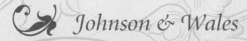 Johnson & Wales

*B*usy people seeking to expand their culinary knowledge and skills might want to consider Johnson & Wales University in Providence, Rhode Island. Like the Culinary Institute of America and the Institute of Culinary Education in New York, it is considered one of the leading culinary schools, and like those two schools, it also provides special classes that are suitable for recreational cooks. The weekend getaway program that Johnson & Wales offers is called the Chef's Choice, and it is held on three of its four campuses (Providence, Rhode Island; North Miami, Florida; and Charlotte, North Carolina).

Two types of Chef's Choice classes are offered, and each requires different levels of knowledge and skill. Level 1, for example, is for beginners, and it includes a three-hour hands-on/demonstration class. (One such class might be on Venetian cuisine, including the preparation and tasting of different foods of this city.) Level 2 is aimed at more advanced students, and it requires a grasp of essential culinary techniques. (One such class might be the All-American Thanksgiving Dinner, in which students learn to prepare all parts of the meal, from appetizers to desserts.)

Students at the Providence campus may take advantage of a two-day package, which includes a three- to four-hour Saturday cooking class for adults and children, a night of your choice at the Johnson & Wales Inn, a $50 gift certificate for dinner at Audrey's Restaurant (a campus restaurant), and a full breakfast for two at Audrey's. It starts at $369 per couple.

For more information contact: Johnson & Wales Inn, 213 Taunton Avenue, Seekonk, MA 02771; (800) 232-1772; www.jwu.edu.

SOUTHEAST

The Greenbrier. PHOTO COURTESY OF THE GREENBRIER

GEORGIA

Jekyll Island Club Hotel
Jekyll Island, Georgia

*M*any disparate flavors have found their way into Southern cuisine (such as Vietnamese, French, Middle Eastern, and more), sometimes with a distinctively Southern touch. Such legendary favorites as buttermilk biscuits, fried chicken, turtle soup, corn fritters, shrimp Creole, yams, grits, and hush puppies have become so popular, however, that they have lost their Southern identity.

To experience true Southern cooking, visitors may have to visit a Southern kitchen where they still hand-churn ice cream, glaze pecans, and make sweet potato pies. The South may have lost some of its unique culinary identity by melting into the international community, but for those willing to explore, surprises still abound.

The historic Jekyll Island Club Hotel may not limit its menu to just Southern food, but it does maintain the spirit of the South by using only Southern-grown products and foods. The executive chef is a true Southerner, born and educated in North Carolina, who trained at some of the finer kitchens in the South. As a result, she brings to the kitchen her contemporary vision of Southern cuisine.

As expected of a Georgia shoreline property, the food at the hotel is fresh and seasonal, mostly from the nearby waters and the hotel's gardens, and it includes an abundance of oysters, crabs, squash, eggplant, and much more. The cooking-class program, which is under the supervision of Executive Chef Abigail Hutchinson and Pastry Chef Carl Sears, includes tasty international treats made with these local ingredients.

The Jekyll Island Club buildings are located on the Georgia shoreline.
PHOTO COURTESY OF JEKYLL ISLAND CLUB HOTEL

ABOUT THE CHEF

Chef Hutchinson, a graduate of a culinary program at an Asheville, North Carolina, community college, rose to her executive position at the Jekyll Island Club Hotel quickly, five years after graduation. Her positions at the Biltmore Estates as demi-chef, the Country Club of Asheville as PM sous chef, and the Ocean Club at Amelia Island (Florida) as executive sous chef prepared her. While working at these jobs, she showed a tireless commitment to learning and mastering everything she could, which paid off well. In 2005, she joined the staff at Jekyll Island Club Hotel as executive chef, and in 2006 distinguished herself and the hotel by becoming one of the four chefs chosen from the 213 historic hotels in America to prepare a meal at the James Beard House in New York City.

Her goal as a teacher is to help students achieve excellence in the kitchen by sharing with them some of the secrets that make her cuisine at the Jekyll Island Club Hotel noteworthy.

ABOUT THE COOKING CLASSES

The hotel offers a four-day package of cooking lessons at manageable prices, three times a year, carefully overseen by both the executive and pastry chefs. Each package includes lessons on preparing tasty meals, pairing food with wine, plating meals attractively, creating irresistible pastries, and mastering efficient cooking and food safety skills. Students will also learn what should be made ahead versus what should be made

Smoked Summer Corn Bisque with Beer-Batter Okra

Compliments of Chef Abigail Hutchinson, Jekyll Island Club Hotel

A popular recipe at Jekyll Island Club is this tasty corn bisque, which is made a little fancy by smoking rather roasting the corn. Enjoy it with a glass of full-bodied chardonnay.

Smoked Summer Corn Bisque

Ingredients
- 1 bag hickory smoking chips
- 10 ears fresh summer corn (slightly open husk; soak in water for 30 minutes)
- 3 quarts corn stock
- 1–2 tablespoons butter
- 2 Vidalia onions, diced
- 3 cloves garlic, minced
- $1/2$ bunch celery, washed and diced
- 3 Idaho potatoes, peeled and diced
- 1 cup white wine
- 1 quart heavy cream
- 1 bay leaf
- 3 sprigs fresh thyme, minced
- Kosher salt and pepper to taste

1. For the corn: Add hickory smoking chips to a barbecue pit, and get it smoking at a medium heat. Add the corn, spaced out, and smoke it for up to 30 minutes. Pull out and let cool. Shuck the corn and cut the kernels off the cobs; set aside. Save the cobs for the corn stock.

last minute, how to prioritize menu items, and more. To lock the techniques into memory, at the end of the program students create a five-course meal using all the information that they have mastered.

One of the important goals of the program is to provide students with new ways to prepare basic foods. "The trick," Chef Hutchinson says, "is to give familiar food an elegant twist by the way you prepare and present it. One example is to make your salsa with roasted tomatillos instead

2. For the stock: Add the cobs to a stock pot and cover with water. Simmer over medium heat for about an hour. Strain the stock and set aside until needed.
3. For the soup: Melt the butter in a medium stock pot. Add the onions, garlic, and celery. Sauté for about 5 minutes over medium heat. Add the potatoes and mix well. Cook for about 10 minutes. Deglaze the pot with the wine and let cook down for about 5 minutes over medium heat. Add the corn stock and kernels, and simmer for about 45 minutes. Pull off the heat and puree with a handheld mixer. Place back over the heat and add the cream, bay leaf, and thyme. Let simmer for 10 minutes. Adjust seasonings with salt and pepper.

Beer-Batter Okra

Ingredients
- 1 egg
- 1^1/$_2$ cups flour
- 1 teaspoon baking powder
- 1^1/$_2$ cups beer (not light)
- 2 teaspoons kosher salt
- 16–20 pieces okra

1. In a small mixing bowl, beat the egg. Sift in 1 cup of the flour and the baking powder. Mix well. Add the beer and salt. Mix until smooth, but don't over-mix.
2. Dip the okra into the remaining flour and then into the batter. Fry in a deep-fat fryer for 2 minutes. Place okra into a cup of the soup and enjoy.

Makes 18 7-ounce servings.

 The Ruling Class

In 1886, a group of wealthy American businessmen discreetly purchased a lonely barrier island off the coast of Georgia and turned it into their exclusive hunting retreat. The abundance of wildlife, natural beauty, and temperate climate made it the perfect choice for their in-season visits. A turreted Victorian clubhouse, surrounded by elegant mansions euphemistically called "cottages," became their center for social activities.

For nearly fifty years, America's elite packed their summer clothes, boarded their private rail cars or luxury yachts, and migrated South, leaving behind the snow and ice storms. During their winter frolic in the Georgia sun, they brought with them their favorite luxuries and occupied their time with morning hunts, lawn parties, carriage rides, swimming, horseback riding, and other amusements. The businessmen responsible for creating this exclusive hideaway were William Rockefeller, Joseph Pulitzer, J. P. Morgan, William K. Vanderbilt, and over fifty of their closest friends.

Until the late 1930s, their hideaway, which they called the Jekyll Island Club, remained private. Fear of possible coastal attack during the impending war with Germany changed everything and led to the club's abandonment and eventual decay. In 1978, it was saved from destruction when it was recognized as National Historic Landmark and later restored to its original glory. Today the Jekyll Island Club Hotel is no longer private; instead, it has become an important historic hotel where tourists can stay and sample a little of what America's most powerful tycoons knew during their visits.

Some of the pleasures that were once only enjoyed by club members are offered to visitors of the island today—sandy beaches, horseback riding trails, golf, indoor and outdoor tennis, fishing, and even carriage rides under oak trees festooned with Spanish moss. To rekindle the feel of yesteryear, the main clubhouse and the surrounding cottages have all been faithfully restored. Although it doesn't have the world-class distinction, for example, of the Cloisters (Sea Island, Georgia), it still manages to successfully capitalize on its past and give visitors one big thrill for their dollar.

of tomatoes and to serve the salsa in hollowed cucumbers."

Other tricks and techniques that she teaches include using citrus juices and zest for flavors in lieu of salt, serving mashed cauliflower as a substitute for mashed potatoes, and arranging food artfully (for example, turning a tomato into a rose garnish for a platter).

The package includes meals (breakfast and food samplings for lunch), superior accommodations, and extras (such as a hotel logo chef's jacket, gift basket, and a dinner dance on the first evening).

Class Costs: From $1,109 (single) to $1,595 (double) for four days, beginning on a Monday and ending on a Thursday.

Class Frequency: Classes are held three times a year, in August, October, and February.

Class Length: Three hours for each session.

Class Type: Demonstrations/hands-on.

Class Size: Eight students minimum, twenty-six students maximum.

Lodging: Rooms are reserved for participants in the Crane "cottage," an Italian Renaissance villalike property built by Richard Teller Crane Jr., scion of the Crane Company. The rooms, handsomely furnished in a blend of sea and marsh colors, include such amenities as Jacuzzi tubs, fireplaces, balconies, and sun porches.

Activities: Naturalists who want to glimpse nature's drama may creep along the shores at night and watch female loggerhead sea turtles making their way surreptitiously onto the beach to lay their eggs in the sand (May to August).

Other pastimes include continental dinner in the hotel's Grand Dining Room, which has not changed significantly since its creation. White Ionic columns still border the walkway, leading to a Victorian fireplace, and the hotel still serves an assortment of seafood and regional cuisine daily. In this elegant, late-nineteenth-century setting, you will dine where great American leaders once ate ten-course meals while settling major issues that would determine the financial and political course of America.

About an hour drive away, visitors may tour the Okefenokee Swamp, a wonderland of wild vegetation and swamp grass grottoes. For $9 to $12 per person, you can take a guided tour through curving, black waters and observe the wildlife close up. Other areas of interest include Cumberland Island (once the island home of the Carnegies) and Sapelo Island (once an island plantation for Thomas Spalding).

For more information contact: Jekyll Island Club Hotel, 371 Riverview Drive, Jekyll Island, GA 31527; (800) 535-9547; www.jekyllclub.com.

Chef Joe Randall's Cooking School
Savannah, Georgia

*L*ow-country food is a spicy mix of cultures and flavors blended together to create a unique culinary taste. Many of Savannah's prized heritage dishes include ingredients brought to the South by African slaves and early Europeans. Enlivened with a sprinkling of spices from the West Indies, these ingredients, when mixed with local meats and seafood, give the food a distinct and seductive personality all its own.

Perhaps one of the most famous low-country dishes is Hoppin' John. Although its origin is a culinary enigma, it remains one of those special meals enjoyed by die-hard Southerners who like to serve it first thing on New Year's Day (ideally with corn bread and sometimes champagne) to bring good luck to the New Year. But the South—or more specifically, the low country—has other noteworthy foods, each with its own unique history, as refreshing and traditionally Southern as a mint julep at Churchill Downs.

To learn about these foods and their history, you can't find a better and more passionate cook than Savannah's star chef, Joe Randall. Some of his most memorable Southern foods are adaptations of low-country favorites, like his Southern Peach in Puff Pastry with Bourbon Custard Sauce or his Steamed Pecan Rice.

ABOUT THE CHEF

Chef Randall has accumulated enormous experience and knowledge from his time spent in the hospitality and food service industry. His food career began in the Air Force flight-line kitchens in 1963. What followed were a succession of opportunities that ultimately led to executive chef positions at several award-winning restaurants (such as the now-defunct Cloister in Buffalo and the Fishmarket in Baltimore), and he has won many awards (including recognition for his outstanding contributions to

Chef Joe Randall prepares low-country cuisine. PHOTO COURTESY OF CHEF JOE RANDALL

Southern cuisine and culture from the president and faculty of Georgia Southern University). He has appeared on numerous local and national television shows; been featured in major publications, including *Plate*, *Southern Living*, and *Fancy Foods* magazines; and has served on the faculty of California State Polytechnic University, Pomona. For many years he has operated a consulting company that provides assistance and guidance to restaurateurs striving to offer high-quality food and efficient operational service to their customers.

His goal as a teacher is to share with students the techniques and skills needed to create authentic low-country flavors that have won African-American cuisine a well-deserved place among the great foods of the world.

ABOUT THE CLASSES

Chef Randall offers more than twenty one-day classes (such as the Low Country Dinner, Southern Desserts, and Savannah English Christmas)

Sea Island Smothered Shrimp on Creamy Stone-Ground Grits

Compliments of Chef Joseph G. Randall

The following recipe may be enjoyed as an appetizer or a main course.

Sea Island Smothered Shrimp

Ingredients
- 2 pounds of medium-size shrimp, peeled and deveined
- 1 cup all-purpose flour
- 4 slices slab bacon, diced
- 1 medium Vidalia onion, diced
- 4 cloves of garlic, minced
- 1 tablespoon paprika
- 3 cups shrimp stock (see recipe)
- 3 tablespoons fresh chopped chives
- $1/2$ cup thinly sliced scallions
- $1/2$ teaspoon cayenne pepper
- Salt and pepper to taste

1. Rinse the shrimp and pat dry. Dredge shrimp in flour, shaking off excess.
2. In a large skillet, fry the bacon until brown. Add the onion and sauté for 2 minutes over medium-high heat. Add garlic and paprika.
3. Stir and add the shrimp; cook 2 to 3 minutes until shrimp turn pink. Add the shrimp stock and chives, then stir and reduce heat. Simmer for 10 minutes.

---

per month, and a quarterly six-part Basic Cooking Series designed to provide students with the opportunity to perfect essential skills (from creating sauces to cooking meats).

His weekend class, A Taste of Savannah Dinner, is popular with out-of-towners seeking a culinary getaway. The three-day program is offered monthly and is held on Friday and Saturday nights and Sunday morning. In each class, he mixes in a little whimsy with his Southern feast.

On Friday evening, the weekend class begins with students learning different ways to create Southern dishes such as Savannah Red Rice. On

4. Add scallions and cayenne pepper, stir, and season to taste with salt and pepper. Heat for an additional 2 to 3 minutes.
5. Serve with the Creamy Stone-Ground Grits (see recipe) by dividing the grits into the center of eight warm soup bowls, then spooning the smothered shrimp over the grits. Serve immediately.

Serves 8.

Creamy Stone-Ground Grits

Ingredients
- 3^1/$_2$ cups water
- 1 tablespoon butter
- ^{1}/$_2$ teaspoon salt
- ^{1}/$_4$ teaspoon white pepper
- 1 cup stone-ground or quick grits
- ^{1}/$_2$ cup heavy cream

1. Bring water to a boil. Add butter, salt, and pepper, then gradually stir in grits.
2. Cover and simmer for 20–25 minutes, or until water has been absorbed, stirring frequently.
3. Remove from heat and stir in the heavy cream. Serve hot.

Shrimp Stock

Compliments of Chef Joseph G. Randall

This stock can be refrigerated for two to three days and frozen up to six months.

Ingredients
- $1/8$ cup peanut oil
- $3/4$ pound shrimp shells
- 1 rib celery, coarsely chopped
- 1 small carrot, coarsely chopped
- 1 small onion, coarsely chopped
- 2 cloves garlic, chopped
- 1 quart water
- $1/8$ cup dry white wine
- 1 tablespoon tomato paste
- 1 sprig parsley
- 1 sprig thyme
- 2 black peppercorns
- 1 bay leaf

1. Heat the oil in a stockpot over medium heat. Add the shrimp shells and sauté for 3 to 4 minutes, stirring until the shells look dry. Add the celery, carrot, onion, and garlic, and continue to sauté for 2 to 3 minutes.
2. Add remaining ingredients. Bring the stock to a boil, then reduce the heat and simmer for 1 hour.
3. Strain the stock through a fine mesh strainer. Return to the heat and boil until reduced to $1/2$ quart.

Saturday students are free to enjoy the pleasures of historic Savannah, and in the evening they meet with Chef Randall to prepare the Dinner Party, which they will afterward enjoy together around the table. The Southern weekend ends with a Low Country Brunch on Sunday, with everyone joining together to prepare a genuine low-country meal, such as Southern Fried Quail.

Class Costs: A six-part-series program costs $325 for all six classes per person; the Friday-night Taste of Savannah class is $65 per person; the Dinner Party is $65 per person; and the Low Country Brunch is $65 per person. The total cost for the weekend program is $195 per person. Evening classes during the week may run anywhere from $60 to $85, depending on the menu.

Class Frequency: The six-part series meets six consecutive Tuesdays four times per year; A Taste of Savannah is offered monthly on weekends.

Class Length: Most classes run three hours, 6:30 to 9:30 p.m. Wednesday through Saturday; Sunday brunch is from 10:30 a.m. to 1:30 p.m.

Class Type: The cooking series are hands-on/demonstration; other classes are strictly demonstration.

Class Size: Minimum of eight, maximum of twenty students.

Lodging: DoubleTree Hotel Historic Savannah, 411 West Bay Street, Savannah, GA 31401; (912) 790-7000; www.stayinsavannah.com. The hotel is located in historic Savannah within blocks of major attractions. Rooms are furnished with antique reproductions and have all the modern amenities needed for a comfortable stay. Hamilton-Turner Inn, 330 Abercorn Street, Savannah, GA 31401; (912) 233-1833; www.hamilton-turnerinn.com. This circa-1873 four-story mid-Victorian mansion offers seventeen luxurious suites with traditional furnishings mixed with antiques.

Amenities: DoubleTree: secure valet parking, fitness center, complimentary twenty-four-hour business center, secretarial and concierge services, and much more; Hamilton-Turner Inn: Gilchrist and Soames bathroom amenities, British-made Christy towels, fireplaces, triple-sheeted bedding, quality linens, and more. For more information contact: Chef Joe Randall's Cooking School, 5409 Waters Avenue, Savannah, GA 31404; (912) 303-0409; www.chefjoerandall.com.

LOUISIANA

New Orleans Cooking Experience
New Orleans, Louisiana

*C*ajun *and Creole foods are unmistakably special, each with their own personality; some consider them to be the best cuisine in the world. The reason for their excellence is because of the considerable attention given to the preparation—and the taste. Although they are two different types of foods, they have similar ingredients, such as rice, crabs, oyster, pork, okra, and yams. What distinguishes the two cuisines is what they do with the ingredients.*

In Creole cuisine, for example, which has strong French and Spanish influences, food preparation is more refined, with sophisticated and complex layers of flavors. This style of cooking began in the kitchens of wealthy planters and families whose European chefs brought to the American table the European style of cooking so popular in the eighteenth and nineteenth centuries. These recipes were adapted to take advantage of locally available ingredients and given a new character by fusing African and Caribbean cooking styles. Since New Orleans was the second-largest immigration port in the country next to Ellis Island, new arrivals (including Italians, Germans, and others) made their contributions as well, turning Creole cuisine into a truly fusion cuisine.

Cajun food, on the other hand, has strong Native American and French Acadian influences; it is usually made in one pot, and it is basic, spicy, and hearty, without the gentle, urbane touches of Creole cooking. It is food from the bayou, created by people who had to make do with what was available— and because of their deep love of food, they made do very well.

The best place to acquaint yourself with Creole and Cajun cooking— and the history of both—is at the New Orleans Cooking Experience. This respected cooking school has attracted its share of prominent teachers who have dazzled student palates.

Chef Frank Brigtsen conducts a Cajun cooking class.
PHOTO COURTESY OF NEW ORLEANS COOKING EXPERIENCE

ABOUT THE CHEFS

Chef Frank Brigtsen designed the curriculum at the cooking school, and he brings to the program a respect for the best of Cajun and Creole foods. His early training was working in the kitchen with world-renowned chef Paul Prudhomme at Commander's Palace Restaurant and K-Paul's Louisiana Kitchen. In 1986, after seven years working with Chef Prudhomme, he and his wife, Marna, opened Brigtsen's Restaurant in New Orleans. Today he is considered one of Louisiana's top chefs and one of the school's top teachers. He has been featured in leading publications (*Gourmet, Food and Wine,* and *Chef* magazines) and on the PBS series *Great Chefs of New Orleans.*

Over the years, Chef Brigtsen has won many awards for his stylized and unpretentious Louisiana cooking, created with seasonal and local ingredients. Some of the recipes that have distinguished him include his Filé Gumbo with Chicken and Andouille (see recipe) and his shrimp étouffée.

Filé Gumbo with Chicken and Andouille

Compliments of Frank Brigtsen, Brigtsen's Restaurant

There are many ways to make gumbo, but all gumbos have one thing in common: a brown roux. To make a flavorful roux, Chef Brigtsen uses the oil that was used to brown the chicken. The seasoning and vegetables are added in two stages to provide different levels of taste and texture, and then filé powder (ground sassafras leaves) is added to the vegetables and cooked until most of the stringiness disappears. This gumbo recipe can be made year-round because it doesn't require any seasonal ingredients.

Gumbo, when made as a main course, is often served with a salad with crabmeat and Creole vinaigrette, or potato salad, and a hot crusty French bread. Dessert may be a bread pudding with hard sauce (i.e., hard liquor like bourbon and whiskey) or Louisiana strawberry shortcake. A good beer or a heavy white or light red wine makes a nice addition.

Ingredients

- 1 pound andouille sausage, sliced into half-rounds $1/4$ inch thick
- 2 tablespoons pomace olive oil
- 4 cups diced yellow onions ($1/2$-inch pieces)
- 3 cups diced celery ($1/2$-inch pieces)
- 2 cups diced green, red, and yellow bell peppers ($1/2$-inch pieces)
- 2 bay leaves
- 1 tablespoon minced fresh garlic
- 4 teaspoons salt
- $1/4$ teaspoon whole-leaf dried thyme
- $1/2$ teaspoon ground black pepper
- $1/4$ teaspoon ground white pepper
- $1/4$ teaspoon ground cayenne pepper
- 3 tablespoons gumbo filé powder
- 12 cups chicken stock or water
- 1 chicken, cut into 8 pieces (or 3–4 pounds bone-in chicken pieces)
- 4 cups vegetable or peanut oil
- 3 cups all-purpose white flour
- About 4 tablespoons Chef Paul Prudhomme's Meat Magic seasoning*

* Chef Paul Prudhomme's Magic Seasonings are available in most grocery stores throughout the United States and in many other countries. It can also be ordered online at www .chefpaul.com.

1. Preheat oven to 350°F. Place the andouille sausage in a shallow baking pan and bake until the edges turn brown, about 40–45 minutes. Remove from the oven and set aside.

2. Heat the olive oil in a large pot over high heat. Add 3 cups of the onion, 2 cups of the celery, 1½ cups of the bell pepper, and the bay leaves. Cook, stirring occasionally, until the onions begin to turn brown, 12–15 minutes.

3. Add the remaining onion, celery, and bell pepper and reduce heat to medium. Cook, stirring occasionally, until the second stage of onions turns clear, 2–3 minutes.

4. Add the garlic, salt, thyme, black pepper, white pepper, cayenne, and filé powder. Reduce heat to low. Cook, stirring constantly, for 3–4 minutes.

5. Add the chicken stock and bring to a boil. Add the cooked andouille sausage. Reduce heat to low and simmer, stirring occasionally, for 1 hour. Skim off any excess oil that rises to the surface and discard.

6. While the broth is simmering, brown the chicken: Heat two frying pans over medium heat (preferably cast-iron skillets). Add enough vegetable or peanut oil to be about ½ inch deep (about 2 cups per skillet).

7. To make seasoned flour, in a shallow baking pan add 2 cups of the flour and 4 teaspoons of the Meat Magic seasoning. Blend well.

8. Season the chicken pieces lightly and evenly with the remainder of the Meat Magic seasoning. When the oil is hot, but slightly below frying temperature (about 350°F), dredge the seasoned chicken pieces in the seasoned flour and fry the chicken on both sides until brown and crispy, about 5 minutes per side. Remove the chicken from the oil and set on paper towels to drain. Add the browned chicken pieces to the simmering broth and cook, stirring occasionally, until the chicken is fully cooked and tender, 35–40 minutes.

9. Remove the chicken from the gumbo and place it on a shallow pan to cool. When the chicken is cool enough to handle, take the meat off the bones and set aside. Discard the chicken bones and skin.

10. To make a roux, after the frying oil has cooled off a bit, slowly and carefully pour some of the frying oil into a heatproof glass measuring cup. (You just want the clear oil, with no browned bits of flour.) You will need ¾ cup plus 2 tablespoons of oil to make the roux.

11. Heat a cast-iron skillet over high heat. Add the oil you reserved from frying the chicken. When the oil is hot, gradually add 1 cup of flour, whisking or stirring constantly. Cook, whisking constantly, until the roux becomes the color of peanut butter. Reduce heat to medium and continue cooking, whisking constantly, until the roux is deep reddish brown (chocolate brown). Remove from heat and set aside to cool for 15 minutes.

12. Bring the gumbo broth to a boil. Carefully pour off any excess oil that may have risen to the top of the roux and discard. Slowly and carefully add the roux to the boiling broth, a little bit at a time, stirring constantly. Reduce heat to low and simmer, stirring occasionally, for 25–30 minutes. Skim off any excess oil that rises to the surface and discard. Add the chicken meat, increase heat to medium, and cook, stirring gently, until the chicken is heated through. Serve immediately with cooked rice.

Yields 12 bowl-size portions.

Judy Jurisich, founder of the school, has created a program that provides an authentic culinary experience reflecting the culture of New Orleans. Each class offers a mix of local history and flavors for students to enjoy and take home with them. In general, her goal is to teach "authentic Creole with a dash of Cajun."

ABOUT THE COOKING PROGRAM

The test of a meal is how it tastes—and creating a good taste means mastering the art of developing deep flavors. To achieve layers of flavor, Chef Brigtsen gives careful attention to each step of preparation. The trick is to maximize the special flavors of each ingredient so that when they are united with the other ingredients, they will provide the rich depth that makes good food taste so special.

In teaching his students, for example, Chef Brigtsen introduces them to techniques that can be applied to any cuisine (like mirepoix and sautéing), and he carefully develops each ingredient by using whatever cooking method he feels is appropriate (for example, browning onions to release their essential flavor before introducing them to the other ingredients, or adding ingredients in stages to the recipe to enhance taste and texture).

By giving special attention to each step of the recipe, he not only eliminates the mystery of creating good food, but he also explains how these techniques may be applied to other recipes. Since he believes that cooking, like eating, should be enjoyable, he strives to bring this joy to the learning process with easy-to-understand information presented in an orderly and pleasant manner.

The school offers a choice of classes:

Half-day classes run about two and a half hours and are usually demonstrations. About five or eight recipes are taught. After food preparation, students gather around the table for a four-course dinner.

The immersion series runs two or three days, and classes may be taken sequentially or over the period of a year.

Two vacation programs are offered (a three-day and a four-day program). The four-day program includes a Thursday-night dinner at

Brigtsen's Restaurant, a Friday-night dinner class, and a Saturday lunch class. The three-day program is the same, but without the Thursday dinner.

On Thursday and Friday evenings, and Saturday lunch, they have open classes weekly. These can be taken as half-day classes individually or packaged into the three- or four-day vacation program. Chef Brigtsen teaches three or four times a month, usually on Thursday evenings. In the summer, they often have guest chefs from noted New Orleans Restaurants, usually on Wednesday or Thursday.

Private classes can be arranged for small groups under sixteen and for larger groups over nineteen; minimum class size is five. These classes are customized to student needs—weddings, rehearsal parties, or birthdays. Large classes are held at the nearby Restaurant Indigo, and several different chefs are used.

Class Costs: Single classes are $150 per person, three-day vacation classes are $290 per person, and four-day vacation classes are $385 per person. Lodging isn't included, but the House on Bayou Road (which is located in the same compound as the cooking school) offers discounts for New Orleans Cooking Experience guests. There are also discount rates for small and large groups, private classes, series classes, and for House on Bayou Road guests. Call for information.

Class Frequency: Weekly.

Class Length: Two and a half hours per class.

Class Type: Demonstration and some "modified" hands-on classes.

Class Size: Maximum twelve students, minimum six per class.

Lodging: The inn and the culinary school are located about twelve blocks from the French Quarter (halfway between the French Quarter and the New Orleans Museum of Fine Arts) on the same two-acre site of a 1798 plantation. This small Creole plantation compound (known as the House on Bayou Road) is filled with charming touches, from its many antiques to its attractive gardens, ponds, and courtyard.

Amenities: Tasty Southern breakfast, concierge service, off-street parking.

For more information contact: The New Orleans Cooking Experience, 2275 Bayou Road, New Orleans, LA 70119; (504) 945-9104; www.neworleanscookingexperience .com.

SOUTH CAROLINA

Woodlands Resort & Inn
Summerville, South Carolina

*A*mid magnolia and oak trees on forty-two acres of parkland grounds, the Woodlands Resort & Inn stands proudly, a reminder of a South that for the most part has gone with the wind. Once the winter home of a Pennsylvania railroad tycoon, it is today an elegant AAA Five Diamond, Mobil Five-Star award-winning resort and a Relais & Châteaux member property.

About twenty-five minutes from Charleston and the Ashley River Road plantations, this stunningly maintained 1906 Greek Revival mansion immediately conjures up images of a privileged past, nestled in a historic low-country community surrounded by eighteenth- and nineteenth-century mansions.

To enhance the experience of sheer luxury, great attention has been given to the resort's cuisine. The Woodlands' executive chef, Nate Whiting, in the tradition of his predecessor, Chef Tarver King, brings to each meal a delicate style that is quietly infused with memorably rich flavors.

In his quest for perfection, he is forever searching for succulent, sun-ripened ingredients to bring fresh flavor to his meals. Many of the ingredients he depends upon are so fresh that they have never known refrigeration. Special cheeses, dry-aged beef, and milk-fed poussin are sent to him overnight from Di Bruno Brothers in Philadelphia, and his seafood is served the same day it is caught. Two of his signature dishes include Roast 'N Toast Swordfish (see recipe) and Lobster "Cappuccino" (a frothy soup with knuckles of lobster for flavor).

Students who visit the Woodlands to take a culinary class from Chef Whiting will not only enjoy one of the most romantic settings in the South, but they will also learn the chef's simple and elegant cooking style.

Woodlands Resort & Inn's 1906 Greek Revival mansion.
PHOTO COURTESY OF WOODLANDS RESORT & INN

ABOUT THE CHEF

Chef Whiting has been the Woodlands's sous chef since 2004 and learned much of what he knows under the tutelage of Chef King, a protégé of Patrick O'Connell.

In each of his classes, Chef Whiting strives to teach students how to prepare food that will appeal to them and others on all levels—from the way it is presented to the way it tastes—using the highest quality ingredients enhanced with organically grown herbs and vegetables.

ABOUT THE CLASSES

The culinary programs at the Woodlands are a little more private and stylish than some other culinary getaways. Three types of programs are offered: cooking demonstrations, the Chef's Table Dinner, and the Chef du Jour program.

Roast 'N Toast Swordfish

Compliments of Woodlands Resort & Inn

To prepare this recipe, Chef Whiting recommends that you use the freshest fish and the best ingredients available, and that you select sourdough bread without big holes. You should also add a little salt to the fish to get it to sweat before wrapping a slice of bread around it. This will make it possible for the bread to adhere to the fish more securely during cooking.

Ingredients
- 2 tablespoons extra virgin olive oil
- 3 cloves garlic (peeled and left whole)
- ³/₄ cup lucques olives (pitted) or a mellow-flavored olive, preferably green
- 1 cup pine nuts
- Salt and white pepper to taste
- 1 tablespoon finely chopped rosemary
- 3 tablespoons finely chopped flat leaf parsley
- 6 ounces swordfish (or other white-flesh fish, such as grouper, snapper, etc.)
- Thinly sliced sourdough bread for each portion of fish
- Large knob French butter
- 2 sprigs rosemary
- Olive Vinaigrette (see recipe)
- 10 large green grapes, peeled

1. Warm the olive oil and garlic in a sauté pan until the garlic becomes golden brown and smells fragrant. Add the olives and fry until they begin to wrinkle and change color. Add the pine nuts, stirring constantly until they become golden brown. Add salt and pepper to taste, and add the chopped herbs. Spread the pine nut mixture out on paper towels to cool; set aside.
2. Bring the fish up to room temperature and season with salt and pepper. Let the fish rest on a plate. When the fish begins to "sweat," wrap each piece with a slice of sourdough.
3. Melt the butter on medium-high heat in an iron skillet or a nonstick pan. When the butter becomes "foamy," add the wrapped fish and rosemary sprigs. Sauté for about 3 minutes or until toasty brown. Flip the fish only once, as it will become soggy if rolled around too much.
4. Drain the fish on a paper towel and keep warm (the longer the fish rests, the less crispy the final dish will be).
5. When ready to "plate up," warm the pine nut mixture and add the grapes. Spoon onto the middle of the plate and place the crispy fish on top. Spoon some Olive Vinaigrette around the dish and serve.

Serves 2.

Olive Vinaigrette

Compliments of Woodlands Resort & Inn

Ingredients
- 1 cup black olive brine
- 1 tablespoon red wine vinegar
- $^1/_2$ teaspoon sugar
- 1 tablespoon Dijon mustard
- 2 teaspoons extra virgin olive oil
- 1 tablespoon lemon juice
- 1 tablespoon minced olives

Mix all ingredients together and keep cold in a sealed container until ready to use.

Roast 'N Toast Swordfish PHOTO COURTESY OF WOODLANDS RESORT & INN

During the once-a-month cooking demonstration, students learn the chef's secrets to cooking. Each demonstration focuses on a specific theme, such as how to use artisanal salts and exotic peppercorns from around the world to enlarge flavor. These demonstrations are free for guests who stay for dinner, and they are modestly priced for those who only want to attend the demonstration. Guests have the opportunity to ask questions, sample the foods, and receive recipes and helpful hints during the demonstration.

With advance reservations, up to eight guests can partake in the Chef's Table Dinner. Guests have the opportunity to enjoy personalized attention from the chef, the sommelier, and the culinary team while they learn the secrets behind the one-of-a-kind meal that they are being served. This intimate dinner party with the staff is a sophisticated and exclusive dining experience that will broaden the guests' knowledge.

For the ultimate experience, the inn offers a private cooking class called Chef du Jour. The student works alongside the chef and his kitchen staff to prepare some of the menu items for the evening meal, using cooking methods such as roasting, braising, sautéing, and baking. Each of these classes is tailored to the particular interests of the student. The class includes a three-course lunch, paired with wine; a chef's jacket; and printed recipes. A spouse or a friend may be included in the class for an additional fee.

Class Costs: Demonstration class: $45 per person, $95 per person for the five-course meal, $49 per person for a wine pairing; Chef's Table: $175 per person; Chef du Jour: $600 per person, $300 for a spouse or friend; special weekend/weekday gourmet package: starts at $540 per person and includes two nights' accommodations, a half bottle of wine upon arrival, a four-course dinner on the night of your choosing, and a full country breakfast for two each morning.

Class Frequency: Demonstration class: held the first Tuesday of the month in a private dining room; Chef's Table: offered weeknights, when available, starting at 6:30 p.m. in the main kitchen; Chef du Jour: schedule depends upon the chef's availability.

Class Length: Demonstration class: forty-five minutes, beginning at 5:30 p.m.; Chef's Table: about four hours; Chef du Jour: eight hours, from 10:00 a.m. to 6:00 p.m.

Class Type: Primarily demonstration. Chef du Jour is strictly hands-on.

Class Size: Demonstration class: maximum of twelve, minimum of two students; Chef's Table: maximum of eight, minimum of two per table; Chef du Jour: private one-on-one class that may be extended to include a friend or spouse.

Lodging: The Woodlands has eighteen guest rooms and a one-bedroom country cottage. Each room has a mix of period furniture, selected for comfort and style. All rooms have Bose CD stereos, lavish bathrooms, and more. (Some have sitting areas; others have fireplaces; many have heated towel racks and soothing whirl-pool baths.)

Amenities: Goose down feather beds, fine Frette linens, terry-cloth robes, flat-panel HDTVs, wireless Internet access, and whirlpool baths.

Activities: Swimming, tennis, croquet, day spa, hiking, golf, carriage rides, and guided hunting and fishing excursions; shopping and fine dining in Charleston; and tours of the historic plantations and gardens along the Ashley River Road. For more information contact: Woodlands Resort & Inn, 125 Parsons Road, Summerville, SC 29483; (843) 875-2600; www.woodlandsinn.com.

VIRGINIA

Clifton Inn
Charlottesville, Virginia

At the edge of Charlottesville, a pleasant surprise awaits visitors seeking fine dining and lodging. Raised on a hill overlooking the Rivanna River is an eighteenth-century house once owned by Thomas Jefferson's daughter Martha and her husband. It was on this land several hundred years ago that Martha entertained and dined with friends in old Virginia style. Today, it is a stunning and intimate eighteen-room Relais & Châteaux inn.

Food is taken very seriously at Clifton Inn. A winner of the AAA Four Diamond Award and the Wine Spectator *Award of Excellence, the restaurant is best known for what has become identified as American food, a subtle fusion of world flavors, innovatively prepared with an avant-garde mix of local ingredients. According to Chef Dean Maupin, a graduate of Greenbrier Resort Hotel's three-year apprenticeship program, this is achieved by presenting food with "honesty" ("high-end, quality ingredients that are unmasked and allowed the freedom to speak for themselves").*

ABOUT THE CHEF

Dean Maupin mastered the fundamentals (how to make stock, sauces, and more) at the Greenbrier. But it was while working under two acclaimed chefs, Carmen Quagliata (Union Square Café, New York City) and Fortunato Nicotra (Felidia Restaurant, New York City), that he learned to strip food of its decoration and turn it into a clean eating experience. He became skilled at emphasizing all the things that make a meal special, such as taste, appeal, freshness, and smell. Today, thanks to their guidance, he has evolved into a serious and skilled culinary artist.

The Clifton Inn is on a hill overlooking the Rivanna River. PHOTO COURTESY OF JOE DAVID

ABOUT THE CLASSES

For private groups interested in polishing their cooking skills, Chef Maupin provides a relaxed program, and each class begins after it is determined what the students want to focus on (e.g., an executive- or family-bonding program, some hands-on experience, or just a watch-and-listen lesson). Once the purpose is understood, together, side by side, students and teacher will prepare the meal. A sommelier provides wine and champagne, and when the meal is ready, the students enjoy the three-course lunch they have prepared.

Weekend packages are also offered, and these also have a specific focus. One, for example, might introduce students to some of the foods that have become inn specialties, while another might be a mind-and-body weekend that introduces guests to spa cooking and includes massage and yoga. All weekend programs include a two-night stay, breakfast, cooking classes, a five-course dinner, and more.

Class Costs: $890 for a weekend package for two; $85 per person for a day class.

Class Frequency: Depends on the chef's schedule.

Class Length: Two hours per day, from noon to 2:00 p.m.

Class Type: Hands-on/demonstration.

Class Size: Maximum ten students; minimum two.

Lodging: Like all Relais & Châteaux hotels and inns around the world, visitors to this property will step into a world of pampered luxury. Each room, uniquely appointed, provides fine touches that make a stay special: Mascioni linens, fresh-

Albemarle Apple Butter Doughnuts

Compliments of Chef Dean Maupin

These are a pleasant treat with your morning coffee.

Apple Butter Doughnuts

Ingredients
- $1/4$ ounce dry yeast
- 3 tablespoons warm water
- $3/4$ cup lukewarm milk
- $1/4$ cup sugar
- 1 teaspoon salt
- 1 egg
- 3 tablespoons butter
- $2^1/2$ cups all-purpose flour
- Apple butter (for filling)

1. In a mixing bowl, dissolve yeast in water. Once dissolved, add milk, sugar, salt, egg, butter, and half of the flour. Mix until smooth.
2. Add the remaining flour and mix until blended. In a greased bowl, let the dough rise until it doubles in size.
3. After the dough has risen, punch it down. It can be refrigerated for up to three days until ready to use.
4. Generously dust a table with flour. Roll out dough to $1/2$-inch thickness. Use $1^1/2$-inch round cutters to cut the dough into rounds. Place each round on a lightly floured sheet. (Excess dough that has been collected after shaping the

cut flowers, Waterworks bath fixtures, Molton Brown soaps and lotions, and much more.

Activities: The inn has its own private lake, a swimming pool, and tennis courts, and it's all within easy access to everything that matters: three presidents' homes, the University of Virginia, and enough historic properties, wineries, and other distractions to satisfy even the most blasé.

For more information contact: Clifton Inn, 1296 Clifton Inn Drive, Charlottesville, VA 22911; (434) 971-1800; www.cliftoninn.net.

doughnuts should be allowed to rest for about 10 minutes, then rolled out again to create more doughnuts.)

5. Let the dough rounds rise and double in size in a warm place. Once they have risen and are soft, deep fry (at 325°F) until golden brown on both sides.

6. Drain doughnuts on a paper towel, then gently use a small knife to make a hole in the center of each. Pipe a little bit of apple butter into the hole. (Chef Maupin uses a local Albemarle County apple butter, though Pennsylvania Dutch apple butter is delicious as well.)

Vanilla Glaze

Ingredients
- ¹/₂ cup butter, softened at room temperature
- 3 cups powdered sugar
- Pinch of salt
- 1¹/₂ teaspoons vanilla extract
- 2–3 tablespoons warm milk

1. Blend the butter, powdered sugar, salt, and vanilla in a bowl with a whisk. Add milk as needed. The glaze should be the consistency of heavy cream. Leave at room temperature, preferably in a warm place like the top of the oven. Stir before using.

2. To serve, dip one side of the warm doughnut in the vanilla glaze.

Makes 12 medium-size doughnuts.

The Inn at Meander Plantation
Locust Dale, Virginia

*A*way from the noise and excitement of city life, hidden in the center *of historic Virginia's countryside, is the Inn at Meander Plantation, an eighty-acre, eighteenth-century inn. Built in 1766, the plantation is a*

 The Hub of Early America

*T*hree English ships sailed into the Chesapeake Bay in 1607 and up *the James River, where they anchored at a site known as Jamestown. Despite disease, hostile Indians, and food shortages, these courageous explorers survived—turning Jamestown into the first successful English colony in America. From there they expanded along the James and Rivanna Rivers into what was later called Albemarle County.*

Over the years, many prominent Americans have lived in the county, including American presidents Thomas Jefferson, James Monroe, and James Madison; novelist John Grisham; actress Sissy Spacek; and television sports personality Howie Long. Newcomers to the area are drawn by the rolling hills, fertile land, and the eighteenth-century spirit and Southern hospitality evident almost everywhere.

Although the county has adapted to modern conveniences, it still proudly displays its early American roots by preserving important properties, erecting plaques, and even celebrating local historic moments. The major hub of this beautiful county is Charlottesville, a pleasant mix of the old and new.

To dip into Charlottesville's past, visitors should begin their tour at Court Historic Square, which was once the original downtown, made up

charming reminder of the Old South, faithfully restored and maintained by two dedicated preservationists, owners Suzanne Thomas and Suzie Blanchard. Their goal was to preserve its original charm without sacrificing modern conveniences, and each update was undertaken with complete respect for the property's historical value.

Although new development is pushing its way into the area, plantation guests won't notice: The property is bordered by land largely untouched by

of a "court-house, one tavern, and about a dozen houses." It was here that the early shops and taverns, frequented by the three early presidents, were located. (Albemarle County Historical Society provides walking tours for a $5 donation; visit www.albemarlehistory.org. To experience the tempo of earlier times, the historical society also arranges free trips on the century-old Hatton Ferry.)

Visitors to Charlottesville can't avoid the strong influences of Thomas Jefferson, especially at the University of Virginia, which he founded in 1825. Thanks to his foresight, this well-respected university has become a major cultural center in the Virginia hills. A variety of events are presented at the university throughout the year, many of which are open to the general public. For details see the calendar on the school's Web site: www.virginia.edu/calendar.

Those who prefer their entertainment in iambic pentameter may want to head to the ruins of the Jefferson-designed Barbour Mansion, where each summer plays by William Shakespeare are performed by the Four County Players (www.b-ville.net). Those who prefer their drama or comedy sung in full voice may want to visit the grounds of James Monroe's Ash Lawn Plantation, where each summer a music festival is scheduled (www.ash lawnopera.org).

time. For the duration of their stay, they will walk in the footsteps of histori-
cal giants like Thomas Jefferson and General Lafayette, both frequent guests
at the property when it was known as the Joshua Fry home.

What has changed noticeably over the years is the food. Like most of
America, Virginia has been invaded by fast-food giants, which have nega-
tively impacted regional cuisine with their tasteless imitation of time-honored
Southern foods. At the Meander Plantation, you will escape such culinary
bedlam. Here, during select seasons, the chef re-creates with originality and
skill some of the traditional flavors that Southerners so dearly love. One way
he achieves this is by maintaining a strong bond with the local market.

ABOUT THE CHEFS

Under the able guidance of Suzie Blanchard, director of the Meander
County Inn Cooking School, Executive Chef David Scales enthusiastically

Suzie Blanchard is the director of the cooking school.
PHOTO COURTESY OF TIMBERWOLF CREEK

shares his knowledge during a two-day, hands-on class once a month. A graduate of L'Academie de Cuisine in Maryland, where he taught briefly, David has almost two decades of restaurant experience. Suzie is a veteran instructor and former food editor for forty suburban Chicago weekly newspapers. Most of what she knows, which is considerable, has been learned on the job and by working alongside respected cooks.

Sweet Potato Scales Crusted Grouper

Compliments of Executive Chef David Scales, the Inn at Meander Plantation

Chef Scales created this recipe when he arrived at the Inn at Meander Plantation, and it celebrates the inn's sophisticated Southern food traditions, his love of fish, and his name. This recipe pairs nicely with Horton Petite Mansing and fresh asparagus spears.

Ingredients
- 1 sweet potato
- 2 cups canola oil
- $1^1/_2$ pounds grouper, portioned into 4 6-ounce fillets
- Salt and pepper to taste
- 1 sweet onion, sliced
- 4 ounces white wine (viognier is recommended)
- 3 ounces olive oil
- Tequila Sunrise Beurre Blanc (see recipe)

1. Cut and turn the sweet potato into four circular batons. With a mandoline, thinly slice the sweet potato sections so that they resemble fish scales.
2. Blanch (simmer) the sweet potato scales in hot oil until they are translucent, about 5–7 minutes. Strain and cool to room temperature.
3. Place the sweet potato scales on the grouper fillets, overlapping them to look like fish scales. Season with salt and pepper. On a bed of onions drizzled with wine and olive oil, roast the fish for about 6–8 minutes. (The fish will be done when it excretes white oil.)
4. Prior to service, place each fillet in the center of a plate. Lightly brown the sweet potato scales with a kitchen blow torch for color, and drizzle Tequila Sunrise Beurre Blanc around the edge of the plate.

Serves 4.

Made-in-Virginia ingredients make tasty meals at Meander Plantation's restaurant.
PHOTO COURTESY OF TIMBERWOLF CREEK

Trained in classic French cooking, David's goal is to create new and tasty meals with made-in-Virginia ingredients. He refers to his style of cooking as Modern American with a Southern Accent. He has been known to slip such ingredients as country ham, collards, or even grits into an entree (like his Sweet Potato Scales Crusted Grouper—see recipe), and he strives to maintain a lightness and purity of flavor that will permit the natural taste of the ingredients to shine.

ABOUT THE CLASSES

Each class, which the two chefs teach together, has a slightly different focus. So much of what they share with the students is dependent on what's in season at that time. One month, for example, they may feature seafood, another month summer crops (like corn, berries, tomatoes, and zucchini), and during the winter holiday months, bite-size hors d'oeuvres.

A two-day cooking lesson for two includes two nights' lodging, all meals, side trips to local food producers, two hands-on/demonstration classes, and a few favors to take home (such as recipes, cooking tips, and an apron). A one-day class includes lunch and dinner. Classes are held in the kitchen and library of the old plantation.

Tequila Sunrise Beurre Blanc

Compliments of Executive Chef David Scales, the Inn at Meander Plantation

This sauce can be stored in the refrigerator and served the next day, if careful. Chef Scales recommends that you let it sit for about three hours at room temperature, then revive it by gently heating it until it is warm. Unfortunately, the flavor of the reheated serving won't be as intense as the original.

Ingredients
- ¹/₂ cup tequila
- ¹/₂ cup red wine vinegar
- ¹/₂ cup orange juice
- 2 sprigs tarragon
- 12 peppercorns
- 1 bay leaf
- 1 shallot, sliced
- 2 ounces cream
- 1 pound cold unsalted butter, cut into 1-inch cubes
- Salt and pepper to taste
- Few drops of grenadine

1. Combine the first seven ingredients in a medium saucepan and reduce over low heat to syrup consistency. After the sauce is reduced, add cream, and then slowly add the butter. Stir constantly to emulsify. (The cream acts as a stabilizer.) Season with salt and pepper to taste.
2. Strain the sauce and keep warm, about 100–120°F. If it is too hot or too cold, the sauce will break.
3. Finish with grenadine just prior to serving.

Makes 16 1-tablespoon servings.

Class Costs: Two-day lesson: about $850 per couple; one-day class: $150 per person.

Class Frequency: Two-day lesson: Monday and Tuesday once a month, year-round.

Class Length: Two-day lesson: two hours on Monday (in the morning and in the afternoon) and two hours on Tuesday (in the morning).

Class Size: Maximum twenty-four students, broken into two groups.

Class Type: Hands-on/demonstration.

Lodging: Students stay either at the manor house or in one of the updated historic buildings footsteps away, all with tasteful antiques selected to match the character of the property. Each of the ten guest rooms has a private bathroom with tub and shower, gas or wood-burning fireplace, window air conditioner, and more. The two-level colonial kitchen house, which has the original hearth and oven, is the most expensive suite.

Dinner Only: Visitors who just want to sample the food may enjoy a five-course dinner at the restaurant Thursday through Saturday. The per-person price is $65, not including wine, taxes, and gratuities. Dinner begins at 6:00 p.m. with hors d'oeuvres and cocktails, followed at 7:00 with a choice of entrees. (Past dinners have included ginger salmon wontons, roasted rosemary pork loin brochette, baked Gruyère cheese grits, caramelized brussels sprouts, and sweet potato pound cake.) Guests who stay at the plantation Sunday through Wednesday are served a dinner basket in their room ($60 per couple).

Activities: In this idyllic setting, with its gentle hills that roll lazily toward the Blue Ridge Mountains, guests are free to while away their spare time horseback riding (about $40), hot-air ballooning (about $175), or enjoying a massage (about $95). (It is strongly recommended that such special amenities or services be arranged in advance.)

For more information contact: The Inn at Meander Plantation, 2333 North James Madison Highway, Locust Dale, VA 22948; (800) 385-4936; www.meander.net.

Briar Patch Bed and Breakfast
Middleburg, Virginia

In the heart of Virginia's horse and wine country, what was a one-room log cabin in 1805 has grown into a cozy and comfortable nine-bedroom inn today. The cabin's origin has been blurred by time, but according to one historian, it may have once been a tenant house on the 1,200-acre property belonging to eighteenth-century Virginia statesman Charles Fenton Mercer.

Briar Patch Inn. PHOTO COURTESY OF JOE DAVID

Virginia's Jodhpur-
and-Riding-Helmet Haunt

The idle rich have always had special playgrounds, and in northern Virginia it's Middleburg, a charming eighteenth-century community with a mix of historic homes and inns, old money and new, and well-tended stables and thoroughbreds. Although the residents only number in the hundreds, their combined worth is in the billions.

A longtime hangout for the horsey set, Middleburg has always attracted its share of celebrities. John F. Kennedy spent weekends here, and Jackie rode in the local fox hunts. Elizabeth Taylor and Senator John Warner exchanged wedding vows in his Middleburg home, and Linda Tripp (of Clinton scandal fame) served hungry travelers at her husband's Washington Street market, the Christmas Sleigh. Personal pleasure often comes first in Middleburg, and as a result the community has had its share of "embarrassments." The most famous in recent years was when the Arms heiress Susan Cummings made international headlines after shooting her two-timing, polo-playing lover. (For some local lore e-mail Vicky Moon at info@vickymoon.com. She provides insider tours of Middleburg for $68 per person.)

Founded in 1787, Middleburg got its name by being located midway between Alexandria and Winchester on the Ashby Gap (currently Virginia Highway 50). Travelers who made the long horse and carriage ride between the two cities would overnight at Middleburg's Red Fox Inn and Tavern (www.redfox.com); today's travelers continue to find cozy accommodations and hearty meals there. The Red Fox is a strong draw, and it's so popular that you may even see a few famous faces there.

Briar Patch Bed and Breakfast's location in the foothills of the Blue Ridge and Shenandoah Mountains offers panoramic mountain views and direct access to Dulles Airport (twenty minutes away), Washington, D.C. (about an hour away), and the charming village of Middleburg (minutes away). Although this property is in transition, it is being restored and updated with an eye toward maintaining it as an unpretentious getaway from Washington, D.C.

Like so many historic inns around the country, the inn offers a three-day cooking getaway. It begins on a Friday night with an appetizer and local wine greeting, and it ends on Sunday morning with a country breakfast of home-baked pastries, pancakes, quiche, or other tasty foods.

ABOUT THE CHEF

Chef Becky Croft, a former culinary student at Johnson & Wales University in Norfolk, teaches part time at Briar Patch Bed and Breakfast, where she was once the full-time chef.

PHILOSOPHY

Becky refers to her taste in food as being "upscale, but upscale without being snobby." Although she prefers to prepare international meals with zesty spices and herbs, they are always meals that aren't outlandish in their presentation or use of ingredients. Some of her guests are the meat-and-potatoes crowd who tend not to be too experimental, so she serves them more familiar foods made from locally grown, fresh ingredients instead.

Weight Watchers might be horrified by her sometimes-generous use of real butter and whipped cream, but she justifies her decision: "Most people on vacation don't want to lighten up with healthier foods. For this reason I always go for flavor, using healthier combinations only when appropriate."

Brie and Dried Cherry Stuffed Chicken Breast with Fontina Risotto and Roasted Asparagus

Compliments of Chef Becky Croft

This recipe is best enjoyed with a bottle of Three Fox's Classico Cabernet Franc. You may want to start the meal with a salad and end it with something traditional like a slice of chocolate cake.

Brie and Dried Cherry Chicken Ingredients
- 4 boneless, skinless chicken breasts
- 4 ounces Brie, sliced
- $^1/_2$ cup dried cherries
- Salt and pepper to taste

Cherry Gastric Ingredients
- 1 cup sugar
- $^1/_2$ cup vinegar
- $^1/_4$ cup Chambord or cherry brandy

Fontina Risotto Ingredients
- 10 ounces Arborio rice
- $1^1/_2$ quarts chicken stock
- 8 ounces grated fontina
- Salt and pepper to taste

Roasted Asparagus Ingredients
- 1 pound asparagus, trimmed
- 2 ounces extra virgin olive oil
- Salt and pepper to taste

1. Slice a "pocket" in each chicken breast and stuff with Brie and cherries. Sauté on one side. Place on a sheet pan and bake in a 350°F oven for 15 minutes or until juices run clear.
2. For the gastric, combine all ingredients in a nonreactive pan. Cook until the mixture is reduced by three-quarters and the consistency of a thick syrup. Pour the sauce over the chicken breasts before serving.
3. For the risotto, sauté the Arborio rice in a small amount of oil until roasted. Gradually add stock and stir until it is all absorbed. Add fontina at the very end and season with salt and pepper.
4. For the asparagus, place the asparagus on a sheet pan. Drizzle with olive oil and sprinkle with salt and pepper. Roast in a 400°F oven, turning a few times, until it is bright green and tender, about 10–12 minutes.

Serves 4.

ABOUT THE CLASSES

Cooking lessons are offered once a month, November through March; special culinary programs are available during the weekday for private groups and corporate team-building parties. During the three-hour, five-course lesson, Becky introduces students to the importance of proper prepping, precooking, and the art of presentation. Each lesson comes with a recipe for students to take home, and each meal is matched with a suitable local wine.

Class Costs: $75 per person for a lesson and tasting.

Class Frequency: Once a month, November through March, on Saturday evening.

Class Length: Each class runs about three hours, from 6:00 to 9:00 p.m.

Class Type: Mostly demonstration, with some hands-on.

Class Size: Not to exceed twenty-five students.

Lodging: The eight-bedroom house and one-bedroom cottage are cozy and have all the creaks and cracks expected from nineteenth-century buildings. It is almost as pleasant as visiting Grandma's house.

Amenities: Private and shared baths, free wireless, free drinks and snacks, hot tub, and more.

Activities: A broad choice of activities is available, and guests may put together any combination that works best for them. Nearby there are Civil War battlefields, three historic towns (Aldie, Middleburg, and Leesburg), antiques shops, restaurants, mountain hiking trails, wineries (wine-tasting tours using the inn's for-hire limousine are about $50 per person), horseback riding (about $36 per person for a trail ride and $99 for a twilight dinner ride at the Marriott Ranch; www.marriott ranch.com/horse.html), golf (from about $57 for nine holes to $99 for eighteen holes; www.raspberryfalls.com), and horse races/horse shows/polo tournaments, such as the Gold Cup at the polo grounds in the Middleburg/Plains area.

For more information contact: Briar Patch Bed and Breakfast, 23130 Briar Patch Lane, Middleburg, VA 20117; (703) 327-5911; www.briarpatchbandb.com.

The Inn at Little Washington
Washington, Virginia

*T*he Inn at Little Washington is an impressive property that began humbly as a garage and evolved over the years into a one-of-a-kind inn. Set in picturesque rural Virginia sixty miles south of Washington, D.C., the inn matches the finest in the world, offering guests all the comforts expected at fine lodgings.

Reviewers have gushed about the inn and its food: Gourmet *magazine says it is in a "class of its own"; the* New York Times *says the menu is "state-of-the-art tantalizing"; and Patricia Wells, of the* International Herald Tribune, *says chef-owner Patrick O'Connell has a "sense of near perfect taste, like a musician with perfect pitch."*

There is no question about it—everything about the inn is special. It may be fussy and overdone, but it is luxurious and comfortable. Regardless of who you are, you will always feel like the lord of the manor. The staff make certain of that by providing an abundance of genuinely polite and responsible service.

To the smallest detail, the inn has been designed to look like a French country inn, and everything has an authentic look to it. While some things are obviously genuine, like the seventeenth-century wooden floors from a French château and the sterling silver, fine china, and crystal table settings, others only seem genuine, like some of the professionally antiqued pine and plywood facades. What holds it all together, turning it into one extraordinary wow, is the tone and the lighting.

To make certain you don't take your surroundings too seriously, you will find touches of wit everywhere, from the frieze in the kitchen of the "five stages of dining" (a Patrick O'Connell takeoff of what Elisabeth Kübler-Ross identified as the five stages of grief) to the hand-painted trompe l'oeil murals of monkeys at play in the intimate bar off the lobby.

Chef Patrick O'Connell has been lauded for having near perfect taste.
PHOTO COURTESY OF THE INN AT LITTLE WASHINGTON

ABOUT THE CHEF

Chef Patrick O'Connell, a college dropout trained in the theatrical arts, has culinary skills that have been honed to near perfection. What is especially remarkable is that he is self-taught, and he has learned everything he knows by reading and practicing. Cooks like Julia Child were his inspiration, and her books provided him with the background to create his special culinary style.

Chef O'Connell's significant rise to stardom proves an important point. No matter what circuitous way a person travels to the top, all truly successful people must share three important traits: a passion for their work, a drive for excellence, and a fresh concept polished to blinding brightness.

In Chef O'Connell's case, this fresh concept was to create a French inn in the country that would be so special that people would be willing to travel miles to visit. It must be an inn that offered a sense of place unlike anything, anywhere. But more importantly, it had to be an inn that served food with the refined flavors he knew growing up.

PHILOSOPHY

Chef O'Connell is committed to instilling in each student a desire to achieve perfection. He does this by introducing them to the best foods

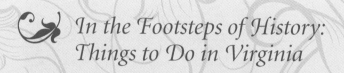

In the Footsteps of History: Things to Do in Virginia

Virginia may not have the Liberty Bell or Plymouth Rock, but it certainly has its share of plantations. The most noteworthy are the homes of the founding fathers: George Washington (Mount Vernon; www.mountvernon .org), James Madison (Montpelier; www.montpelier.org), Thomas Jefferson (Monticello; www.monticello.org), and James Monroe (Ash Lawn–Highland; www.ashlawnhighland.org). The latter three are in the Charlottesville area.

For a living-history experience, begin your travels in Richmond by visiting the Virginia House (www.vahistorical.org/vh/virginia_house01.htm), a Tudor mansion exported to America in pieces and reassembled. After leisurely touring the property and enjoying tea in its noble setting, head south to Williamsburg on Virginia Highway 5.

On VA 5, there is a small stretch of land wedged between the James and Chickahominy Rivers (between Richmond and Williamsburg) that overflows with historic plantations and farms. Known as Charles City County, an area with no city center, its main marker is a 250-plus-year-old courthouse. Unchanged by time, it was once the home to early American settlers, Indians, planters, slaves, and even U.S. presidents; today, like Williamsburg,

available, which he encourages them to create, one food at a time (a salad, a stew, a brioche), over and over again, until they achieve perfection. Once mastered, he recommends they try another recipe—and then another. He believes culinary perfection only occurs after repeated performance, using the finest example available as a benchmark to measure success.

ABOUT THE CLASS

The class, which is open only to culinary nonprofessionals, is a perfect getaway for anyone who wants to work alongside Chef O'Connell and

it is a pleasant area to visit to experience the past. For more information visit www.charlescity.org.

For those who prefer food and wine over history, the area has much to offer. Although Virginia wines tend to be more expensive than those from California, few of them are disappointing. If you are in the area during the Virginia Wine Festival, you may want to reserve some time to sample regional wines. Most of the major wineries in the state are represented. For more information visit www.virginiawinefestival.org.

There are also many wonderful food festivals throughout the state, and each has its own focus—the oyster festivals in Urbana (www.urbana oysterfestival.com) or Chincoteague (www.chincoteaguechamber.com/oyster-festival/index.html), the apple festivals throughout the state (www.virginiaapples.org/events/index.html), and, of course, the beloved but wacky peanut festival in Suffolk (www.suffolkfest.org).

Michie Tavern (www.michietavern.com) is a wonderful place to pause for an early-American lunch en route to Monticello near Charlottesville. You can eat your fill of tasty Southern specialties (colonial fried chicken, black-eyed peas, biscuits, hickory smoked pork barbecue, corn bread, and much more) in an eighteenth-century tavern setting at a fair price.

Apple Rutabaga Soup

Compliments of Chef Patrick O'Connell, the Inn at Little Washington

Rutabagas bring back childhood memories for Chef O'Connell, whose mother often prepared them during his early years—usually as a puree. Despite their "weird" taste, he found the gorgeous golden color seductive.

This soup recipe he created from rutabaga looks and tastes like liquid autumn. What's so wonderful about it is that it's simple to prepare, and it can be made in advance and even frozen. The elusive secret ingredient is a bit of maple syrup, which enhances the natural sweetness of the rutabaga.

Water or vegetable stock may be successfully substituted for the chicken stock if you wish to make this soup vegetarian, or if you want to avoid making chicken stock.

Ingredients
- 1 stick (¹/₄ pound) butter
- 1 cup roughly chopped onion
- 1 cup peeled, cored, and roughly chopped Granny Smith apple
- 1 cup peeled and roughly chopped rutabaga
- 1 cup peeled, seeded, and roughly chopped butternut squash
- 1 cup peeled and roughly chopped carrots
- 1 cup peeled and roughly chopped sweet potato
- 1 quart good chicken stock
- 2 cups heavy cream
- ¹/₄ cup maple syrup
- Salt and cayenne pepper to taste

Apple Rutabaga Soup
PHOTO COURTESY OF THE INN AT LITTLE WASHINGTON

1. In a large saucepan over medium-high heat, melt the butter. Add the onion, apple, rutabaga, squash, carrots, and sweet potato and cook, stirring occasionally, until the onions are translucent.
2. Add the chicken stock and bring to a boil. Simmer for 20 to 25 minutes or until all of the vegetables are cooked through and tender.
3. Puree the vegetables in a blender or food processor. Strain through a fine mesh strainer into the same pot you used to cook the vegetables. Add the cream, maple syrup, salt, and cayenne pepper.
4. Return the pot to the stove and bring the soup to a simmer. Serve.

Makes 2 quarts (6–8 servings).

The inn's kitchen has been referred to as the most beautiful in the world.
PHOTO COURTESY OF JOE DAVID

his award-winning team in what has sometimes been referred to as the world's most beautiful kitchen. The class is taught like the traditional French apprentice program, the *Stagière,* in which students observe the professionals and work next to them. Students will be introduced to every stage of preparation, discovering ways to evaluate fish, meat, and produce; learning organizational skills; and learning essential techniques for cooking and entertaining.

Each class is customized to a student's individual taste and includes two or three eight-hour days in the kitchen (including lunch). Also offered are some nice extras: the inn's trademark kitchen uniform (a pair of Dalmatian-spotted chef's pants and matching apron that reflect the inn's Dalmatian mascot), a photo with the staff and Chef O'Connell, a copy of the book *Patrick O'Connell's Refined American Cuisine*, and a guaranteed dinner reservation for the nights of your stay.

During certain holidays, Chef O'Connell provides demonstration classes. Guests sit around a large table, and he performs. Contact the inn for prices.

Class Costs: $1,800 per person for two-day class; $2,400 per person for a three-day class. Dinner and accommodations are extra.

Class Frequency: Private classes (*Stagière*) with the chef are arranged to fit everyone's schedule; demonstration classes are arranged on a first-come, first-served basis.

Class Length: Eight hours each day for the *Stagière;* demonstration classes run one-and-a-half hours.

Class Type: Demonstration/hands-on.

Class Size: One person or couple per class for individual classes (*Stagière*); forty students for the holiday demonstration.

Lodging: The inn's rooms were imaginatively created by Joyce Evans, a London stage and set designer. She created each room without visiting the property, arranging for the furniture to be shipped from England to Virginia, where it was assembled. The end result is a luxurious fantasy against a backdrop of striking authentic and reproduction antiques, which leaves visitors feeling like guests in the home of American nobility.

Amenities: Fireplaces, Jacuzzi, twenty-four-hour room service, and much more.

Activities: The area has its share of wineries and interesting communities, but Washington and the inn are so comfortable and special, it is unlikely that you will want to drift far from them. There is a small theater in town and a few shops, and some spectacularly restored eighteenth-century homes, but not much more. Yet, you won't be bored. It is too beautiful to be bored.

If you want to tour the nearby Shenandoah Valley, the staff can arrange an unforgettable picnic lunch—and a map. If you want to linger at the hotel and be pampered, an English tea is served each day between 3:00 and 5:00 p.m. What sets this Relais & Châteaux inn apart from so many other fine inns is that here nothing is impossible. *Everything* is only a request away.

For more information contact The Inn at Little Washington, Washington, VA 22747; (540) 675-3800; www.theinnatlittlewashington.com.

WEST VIRGINIA

The Greenbrier
White Sulphur Springs, West Virginia

*B*uried in the middle of nowhere is a chic hideaway that has been attract-ing trendsetters and leaders for years. Some flock here to be pampered and to escape their worshiping admirers; others come to drink the mineral water and bathe in the supposedly healing sulfur springs. Surrounded by 6,500 private acres of mountainous West Virginia land, this famous resort, known simply as The Greenbrier, is internationally respected for its AAA Five Diamond and Mobil Four Star Award-wining service, which is almost as perfect as the setting's natural beauty.

Chef Susanne Moats (center) works with students. PHOTO COURTESY OF THE GREENBRIER

Above and beyond the many pleasures available at the resort, the most favorably regarded is the food, a blend of classic international, continental, and American cuisine. Renowned for keeping pace with the times and even breaking into new culinary frontiers, the resort has earned a stellar reputation in the culinary world for attracting new young chefs. Its three-year apprenticeship program has trained many of tomorrow's great chefs.

In return for the opportunity to learn at The Greenbrier, many of these new chefs have left behind something truly generous: fresh ideas that have led to tomorrow's culinary rage. Some students who have gone on to successful careers include: I. Pano Karatassos (president, Buckhead Life Restaurant Group), Lawrence T. McFadden (CMC, food and beverage director, the Ritz-Carlton, Naples, Florida), Russell Scott (instructor, the Culinary Institute of America, Hyde Park, New York), and Dean Maupin (Clifton Inn, Charlottesville, Virginia).

Like other world-class resorts sensitive to public needs, The Greenbrier has always been in the vanguard for serving healthier foods. Although the Southern influence is noticeable in favorites like Southern fried chicken, buttermilk biscuits, and corn pudding, what makes these foods unique is the chef's dedication to lightening them up and giving them special Greenbrier distinction.

ABOUT THE CHEF

All hands-on classes are conducted by Susanne Moats, a graduate of the Pennsylvania Institute of Culinary Arts and a former extern at the White Elephant Resort in Nantucket. Her primary responsibility is to instruct adults and children, and to test and write cooking school recipes.

ABOUT THE CLASSES

Aspiring gourmets not interested in a professional program may take a series of receational classes. Designed to meet the resort's high standards, these classes are either demonstration or hands-on. Special demonstration classes are only held when the resort hotel has a visiting celebrity chef (such as Steven Raichlen, John Ash, or Anne Willan). For the general benefit of guests, there are also free demonstrations of the resort's signature dishes at The Greenbrier Gourmet Shop daily at 11:00 a.m. and 2:00 p.m.

Each adult hands-on class offers a unique lesson about the latest culinary trends and has its own theme, so it is possible to attend as many or as few classes as you wish. Past themes have included cooking for picnics, home entertaining, cocktail parties, and more.

The instructor begins each class with a demonstration, and afterward the students prepare the day's menu. Students are taught basic techniques (such as baking, roasting, frying, and so on), how to create sauces, how to present the food, and more. When the food is ready, the class enjoys the meal with a suitably paired wine. The adult class is limited to students age seventeen and older, but children between the ages of thirteen and sixteen may attend if accompanied by an adult.

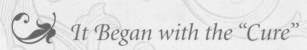

It Began with the "Cure"

What began in 1778 as a place to enjoy the "cure" evolved into a very elegant resort in the nineteenth century that hosted kings, presidents, generals, and, of course, its share of commoners. By the eve of the Civil War, it was so successfully established among Southern aristocrats and the very fashionable that it was simply referred to as "the old white hotel," the place to go for the "cure."

The Civil War brought a temporary halt to its popularity, but that all changed when the Chesapeake and Ohio railroad reopened it in 1914 and renamed it The Greenbrier. Almost overnight, the resort soared to world-class heights, becoming a year-round playground with a new hotel building and an eighteen-hole golf course. Some years later it distinguished itself once again by becoming a top golf resort when it hired Sam Snead to be its on-site golf pro. In the years that followed, it never lost its position—and it still remains one of West Virginia's best golfing hideaways.

Smoked Salmon BLT

Compliments of Chef Susanne Moats, The Greenbrier

The following canapé recipe is a favorite among many of the cooking school students. Sommelier Lori Deskins recommends a sauvignon blanc wine to go with it, one that isn't too aggressive, and might even have a little Sémillon blended in with it, such as a white bordeaux. For red-wine lovers she suggests an unoaked wine such as a Dolcetto from Italy or a lighter-style pinot noir.

Ingredients
- 6 slices Pullman bread or 12 slices party rye
- $1/4$ cup melted clarified butter
- Salt and pepper
- 4 slices bacon
- 2 tablespoons turbinado sugar
- 12 slices smoked salmon
- 1 small head frisée
- 8 grape tomatoes
- $1/4$ cup mayonnaise

1. Cut the crust off the Pullman bread and cut into triangle-shaped quarters. (If you're using party rye, cut the slices in half on the diagonal.) Place on a sheet tray, brush with butter, and season with salt and pepper. Toast the bread slices in a 350°F oven until golden brown, about 3–5 minutes per side. Set aside until needed.
2. Place the bacon on a sheet pan and put it in the oven until the fat is rendered, about 10 minutes. Remove from the oven and sprinkle with turbinado sugar. Return bacon to the oven and cook until it is crisp and the sugar is brown, about 10–12 minutes. After bacon is cooked and has cooled, dice it into very small pieces. Set aside until needed.
3. To make salmon rosettes, roll one slice of salmon and cut off the dark end of the roll. Cut the roll in half, then fluff the top to create a flower. Repeat with the remaining salmon slices. Refrigerate until needed.
4. Cut the frisée into small pieces. Wash with ice cold water and spin dry with a salad spinner. Refrigerate until needed.
5. Slice the grape tomatoes widthwise. Set aside until needed.
6. To assemble the canapés, place toasted bread on a clean surface and spread a little mayonnaise on top of each slice. Arrange a salmon rosette in the center of the toasted bread. Garnish both sides of the rosette with frisée, tomato, and bacon. Arrange onto a serving platter and enjoy.

Yield: 24 canapés.

Hands-on cooking classes for children are also offered, and students between the ages of six and twelve are taught basic kitchen safety, culinary techniques, and some favorite recipes like pizza, chocolate toffee cookie bars, and quesadillas. The food prepared will be available for parents to sample.

Class Costs: Adult class: $208 per person; children's class: $98 per person (lodging is additional).

Class Frequency: Tuesday through Saturday for the adult class and Tuesday, Wednesday, Friday, and Saturday for the children's class, June through September.

Class Length: Adult classes run four hours (9:30 a.m. to 1:30 p.m.); children's classes run two hours (2:30 to 4:30 p.m.).

Class Type: Hands-on/demonstration.

Class Size: Adult class: minimum four students, maximum twelve; children's class: eight students maximum.

Lodging: The choice of rooms and suites at The Greenbrier is impressive, from a standard room to a two-level presidential suite. All rooms (and guest houses) are decorated with a Dorothy Draper flair, a daring style of decorating that mixes dramatic design and vibrant colors.

Activities: 40,000-square-foot spa, nightly movies, bowling, falconry, kayaking, fishing, swimming, sulfur springs, and more.

Besides the typical resort activities, The Greenbrier also offers something special. Years ago, the U.S. government built within the heart of the resort a bunker to be used for important officials in case of national emergency. For a long time it was a well-kept secret, until the *Washington Post Magazine* spilled the beans and forced the government to seek hiding elsewhere. Today, visitors may take a ninety-minute tour of the bunker—and see how well the powerful live even during national crisis.

For more information contact: The Greenbrier, 300 West Main Street, White Sulphur Springs, WV 24986; (800) 228-5049; www.greenbrier.com.

SOUTHWEST

The Inn on the Alameda is home to the Santa Fe School of Cooking.

SOUTHWEST

NEW MEXICO

Jane Butel Cooking School
Albuquerque, New Mexico

*D*id you know that real women eat hot chiles? Jane Butel, "Queen of Chiles," who has authored eighteen books, including one on chiles, believes so. In fact, she has built a solid reputation convincing people that the chile is more than nature's flame thrower. It is actually a very healthy food.

She started sharing this message with the world through her writings, teachings, and television projects long before torching the palate with spice

Jane Butel, aka "Queen of the Chiles" is an authority on regional Southwest cooking.
PHOTO COURTESY OF JANE BUTEL

became the rage in the States. She even formed her own company, Tex-Mex, Inc. (dba Jane Butel Cooking School), to capitalize on the strong wave of interest she has created.

Regarded as an authority on regional Southwest cooking, Jane's reputation has crossed oceans. A home economics graduate from Kansas State

Santa Fe School of Cooking

You know you have arrived in New Mexico when your cheeseburgers, croissants, and muffins have been kissed by hot chiles. There is nothing like the bliss that comes from tasting familiar foods with a spiced-up kick. Food lovers seldom rebel against this because so many foods—like corn, squash, and black beans—take on an exciting new dimension simply by methodically adding spices.

To create that heavenly depth, which is so evident in traditional New Mexican food, Chef Eddie Lyons at the Santa Fe School of Cooking believes you must begin by toasting the spices. When exposed to direct heat, the spices release the wonderful oils and irresistible aromas that make this regional food so memorable. You can learn more about spicing up your meal at the well-regarded school, where many respected names in the culinary world have taken classes (and then shared what they learned with others). For a list of classes and more information about the cooking program, visit www .santafeschoolofcooking.com.

The Inn on the Alameda offers an attractive culinary getaway package in conjunction with the school called Muy Sabrosa ("very tasty"). Offered year-round, the package price ranges from $332 to $850 for two, including two nights' lodging, a lavish continental breakfast, and an afternoon wine and cheese reception daily. A two-and-a-half-hour cooking class is followed by a spicy lunch at the school. For more information about the Muy Sabrosa getaway package, contact: the Inn on the Alameda, 303 East Alameda, Santa Fe, NM 87501; (800) 289-2122; www.innonthealameda.com.

*University, she is the daughter and granddaughter of respected home econo-
mists. Over the years, through experience and education, she has built on
the knowledge she inherited from her family and turned it into a profitable
career.*

*She offers two weekend and weeklong classes in the Albuquerque area,
plus a choice of three-hour classes and an online program. Her classes, like
those of other serious-minded chefs, go beyond teaching techniques and providing hands-on training; they also reveal the health aspects of certain foods.
She wants her students to understand why some foods are good for you—
and what happens to them when they're mixed with other ingredients.*

*Students who attend one of her classes will learn that those spicy bits of
chile do more than just ignite a fire. They fill you with nutrition (they have
low sodium and minimal fat, and are rich in vitamins A and C), unclog the
vascular system by auguring plaque, decrease appetite, stimulate metabo-
lism, and even strengthen the immune system.*

*A class with Jane is more than just a class in spicy hell. It is a class in
salvation—the art of mixing ingredients to bring about the right chemical
reaction—and an introduction to the many hidden secrets of the chile.*

*For more information, including the latest prices, contact: Jane Butel
Cooking School, 2655 Pan American Northeast, Suite F, Albuquerque, NM
87107; (505) 243-2622; www.janebutel.com.*

TEXAS

Lake Austin Spa Resort Cooking School
Austin, Texas

Spas are notorious for serving starvation-size portions of flavorless foods such as steamed broccoli and mini helpings of boiled fish, stripped completely of creams, cheeses, or excess fat. At Lake Austin Spa Resort, you will never experience such food deprivation. Your stay will be filled with nutritionally balanced food prepared with verve and taste, such as Chicken-Fried Portobello Mushroom Steak with Roasted Garlic Mashers and Cream Gravy (see recipe).

The spa's executive chef, Terry Conlan, has achieved this miracle in culinary refinement by redesigning famous recipes to make them light without abandoning flavor. His trick is to eliminate unneeded calories but retain the original flavor and texture. (For example, he'll sprinkle small pieces of bacon on a salad or froth the top of his fat-free mushroom cappuccino with a little whipping cream.) By accenting the meal with restraint, using such foods as bacon, cream, butter, and cheese, he is able to maintain the familiar flavor and texture without the high fat count.

Every month, this award-winning resort (named by Condé Nast Traveler *as the number one destination spa in North America) offers guests a Culinary Experience that is focused on preparing fine spa food.*

ABOUT THE CHEF

Overseeing the program is Chef Conlan, who has put the spa resort on the culinary map in recent years with his innovative cooking. What is so amazing about this is that he stumbled into cooking accidentally after college, without any formal culinary training, and instantly fell in love with it. A series of well-timed professional moves led him to

Chicken-Fried Portobello Mushroom Steak
with Roasted Garlic Mashers and Cream Gravy

Compliments of Executive Chef Terry Conlan, the Lake Austin Spa Resort

Some Southerners believe everything, not just chicken, tastes good when deep fried. For them, it's that crispy crust that makes a meal so thoroughly enjoyable. Chef Conlan achieves that crispy crust not by frying the food over burners, but by "frying" it in the oven and using toasted whole wheat bread crumbs. Each serving has only 360 calories and 5 grams of fat.

Chicken-Fried Portobello Mushroom Steak

Ingredients
- 1 cup whole wheat bread crumbs
- $1/2$ cup buttermilk
- 1 egg white
- $1/4$ cup flour
- 1 teaspoon paprika
- $1/4$ teaspoon black pepper
- $1/8$ teaspoon cayenne pepper
- $1/2$ teaspoon garlic powder
- $1/2$ teaspoon onion powder
- $1/4$ teaspoon dried thyme
- $1/4$ teaspoon dried leaf oregano
- 2 large portobello mushrooms, stemmed and cut into $1/2$-inch-thick vertical slices

1. Preheat the oven to 275°F. Bake the bread crumbs for several hours until they are dried out, and then grind them in a food processor. Set aside.
2. Whisk the buttermilk and egg white in a large bowl. In a separate bowl, combine the bread crumbs, flour, and spices.
3. Preheat the oven to 400°F. Dip each mushroom piece first into the buttermilk mixture, then into the seasoned bread crumbs. Spray each piece lightly with nonstick cooking spray and arrange in a single layer on a nonstick baking sheet. Bake for 12–15 minutes or until crisp. Serve hot with with Roasted Garlic Mashers and Cream Gravy (see recipes).

Roasted Garlic Mashers

Ingredients
- 4 medium Yukon Gold or Idaho potatoes, peeled and sliced
- 2 roasted garlic bulbs
- $1/2$ cup skim milk
- 2 tablespoons light butter
- Salt and freshly ground pepper to taste

1. Place potatoes in a saucepan with enough cold water to cover. Bring to a boil over high heat and cook until tender.
2. Drain and place the potatoes in a large bowl, then immediately combine them with the garlic pulp, milk, butter, salt, and pepper. Mash with a hand masher until smooth.

Cream Gravy

Ingredients
- $1/2$ cup 1 percent milk
- $1/4$ cup evaporated skim milk
- $1/2$ chicken bouillon cube (or $1/4$ teaspoon salt)
- 2 tablespoons flour dissolved in $1/4$ cup 1 percent milk
- $1/8$ teaspoon black pepper

1. Combine the 1 percent milk and evaporated skim milk in a saucepan over medium heat. Add the bouillon cube and bring to a simmer. Whisk in the flour and milk mixture and season with pepper.
2. Cook, stirring constantly, for 2 minutes. Thin the gravy with additional 1 percent milk if necessary.

Serves 4.

kitchens where he was able to learn and work his way up to his current position at the Lake Austin Spa Resort, where he has been the executive chef since 1992.

Most of his success he owes to the talented chefs he has worked with—and those he admires, like Mario Batali. By combining his taste with what he learned, he re-created famous recipes in his own cooking style. His cookbook *FRESH: Healthy Cooking and Living from Lake*

Austin Spa Resort, which was a finalist in the International Association of Culinary Professionals 2004 Cookbook Awards, illustrates this point by featuring remarkably light, original, and tasty foods from around the world. After it was published, it caught the attention of many respected magazines, such as *Weight Watchers, Bon Appétit,* and *Cooking Light,* which featured him and his cuisine.

 Things to Do in the Green City of Austin

Being a green city, perhaps one of America's greenest, has helped make Austin a tourist mecca. But what pushes it to the top and keeps it there is its natural beauty: the hills, parkland, and lakes scattered throughout the area. In addition to the scenic beauty, visitors have a wide choice of activities to enjoy. Some places worth visiting include the following:

· *Whole Foods's (www.wholefoodsmarket.com) flagship store in Austin is not only the largest high-end grocery store in the chain, but it also provides dining stations serving everything from seafood to barbecue. There are also cooking classes that will take participants on a culinary tour of the world without ever leaving the store. Classes are held Monday through Saturday in the store, as well as online, and these classes cover everything from vegetarian to big-game party menus. Private and public demonstrations, and private hands-on classes, begin as low as $55, depending on the food and the arrangement. For more information about the cooking classes, call (512) 542-2340.*

· *Austin Ghost Story Tour (www.austinghosttours.com) will appeal to those who enjoy the macabre and want to learn about America's first serial killer, the Servant Girl Annihilator. The tour includes visits to some of the historic district's haunted taverns, where you will hear the truth about them from the people who know, the employees.*

· *Austin Museum of Art (www.amoa.org) has two locations, downtown and in Laguna Gloria. The downtown location appeals to the general*

PHILOSOPHY

Chef Conlan's goal is to teach students ways to strip popular regional and international dishes of excess fat without losing the deep flavors. He hopes his unique approach will inspire students to create satisfying and healthy meals without adding unneeded calories.

public with its continually changing exhibits, featuring contemporary art; the Laguna Gloria location, formerly the home of local legend Clara Driscoll, appeals to visitors who prefer intimate art exhibits and informative discussions covering art and nature.

- *The Blanton Museum of Art (www.blantonmuseum.org) has a huge collection of art from Europe and the Americas. Like most popular museums, its exhibitions feature art from a variety of mediums and represent different forms of artistic expression. The museum is located on the campus at the University of Texas–Austin.*
- *The Inner Space Cavern (www.innerspace.com), where ice age animals have been found, has its share of eerie cave formations. A visit includes a narrative about the cavern and its flora and fauna.*
- *Lady Bird Lake provides a relaxing setting for a boat ride on an old-fashioned paddle-wheeler (www.lonestarriverboat.com). On a nice day, you will be able to see the city's downtown skyline.*
- *The Texas Hill Country, with its intense sun and cool nights suitable for growing quality grapes, has several wineries. For a listing visit www.austinwebpage.com.*
- *The Wild Basin Wilderness Preserve (www.wildbasin.org) has three miles of hiking trails through woodlands and past streamside habitats. Concerts, adult workshops, children's programs, and much more are offered here.*

ABOUT THE CLASSES

Classes are offered every second week of the month and last five days. Each program includes daily cooking classes, wine and cheese tastings, top ten foods for good health, and essential information about herbs. Celebrity chefs and successful food artisans will discuss preparing and selecting great-tasting foods. Besides classes in cooking, the program offers a variety of culinary-related activities (such as a tour of the organic garden, a tea party, a cowboy breakfast on the shores of Lake Austin, classes in the art of entertaining, wine seminars, and cheese tastings).

Terry Conlan is executive chef at Lake Austin. PHOTO COURTESY OF LAKE AUSTIN SPA RESORT

Class Costs: $1,705 to $3,870 per person, double occupancy, including lodging, food and fitness classes, cooking program, and spa and fitness allowances. (Rates vary depending on the length of stay, from three to seven nights.)

Class Frequency: Monthly, for five days.

Class Length: Varies one to two hours, depending on the week.

Class Type: Hands-on/demonstration.

Class Size: Minimum two students per class, maximum thirty.

Lodging: Sitting elegantly on sixteen acres on the shores of Lake Austin, this award-winning resort in the Texas Hill Country has won a reputation for being a world-class spa. It has forty guest rooms facing the lakeside with attractive regional decor designed by local artisans. Each room is prepared with your rest and relaxation in mind.

Amenities: Wireless Internet, 300-thread-count Egyptian cotton sheets, down comforters, luxury spa robes; several rooms have fireplaces and private wildflower gardens.

Activities: Guests can choose from over one hundred different types of therapeutic treatments to tone the body (from body scrubs to healing therapies), and there are assorted wellness and discovery programs. The property has nature and wildlife trails and peaceful public areas, and guests can canoe, kayak, hike, and meditate, as well as participate in yoga, Tai Chi, and aquatic and swimming classes.

For more information contact: Lake Austin Spa Resort, 1705 South Quinlan Park Road, Austin, TX 78732; (512) 372-7300; www.lakeaustin.com.

Rosewood Mansion on Turtle Creek

*R*osewood Mansion on Turtle Creek offers children ages five to twelve a little guidance in mastering the art of fine dining. Twice a year (sometimes more frequently), this five-star boutique hotel in the upscale Turtle Creek neighborhood of Dallas opens its private dining room to preteens and serves them a three-course lunch in etiquette. For two hours youngsters are treated like little adults and taught important basic dining skills that will help them handle themselves in social situations with ease.

This youngster is learning the tricky art of eating soup. PHOTO COURTESY OF ROSEWOOD MANSION ON TURTLE CREEK

The classes, which are set up in a question-and-answer format, give the youngsters every opportunity to learn the essentials by encouraging them to express an opinion or ask a question. Each class may vary slightly, depending on the children's ages, but regardless of age, the goal is the same: to turn youngsters into young ladies and gentlemen who can handle a knife and fork, and debone their fish or meat with savoir faire. Should you eat with your left or right hand? What do you do with the bones? Which fork or knife goes with what? These questions, and others, are addressed.

As they enjoy their three-course meal (which consists of a soup, meat or fish entree with vegetables, and a dessert), the children face obstacles, deliberately placed before them, so that they can master such essential skills as how to eat soup, how to cut around a bone, or how to pick up playful little foods like peas. Leading the class is etiquette expert Colleen Rickenbacher and the hotel's renowned executive chef, John Tesar.

All students must attend the class with an adult to assist the child when necessary. The class usually has about forty parents and children, and it costs about $60 per person. Class begins at 11:30 a.m. and ends at 1:30 p.m.

For more information contact: Rosewood Mansion on Turtle Creek, 2821 Turtle Creek Boulevard, Dallas, TX 75219; (214) 559-2100; www .mansiononturtlecreek.com.

Blair House Inn Cooking School
Wimberley, Texas

*T*he Texas Hill Country is a mix of cascading streams and tranquil pools
*of water set amid soaring cedar and oak trees. Each season the area is
awakened by a special greeting, a new splash of color to give the rolling hills
an irresistible freshness.*

*In the heart of this picturesque country, overlooking Paradise Valley, is
the Blair House Inn Cooking School. In this tranquil setting, about an hour
from Austin and minutes away from the quaint town of Wimberley, groups
of students with different cooking skills and goals are brought together and
melted into one family of friends, and they are guided by executive chef/
instructor Joseph "Joey" Kulivan.*

ABOUT THE CHEF

A graduate of the School of Culinary Arts at Chicago's Kendall College,
Chef Kulivan has had considerable experience working in Europe and in
the States under the tutelage of respected chefs. The goal of his hands-on
class is to create for each student a memorable experience and a recognition that good food is learning to prepare in-season meals with fresh,
local ingredients.

PHILOSOPHY

At the Blair House, the goal is to bring pleasure and fun to cooking by
removing the mystery of different cooking techniques and by simplifying
the application of these techniques in various recipes. Since the culinary
program is an intensive examination of some of the most urgent basics,
Chef Kulivan strives to reduce the stress by making the classes as relaxed
and comfortable as possible to allow students and teacher to bond easily.
He finds pleasure in breaking down communication barriers and bring-

ing together people of different backgrounds into one solid unit. This he believes is fundamental for achieving his primary purpose of expanding the student's culinary knowledge. In each class, he systematically follows a basic format (show, tell, do, and review), which he believes facilitates retention and builds the confidence that comes with knowledge.

ABOUT THE COOKING PROGRAM

Although long-lasting friendships have been known to begin here, the Blair House is primarily a place to learn—not just recipes—but food preparation techniques. By focusing on six or seven significant techniques, Chef Kulivan demonstrates how students can prepare not one, but many recipes—whether they require braising, baking, broiling, or sautéing—by simply using a basic recipe formula. For example, when preparing bread, he will talk about yeast and how it grows when mixed with flour and other ingredients; he will demonstrate what bread feels

Twice-Cooked Potatoes with Roasted Garlic

Compliments of the Blair House Inn

Ingredients
- 16 red or white new potatoes, quartered
- 3 tablespoons unsalted butter
- $1/4$ cup fresh chervil leaves
- Roasted minced garlic
- Coarse kosher salt and freshly ground black pepper to taste

1. Cook the potatoes in boiling water until they are just tender, approximately 10 minutes. Drain well.
2. Melt the butter in a large skillet over medium heat. Add the boiled potatoes and sauté just until crispy, about 5 minutes. Sprinkle with chervil and roasted garlic, and season with salt and pepper. Serve hot.

Serves 6.

Beer Can Chicken

Compliments of the Blair House Inn

This recipe, a Blair House Inn specialty, has become a student favorite. Chef Kulivan recommends that you serve it with Twice-Cooked Potatoes with Roasted Garlic (see recipe), and it pairs well with zinfandel or a favorite beer (the one, perhaps, that is used to cook the chicken).

In preparing the chicken, you should use a good beer (the darker it is, the more intense the flavor). The grill should be very hot, and the beer can should be washed well before it is inserted into the cavity of the chicken. (You shouldn't use cans that contain dyes on the outside. Any clean can may be used. By using a high heat, any bacteria should be killed during the cooking.)

Ingredients
- 1 12-ounce can beer
- 1 tablespoon spices (your choice)
- 1 tablespoon compound butter
- 1 2$^1/_2$-pound roasting chicken
- 1$^1/_2$ tablespoons olive oil
- $^1/_2$ tablespoon ground black pepper
- $^1/_2$ tablespoon chopped fresh thyme
- $^1/_2$ tablespoon chopped fresh sage

1. Preheat outside grill (gas or wood) to 400°F.
2. Pour out a quarter of the beer from the can. Add 1 tablespoon of your favorite spices (Cajun, lemon-pepper, curry, etc.) to the remaining beer in the can.
3. Place the compound butter under the skin of the chicken breast, and rub the olive oil, black pepper, thyme, and sage (or substitute your favorite spices) on the outside of the chicken.
4. Insert the entire beer can into the cavity of chicken. Arrange the chicken upright on a cookie sheet and place directly it on the barbecue or smoker grill. Shut the lid and smoke/bake for approximately 1 hour, or until the internal temperature reaches 180°F and the juices run clear when the thigh is pierced with a fork. Remove and let rest for 15 minutes. Carve into 6 serving pieces.
5. Serve with your favorite side dishes, and condiments like jalapeño jelly.

Serves 6.

like and smells like when working it. But most importantly, he will present students with a basic recipe for bread—and he will then show how each loaf changes by making a few additions or alterations to the recipe.

Every class has a unique menu, which changes dramatically for each three-course lunch and five-course dinner. One main course may be a Toulosian Cassoulet Français with Home-Made Lamb Sausage; another may be a Cedar Planked Wild King Salmon with Jerk Spice and Mango Salsa. The menu will always depend on what is fresh and seasonally available.

Classes begin with orientation on Monday evening. During the orientation, students are introduced to the chef and given a syllabus with sixty recipes and some important technique shortcuts. The orientation is followed by a three- or four-course dinner, which the chef prepares for the students.

On Tuesday, the day starts off at 8:00 a.m. with a three-course breakfast; each breakfast is a distinctive culinary treat with French-roast coffee, blended orange juice, and freshly made bread. One morning the main breakfast entree may be huevos rancheros (eggs country style); another morning it may be eggs Benedict. While the chef is preparing the breakfast, students may have the opportunity to observe him—and, when possible, assist in the preparation.

After breakfast the first cooking class commences, an intensive class that continues throughout the day (with a two-hour midday break) until 8:00 p.m. The routine is basic: A four-course lunch is prepared in the morning, with each person assigned a specific responsibility, and it concludes with the class eating what they have just prepared. After the lunch break, students meet to prepare a five-course dinner. They are once again assigned cooking tasks, but they will be different from those performed earlier. The lesson ends with everyone eating what they have created.

Included in the three-day class are visits to wineries, olive orchards, and food markets where students learn about local products and are shown how to buy and store seasonal foods to preserve their freshness. To save money, they are encouraged to purchase large chunks of meat and taught how to butcher, store, and prepare it.

The two types of programs offered are the three- and five-day classes. Offered during the week, both have themes (holidays, Italian, Mediterranean, etc.) and are limited to eight attendees, but the five-day program involves more hands-on cooking and some extra trips to various food-producing locations (such as the local olive vineyard). On weekends, private classes are scheduled for one or two people.

Class Costs: $716 for a single person and $1,220 per couple for the three-day class, including lodging; $160 per person for private weekend classes. For price information for the five-day classes, contact the Blair House.

Class Frequency: About twenty-five themed classes are held throughout the year, usually twice each month, except in December (when there is only one class).

Class Length: About eight class hours each day.

Class Type: Mostly hands-on, with demonstrations, lectures, and reviews.

Class Size: Minimum two, maximum eight students per class. Private classes may include only one student.

Lodging: Each room is individually designed and has a private view of the hills. Students have a choice of eleven rooms, each tastefully decorated with paintings by local artists.

Amenities: Fresh flowers, Internet access, whirlpool tub, guest robes, stone fireplace, and more. Each night a special dessert and beverage are delivered to your room.

Activities: Perhaps the biggest attraction in the area is the Village of Wimberley. Dubbed Texas's most scenic community, Wimberley is a 150-year-old treasure that offers many enjoyable sights (including cascading lakes and rippling creeks, and exotic birds and butterflies). Visitors to the area may take long hikes, swim in clear-water pools, camp, and more. For theater lovers, there is an outdoor theater and an annual Shakespeare festival. A variety of shops and eateries, including those that serve the omnipresent Texas barbecue, are all centrally located. For more information contact: Blair House Inn, 100 West Spoke Hill Road, Wimberley, TX 78676; (877) 549-5450; www.blairhouseinn.com.

Food & Wine Magazine Classic

*T*he annual Food & Wine Magazine Classic in Aspen, Colorado, has
become a star-studded food and wine gala overflowing with big names
like José Andrés, Mario Batali, Emeril Lagasse, Jacques Pépin, and more.
Dubbed by FOX television as a "culinary carnival" and christened by the
New York Times as the "granddaddy of them all," its sheer magnitude and
quality dazzle even jaded food lovers.

Anyone lucky enough to attend will
be privy to culinary secrets and the latest trends, and sample some of the best
wines and artisanal foods available in the
country. Scheduled in June of each year,
the Classic offers nearly a hundred cooking demonstrations, seminars, and wine
tastings, featuring top-name chefs and
industry leaders from around the country. Because of the Classic's significant
corporate backing, it would be difficult to
find any food and wine event anywhere
that could match it.

Jacques Pépin adds a little fire
to the meal at the Food & Wine
Classic in Aspen.

PHOTO COURTESY OF HEEDUM AGENCY

There is nothing cheap about this
getaway weekend. The two more popular
first-class hotels, Little Nell Aspen (675
East Durant Avenue, Aspen, CO 81611; 970-920-4600; www.thelittlenell
.com) and the historic Hotel Jerome Aspen (330 East Main Street, Aspen,
CO 81611; 970-920-1000; www.hoteljerome.rockresorts.com) offer rooms
beginning at about $500 per night, if you are lucky enough to get one. How-
ever, you won't be disappointed. Amenities include a pool, Jacuzzi, spa services, and even pet extras (at the Little Nell), and heated outdoor pools, a
fitness center, and twenty-four-hour in-room dining (at the Hotel Jerome).
Tickets to the Food & Wine Magazine Classic are about $1,000 per per-
son, which includes entry to all tastings and seminars. For tickets and more
information visit www.foodandwine.com/classic.

MIDWEST

Chicago skyline. PHOTO COURTESY OF JOE DAVID

ILLINOIS

The Chopping Block
Chicago, Illinois

*C*hicago is fast becoming America's number-one getaway spot, surpass-
ing even New York City for entertainment and attractiveness. Few cities
anywhere have as much to offer, from the very elegant Lake Shore Drive to
the quirky, bean-shaped Cloud Gate in Millennium Park. If your feet can't
handle all the walking, you can visit two of Chicago's tallest buildings, the
Sears Tower and the John Hancock Center, and take in the entire city all
at once.

Food lovers unacquainted with Chicago's popular restaurants have an
opportunity to learn about them by attending the annual Taste of Chicago
in Grant Park, where local restaurateurs serve their favorite menus. The
millions of visitors who flock there can order anything from chicken California wrap with baby greens salad to Tuscan fried crab cake with basil mayonnaise. If you hate such extravagant events with thick crowds, especially
during the hot summer, you can always take an air-conditioned break from
the city madness and head to the Chopping Block Cooking School, where
you can brush up on your cooking skills in small, comfortable classes.

The Chopping Block's facility at the Merchandise Mart was built by Jill
Prescott (see the Midwest section for more information about her Sheboygan, Wisconsin, school) as a cooking school and as a set for her PBS series
Jill Prescott's Ecole de Cuisine. Today this 8,000-square-foot property has
become the main location for the Chopping Block's cooking programs. (Its
second location is in Lincoln Square, Chicago's Germantown area.)

The Chopping Block, in business since 1997, offers both demonstration
and hands-on classes, all aimed at the home cook. It is considered one of the
larger recreational cooking schools in the United States, offering as many as

Shelley Young (right) works alongside a student.
PHOTO COURTESY OF ALAN KIMREY, © 2007 PIXMISSION, LLC

250 to 300 classes per month, including such novel programs as date night or girls' night, special-events programs, celebrity demonstration classes, birthday-party-planning classes, team-building classes, and even classes on how to have a wine-tasting event at your next social gathering.

ABOUT THE STAFF

All thirty teachers on the staff have been selected because they are inspired cooks. They all are culinary school graduates and have at least five years of professional experience. Since learning techniques are taught at most

Apple Pie

Compliments of the Chopping Block

The signature dish at the Chopping Block is the apple pie. To create a successful pie, Shelley Young recommends the following:
- *Use sugar sparingly. It is a tenderizer, and more than two tablespoons in the recipe will make the dough difficult to roll.*
- *Refrigerate the pie dough for at least twenty-four hours. It will roll out easier, and the colder it is when placed in the oven, the flakier it will become.*
- *Be certain that the fruit filling bubbles before removing the pie from the oven. Flour thickens only at boiling point.*

Pie or Tart Dough

Ingredients
- 2 cups all purpose flour
- 1–2 tablespoons sugar
- Pinch fine sea salt
- 6 ounces (1$^1/_2$ sticks) unsalted butter, chilled and cut into small pieces
- $^1/_4$ cup shortening, chilled and cut into small pieces
- $^1/_4$–$^1/_3$ cup cold water

1. Put flour, sugar, salt, butter, and shortening into the bowl of a food processor fitted with a metal blade. Pulse mixture until crumbly and the butter is in small pieces throughout the flour. Working quickly, restart the processor and add water until the mixture just forms a ball.
2. Place dough onto a work surface and flatten into a disk. Wrap in plastic wrap and refrigerate for at least twenty-four hours.

Makes one double pie crust or two tart crusts, suitable for a 9-inch pie pan.

Pie Filling

Ingredients
- 3$\frac{1}{2}$ pounds apples (Granny Smith or Pippin), peeled, cored, and cut into $\frac{1}{2}$-inch wedges
- $\frac{1}{3}$ cup all-purpose flour
- 1–1$\frac{1}{2}$ cups sugar
- 1 teaspoon cinnamon
- $\frac{1}{2}$ teaspoon fine sea salt
- Pie or tart dough
- 1$\frac{1}{2}$ tablespoons unsalted butter, cut into small pieces
- Heavy whipping cream for garnish
- Sugar for garnish

1. Combine apples, flour, sugar (vary amount depending upon taste of apples), cinnamon, and salt in a large bowl. Set aside.
2. Divide the pie dough into two unequal parts (about two-thirds for bottom crust and one-third for the top). Place the smaller portion of dough in the refrigerator. Lightly dust a clean surface with flour and roll out the bottom crust to $\frac{1}{8}$-inch thick, making certain to lift and turn the dough occasionally to ensure it does not stick. Roll dough onto rolling pin, lift, and place into a 9-inch cast-iron pan. Gently push the dough to fit within the pie dish, allowing the excess to hang over the edge.
3. Pour in filling and sprinkle pieces of butter on top. Remove the smaller portion of dough from the refrigerator and roll into a $\frac{1}{8}$-inch-thick circle. Insert a knife in several places through the top crust to create vents. Place the dough over the filling and trim excess crust, leaving about 1 inch of excess. Close the crust by folding it over and pinching the excess or using a fork to crimp. Brush the top of the pie with heavy cream and sprinkle generously with sugar.
4. Preheat oven to 375°F. Place the pie on a baking sheet covered in parchment and bake until the filling is bubbly in the center, the apples are tender, and the top crust is golden brown, about 1–1$\frac{1}{2}$ hours. Allow the pie to cool before cutting and serving.

Makes one 9-inch pie.

culinary schools, the emphasis isn't placed on where a teacher graduated from, but instead on how passionate he or she is about cooking.

Shelley Young, founder and director of the Chopping Block, is a culinary arts graduate of a Des Moines–area community college. Shelley, who became interested in cooking during her teens, learned her first important lesson in food preparation while working in a nursing home: mastering the ability to adjust each meal to meet the different dietary needs of the patients without sacrificing flavor and appeal. Acquiring such a skill gave her a solid foundation for what would follow in her pursuit of a successful career in the culinary arts. Before founding the Chopping Block, she worked as a chef in Iowa, Southern California, and Chicago for seventeen years.

PHILOSOPHY

There isn't a Chopping Block way of cooking. Instead, each teacher has his or her own teaching style. The goal is to teach the science behind the cooking more than recipes and to encourage students to find and develop their own special style.

ABOUT THE CLASSES

The Chopping Block offers a variety of different classes, including a boot camp series, hands-on classes, demonstration classes, and children's classes. Class topics change from month to month, depending on the demand and the season, and they include classes in everything from vegetarian to French, from wine tasting to social and corporate events.

Each cooking class is planned to provide basic information about preparing a balanced meal. Students will learn to time meals, identify different flavors, cook foods in advance, and other important basics.

During the intensive two-, three-, or five-day boot camp series, classes cover the basics, including knife skills, butchering, braising, roasting, sautéing, poaching, and much more. Classes are held during consecutive days, from 8:00 a.m. to 5:00 p.m., and include a mix of demonstration and hands-on teaching approaches. At the completion of meal preparation, students enjoy what they have prepared and discuss any techniques and culinary concerns that are relevant to their lesson. On the last day of the program, students are all expected to create a menu from a market basket of ingredients without using a recipe.

The purpose is to teach students to cook without recipes, instead using only templates when necessary. Students are encouraged to adjust meals to their tastes—from spicy to rich—and to use cooking techniques that suit them. To help them achieve this end, a different teacher is assigned to each class so students are exposed to as many cooking styles as possible.

Many of the one-day classes are set up with an emphasis on demonstration, based on the belief that students learn more and learn more quickly from demonstrations than they do from hands-on teaching. According to Shelley Young, this is because 90 percent of the cooking techniques are so simple that they rarely require hands-on class time.

Class Costs: Five-day, hands-on boot camp series $1,750; hands-on classes $75; demonstration classes $40; children's classes $25.
Class Frequency: Daily from 8:00 a.m. to 5:00 p.m.
Class Length: Boot camp: five consecutive days, eight hours each day; other classes run from two to two-and-a-half hours each.
Class Type: Mostly demonstration, but some hands-on.
Class Size: Sixteen to twenty students for hands-on classes; fourteen to twenty-five students for demonstration classes; ten students for the children's classes.
For more information contact: The Chopping Block, Merchandise Mart, Suite 107, Chicago, IL 60654; (312) 644-6360; www.thechoppingblock.com. Lincoln Square location: 4747 North Lincoln Avenue, Chicago, IL 60025; (773) 472-6700.

Chefs Jacquy Pfeiffer and Sébastien Canonne create a sweet perfection.

The French Pastry School
Chicago, Illinois

A pastry chef once said that a dessert needs to be more than just the last course—it must be the perfect climax to a delicious meal. Anything less might leave a lingering taste of failure. At the French Pastry School, students are taught how to avoid such failure by a staff of talented pastry chefs, all under the attentive supervision of chefs Jacquy Pfeiffer and Sébastien Canonne, M.O.F., both stars in pastry firmament.

Anyone who has dreams of napoleons, chocolate hazelnut tortes, or wild strawberry jams, or who is forever thinking of ways to make perfect candies—smooth ganaches and shiny chocolates—might want to consider this little gem of a school, hidden in downtown Chicago in the huge shadow of the nearby Sears Tower. Students who attend this privately owned pastry school will enjoy the pleasure of seeing their sweet dreams transformed into delicious realities.

ABOUT THE STAFF
Famous chefs from around the world are regular guests. Some simply come to take brush-up classes, and others teach a few classes. Recreational cooks will have access to the same staff, equipment, and facilities that the professional students and those of the twenty-four-week program do. Those fortunate enough to take a class with Sébastien Canonne (a recipient of France's highest honor for artisans, the Meilleur Ouvrier de France) or Jacquy Pfeiffer will not only learn some of the recipes and techniques that they have mastered over the years, but also some of the unusual ones that give these successful chefs an edge.

PHILOSOPHY
Canonne, strongly believes that a student must show respect for his creation by always using the best ingredients and his most polished skills

to turn his confection into something lofty. He must also know how to layer flavors in proper balance to bring about a compatible taste interaction. The dessert must be "a total sensory experience, engaging more than our sense of taste, but also our sense of sight, smell, touch, and sound (through texture)."

Chocolate Bouchons

Compliments of the French Pastry School

When preparing this recipe, it is important that you always measure your ingredients accurately and avoid making substitutes. It could change the texture and appearance of the bouchon.

Ingredients

- $^1/_2$ cup plus 1 tablespoon Plugra 82 percent fat butter
- 1 cup plus 1 tablespoon confectioner's sugar
- $^1/_2$ cup American Almond almond powder
- $^1/_3$ cup King Arthur pastry flour
- $^1/_8$ cup Cacao Barry cocoa powder
- 3 fresh egg whites
- 1 tablespoon apple compote

Chocolate Bouchons
PHOTO COURTESY OF FRENCH PASTRY SCHOOL,
PHOTOGRAPHY BY PAUL STRABBING

1. Prepare the *beurre noisette* by heating the butter in a saucepan until light brown. Strain and set aside.
2. In a mixing bowl, add all the dry ingredients and combine well. Add the egg whites, the apple compote, and the *beurre noisette*. Let mature overnight in the refrigerator.
3. The next day, pipe the mixture into cupcake molds and garnish with gianduja cubes, candied orange, and cacao nibs.
4. Bake in a 375°F oven with the vent closed for about 8–10 minutes. Let cool. To store, keep in an airtight box or freeze.

Makes 12 bouchons.

Pfeiffer believes that pastry making requires continuous practice and education, and it's not something that can be mastered in a lifetime. Therefore, he encourages his students to continuously refine their skills by attempting to outdo themselves until they have reached their highest level of excellence.

The school's goal is to take whatever raw talent a student has and refine it through repetitious exposure to the best techniques. The end result will be a student who can prepare something special that will look and taste great.

ABOUT THE CLASSES

Established in 1995, the French Pastry School offers three types of programs for students: the twenty-four-week professional program, L'Art de la Pâtisserie; the Continuing Education class series, a two-, three-, or five-day program for professionals who want to brush up on their skills; and a food enthusiast program for cooks who simply want to take two, three, or five days of classes to learn basic professional techniques.

The choices of programs for recreational cooks are irresistible. Some examples include a class in preparing artisanal breads (like a French baguette or a sourdough loaf), and classes in making cakes like raspberry mousse and the ever-popular chocolate hazelnut torte. There is even a Pastry Camp, during which you can spend a week creating everything from sugar candies and breads to petits fours and chocolates.

No prerequisite is necessary for any program, only interest. (However, be aware that this is a school for serious-minded students who have a passion for sweets and want to learn how to be perfect at creating them.) Classes are deliberately taught on consecutive days, because cooking is a craft that requires practice. The recreational classes are condensed versions of what is taught in the professional program. Since there are hundreds of recipes for preparing chocolates or pastries, the program's goal isn't to teach you how to reproduce them all, but to teach you some of the fundamental and important techniques for preparing a few key recipes. Hopefully mastering them will make learning other recipes easier.

In each class, everything is made from scratch. Nothing is packaged or powdered or premixed. Students will be exposed to the slow-food movement and will become aware of the correct use of fats, but no attempt will be made to discuss healthy eating issues (students are encouraged to try small amounts of every creation). The focus is strictly on preparing tantalizing sweets. At the end of each class, you may take your creations home with you.

Students are taught using the artist-apprentice model, employed for centuries in Europe. This is a learning environment in which the student is always in close contact with his instructor. Each class begins with an explanation of procedure, which is followed by the chef-instructor producing the recipe. During the entire hands-on class, while students prepare their food, the instructor observes and works alongside the students, providing constant feedback.

Class Costs: $525 to $955, depending on class length and ingredients.

Class Frequency: Programs are held several times a month, year-round.

Class Length: Four to eight hours per day, varying from class to class.

Class Type: Demonstration/hands-on, using the European artist-apprentice model

Class Size: Sixteen students per class.

Lodging: The French Pastry School doesn't offer lodging, but hotels are plentiful in Chicago. Here are three that the school recommends:

Best Western River North, 125 West Ohio Street, Chicago, IL 60610; (312) 467-0800; www.rivernorthhotel.com. This full-service, conveniently located hotel offers access to year-round swimming, among other amenities. They offer special rates for French Pastry School students.

Holiday Inn Chicago Mart Plaza, 350 West Mart Center Drive, Chicago, IL 60654; (312) 836-5000; www.martplaza.com. This is a typical, comfortable, full-service Holiday Inn with a swimming pool and exercise/steam room.

Club Quarters, 111 West Adams Street, Chicago, IL 60603; (312) 214-6400; www.clubquarters.info. This is a private club available to select people with private club or organization memberships. It's a nice, middle-of-the-road hotel facility with an English pub that serves traditional British food.

For more information contact: The French Pastry School, City Colleges of Chicago, 226 West Jackson Boulevard, Suite 106, Chicago, IL 60606; (312) 726-2419; www.frenchpastryschool.com.

The Wilton School
Darien, Illinois

*T*he Wilton School has been setting standards for cake decorating since 1929, yet it adapts quickly to current trends and teaches students the latest techniques in cake design. The program is suitable for students of all levels of expertise and covers all aspects of cake design, from basic party cakes to elaborate three-tiered wedding cakes.

A two-week master course (eight hours each day), designed for students interested in a career in cake design, is open to beginners and professionals, and it covers the basic skills needed to create sensationally designed cakes. At the end of the course, students will receive a Wilton certificate of completion.

The school also offers practical courses for recreational cooks, and each course is focused on a specific interest. These classes may last anywhere from one to five days. Under the guidance of talented teachers, students will design fantasy cakes, holiday cakes, and even cakes with the elaborate Lambeth decorating method (which involves intricate piping of layer-upon-layer decoration). There are also children's classes, which include gingerbread and haunted house decorating, and cupcake design.

Each year new classes are added to reflect changing public tastes and public demand. For the latest trends and classes, check the school's Web site.

Class Costs: $60 to $850, depending on the length of the course. This doesn't include the $25 to $150 registration fee.
Class Frequency: Daily throughout the year.
Class Length: From about 8:00 a.m. to 3:00 p.m. or 9:00 p.m. to 4:00 p.m.
Class Type: Demonstration/hands-on.
Class Size: Minimum six students, maximum twenty-four.
Lodging: The school suggests that students who need lodging contact the following:
Hickory Ridge Conference Center, 1195 Summerhill Drive, Lisle, IL 60532; (630) 971-5000; www.marriott.com/hotels/travel/chihr-hickory-ridge-marriott-conference-hotel. This resort-style hotel is set on twenty-six wooded acres, and it offers such

Students design cakes for special occasions, like this one for an eightieth birthday.
PHOTO © 2007 BY WILTON PRODUCTS, INC. USED WITH PERMISSION.

extras as tennis, golf, a fitness center, and more. Special rates are available for Wilton School students.

LaQuinta Inn, 855 Seventy-ninth Street, Willowbrook, IL 60527; (630) 654-0077; www.lq.com/lq/properties/propertyProfile.do?ident=LQ1051&propId=1051. This inexpensive inn has basic amenities, including continental breakfast, a laundry facility, and fitness and business centers.

Marriott Towne Place Suites, 455 East Twenty-second Street, Lombard, IL 60148; (630) 932-4400; www.marriott.com/hotels/travel/chitl-towneplace-suites-chicago-lombard. This Marriott offers comfortable one- and two-bedroom suites with full kitchen. Amenities include free Internet access, continental breakfast, outdoor swimming pool, and more. Offers special rates for Wilton School students.

For more information contact: The Wilton School, 7511 Lemont Road, Darien, IL 60561; (800) 772-7111, ext. 2888; www.school.wilton.com.

MICHIGAN

Kirby House
Douglas, Michigan

Saugatuck and Douglas are twin resort villages in what is popularly labeled the Art Coast of Michigan. Splashed with gaiety, the area has been known to be as colorful as a rainbow on summer weekends—with overflowing crowds and NO VACANCY *signs everywhere.*

Saugatuck is part of the Art Coast of Michigan. PHOTO COURTESY OF JOE DAVID

But in the late fall and early spring, when the air has an icy chill to it and the summer excitement is only a memory, the Kirby House, a bed-and-breakfast in Douglas, throws open its doors to food aficionados interested in some fun in the kitchen. Although no promises are made to turn cooks into chefs, or goose liver into delicate pâté, every attempt is made to keep the conversation centered on food—and cooking. Leading the direction is Chef Ray Riker, a self-made culinary maestro who is building a local reputation for his gourmet breakfasts.

Chef Riker purchased the Kirby House in 1998, and since then he has been earning repeat business because of his cooking skill and ability to create memorable flavors. This he attributes to his long-time love affair with food, which began when he was a child under the influence of his mother—and Prosper Montagné's book Larousse Gastronomique.

 A Resort with a Sweet Dream

*T*here is a strip of land along the western shores of Michigan where many Midwesterners migrate each summer. To them, this is more than a place to go to escape the summer heat—it is their ancestral "cottage" or "lodge" inherited from their parents, beautifully wrapped in a blanket of warm memories. Many religiously return year after year to rekindle childhood memories—the frolics along the shore, the spooky camp stories around a bonfire, and the lazy boat rides on a moonlight lake.

Saugatuck is one of those quaint, picturesque summer places. It is about two and a half hours by car from Chicago and about three hours by Amtrak (which arrives in Holland, a neighboring community that is a short cab ride away). A longtime favorite vacation area for Chicagoans, Saugatuck has one-of-a-kind boutiques, art galleries, and artist studios throughout the village, and the sort of activities you might expect at a trendy beach resort

ABOUT THE CHEF

Chef Riker has over twenty-five years of experience working in some of Detroit's better restaurants, as a waiter and as a cook. During this period he became acquainted with important techniques that helped shape his culinary skills. In 2002, he brought all this experience together and refined it with a two-week professional chef program at the Culinary Institute of America in Hyde Park, New York.

ABOUT THE CLASSES

The cooking program is primarily intended to provide a fun-filled get-away for culinary novices interested in learning to work creatively with their hands—and to meet other like-minded people.

(fishing, biking, boating, golfing, swimming, and, for thrill-seekers, wild cruising on schooners over the sandy dunes).

Part of what has been dubbed the Art Coast of Michigan, Saugatuck has a large artist community, about fifty galleries, and a summer school program run by the Chicago Institute of Art (Ox-Bow). To enhance its artsy character, the Mason Street Warehouse Theatre was established, offering the community noteworthy Broadway-quality plays each summer.

Besides the visual and performing arts, Saugatuck is also developing its culinary arts. Once a year all the local establishments that specialize in serving food and selling gourmet products unite to put on the Taste of Saugatuck-Douglas Food Festival. But that isn't all: Saugatuck has ambitions to go a step further and snag a major cooking school. If such a sweet dream is realized, it could enlarge the reputation of Saugatuck by making it even more popular than it already is.

Two weekend culinary packages are offered, one in November and the other in March. The weekend begins on a Friday with hors d'oeuvres and wine at the Butler Pantry (a respected Saugatuck restaurant and cooking store). The hands-on cooking class starts on Saturday after the 10:00 a.m. breakfast, with everyone participating in the food preparation for the evening dinner. Since it is a small kitchen, it sometimes gets a little crowded. To simplify the food preparation, students are broken into small groups, with each group preparing one part of a five-course meal. During class, Chef Riker guides and advises students as needed. This may include teaching basic skills such as chopping, dicing, slicing, and kneading, or anything else relevant to the meal preparation. When the dinner is ready to be served, students are then expected to plate and serve the food, and even pair it with the right wines.

Class Costs: Starts at $500 per couple, which includes two nights' lodging and breakfasts.
Class Frequency: Twice a year, November and March.
Class Length: A weekend package with about four to five hours of class on Saturday.
Class Type: Hands-on/demonstration.
Class Size: Maximum eighteen students.
Lodging: The Kirby House, a restored 1890 Queen Anne Victorian, is located in the historic town of Douglas, a few minutes away from Saugatuck. Established in 1851 as a port town for steamships carrying fruit, lumber, and leather to the Chicago Market, Douglas is known today for its restored houses and shops.
Amenities: Heated seasonal swimming pool, outdoor hot tubs, wireless Internet, free-to-use bicycles, CD players, refrigerator, microwave, and more. A continental breakfast is offered each day for early risers at 8:30 a.m. and a full breakfast for late risers at 10:00 a.m.
Restrictions: No smoking, no pets; children are not encouraged.
For more information contact: The Kirby House, 294 West Center Street, Douglas, MI 49406; (269) 857-2904; www.kirbyhouse.com.

Lake Kalamazoo Crepes Florentine

Compliments of the Kirby House

When making crepes, the first one is rarely as good as the second. The reason for this is that the pan needs to be hot and seasoned, and the oil and heat generated during the preparation of the first crepe prepares the pan for subsequent ones. Don't allow the pan to become too hot, however, or your crepe will become weblike. If the pan is too cool, the crepe will stick.

Crepe Filling

Ingredients
- 1 tablespoon olive oil
- 4 boneless, skinless chicken breasts, chopped into bite-size pieces
- $^1/_2$ teaspoon pepper
- $^1/_2$ teaspoon salt
- $^3/_4$ tablespoon dried basil
- 1 tablespoon dried parsley
- $^1/_4$ tablespoon garlic powder
- $^1/_2$ pound frozen spinach
- $^1/_2$ pound frozen broccoli
- 1 medium onion, peeled and diced
- $1^1/_2$ cups chopped wild mushrooms
- $^1/_2$ cup butter or margarine
- $^3/_4$ cup shredded cheddar cheese
- $^1/_4$ cup grated Parmesan cheese
- $^1/_8$ teaspoon paprika (to sprinkle on crepes after cooking)

1. In a large frying pan over medium heat, heat olive oil. When the oil is hot, add chicken and sauté until the juices run clear. Remove chicken from pan and coat with half the pepper, salt, basil, parsley, and garlic powder on each side. Return to pan and brown on both sides, 5 minutes a side.
2. Boil the spinach and broccoli in boiling water until slightly tender. Avoid overcooking. Drain and let cool.
3. Sauté the onion and mushrooms in butter or margarine over medium heat, stirring often, until the onion is translucent and the mushrooms are soft. Add the remaining pepper, salt, basil, parsley, and garlic powder.
4. Add the cheddar cheese, then the Parmesan, and stir well. Stir in half the Mornay sauce (recipe follows) and set aside.

Mornay Sauce

This may be refrigerated for several days and later reheated on low heat.

Ingredients
- $1/2$ cup butter or margarine
- $1/2$ cup flour
- 4 cups 2 percent or whole milk
- $1/4$ teaspoon garlic powder
- $1/2$ teaspoon salt
- $1/4$ teaspoon pepper
- 1 cup finely shredded cheddar (or other flavorful cheese)

1. In a saucepan over medium heat, melt the butter or margarine. Whisk in the flour until bubbly. Slowly add in enough milk until the sauce begins to thicken.
2. As the sauce thickens, add the spices one at a time, stirring constantly. When the sauce is hot, add the cheese slowly, stirring until melted and blended. Add remaining milk when the sauce once again thickens.
3. As soon as the sauce has a nice thick consistency, taste it and spice it to your liking. Reduce the heat to the lowest possible temperature, stirring ingredients often. If necessary, add more milk to avoid the sauce becoming too thick. The sauce should be about as thick as gravy.

Crepe Batter

Ingredients
- 4 large eggs
- $1/2$ cup vegetable oil
- 1 cup flour
- $3/4$ cup 2 percent or whole milk
- $1/4$ teaspoon garlic powder
- $1/4$ teaspoon salt
- $1/4$ teaspoon pepper

1. Beat eggs until frothy. Slowly whisk in the oil, then the flour, until blended. Add milk slowly, followed by the spices. The batter needs to be thin but not runny. Let it set for at least 15 minutes.
2. Whisk again and check the thickness. Add milk to thin or flour to thicken if necessary. While preparing the filling, it may be necessary to add milk to the batter since it will probably thicken while waiting to be used.

Crepe Cooking and Assembly

1. In a nonstick crepe pan over medium heat, melt some butter. After the pan is hot, lift it from the fire. Using a small ladle, put a thin coat of batter on the pan, just enough to cover it to the edges. Swirl the pan around to coat evenly. Return the pan to the burner and cook until the edges are brown. With a spoon, go around the edge of the crepe to separate it from pan. Carefully insert a spatula under the crepe and flip. Brown the second side. Slide the crepe onto a plate and repeat the process.
2. Preheat an oven to 350°F. To assemble the crepes, place the filling in the center of each crepe shell and roll. In an oven proof dish sprayed with non-stick cooking oil, arrange the assembled crepes in a line. Top with remaining Mornay sauce.
3. Bake for about 45 minutes to one hour, until the sauce is bubbly. Sprinkle with paprika and, using spatula, spoon neatly onto plates. Garnish with fresh parsley or basil.

Note: These crepes freeze well. Remove from the freezer a day in advance and thaw in the refrigerator. Bake about an hour; longer if still semifrozen.

Makes 4–6 servings.

Chateau Chantal
Traverse City, Michigan

A short distance from Traverse City, extending into Grand Traverse Bay like an eighteen-mile-long arm, is Old Mission Peninsula. Traveling along this scenic stretch of land is like taking a slow journey into another world, one of rolling hills and winding roads, of vineyards and cherry orchards. At the end of the journey are spectacular bay views and Chateau Chantal, a sixty-five-acre estate that resembles a medieval French castle.

An American version of a modern Loire Valley chateau, Chateau Chantal is more than just another stunning bed-and-breakfast—it is a retreat for gourmets who seek a food-and-wine holiday. Opened as a winery in 1993 and a cooking school in 2004, this striking property, which is owned and managed by Robert and Nadine Begin and their daughter Marie-Chantal, has handsomely furnished suites named after famous artists.

While their wine (including Riesling, pinot grigio, merlot, and chardonnay), all produced here with meticulous attention to detail, deserves attention, their cooking school does, too.

ABOUT THE STAFF

Heading the cooking school program is Nancy Krcek Allen, a graduate of San Francisco's California Culinary Academy. Nancy is a certified culinary professional, a member of I.A.C.P., Slow Food, and the New York Association of Cooking Teachers. Her many accomplishments include food writing, teaching at the Institute of Culinary Education (ICE) and the Natural Gourmet Institute, and writing ICE's new professional and recreational Asian curriculum.

Allen's goal as a teacher is to encourage students to become experimental, liberated cooks who don't depend on recipes, but on their own judgment instead. She achieves this by focusing on techniques and skills rather than recipes.

Also on staff is Lynne Brach, who has worked with Allen since 2001. Her culinary training began in Sweden, where she attended a Hem Tekniska school. She has worked in a variety of settings, but primarily for a wilderness program in northern Ontario, where she cooks for the camp.

ABOUT THE CLASSES

Students will learn techniques and skills for preparing irresistible foods, but, more importantly, they will learn about basic food preparation (e.g., stock and soup base), the foundation of a successful meal. The same applies to wines, and students will become familiar with the nuances of pairing them with food. One of the first things students will discover is that rules don't always apply: Food flavors change with each new ingredi-

Nancy Krcek Allen (left) oversees student progress. PHOTO COURTESY OF CHATEAU CHANTAL

ent, so what you garnish your food with can determine what wine should be paired with it—even if it's an untraditional choice.

Chateau Chantal, which is open year-round, also has wine seminars led by Mark Johnson, head winemaker. The seminars, which focus on winemaking and grape growing, and the art of correctly tasting wines, include a tour of the vineyard, a pleasant lunch, and a six-course dinner paired with wines.

Caramelized Onions

Both this recipe and the Maple Sweet and Sour Red Jam recipe are versatile and can be added to other foods to enrich the flavor. For example, for onion soup you can mix the onions with broth, or for a quick sauce you can stir them into a little reduced heavy cream or tomato puree, or puree them with chicken stock. You can also make batches to freeze for use later as building blocks in rice, pasta, vegetable, or meat dishes.

Ingredients
- ¼ cup butter or extra virgin olive oil (or a combination of the two)
- 2 pounds red onions, finely sliced
- Sherry, Marsala, port, wine, or pomegranate juice for deglazing
- 1 teaspoon or more salt

1. Heat a heavy casserole (large enough to accommodate the onions) over medium heat. Add the fat. When it is hot, spread the onions evenly in the pot. Turn the heat to low and cover. Cook the onions, stirring occasionally, until they are tender and melting, about 35–45 minutes.
2. Remove the cover and raise the heat. Brown the onions, stirring occasionally. If you haven't used enough fat, they may begin to stick. Add a tablespoon of your chosen alcohol and deglaze/scrape the brown off the bottom. Cook the liquid away and resume cooking until the onions are an even, nut-colored brown. Deglaze as necessary. Season with salt to taste.

Makes 2–3 cups.

Class Costs: Package cooking class: $275 per person (based on double occupancy and double enrollment in the cooking class), including lodging, breakfast each day, and the cooking class; wine seminar: $135 per person, including wine tasting, vineyard tour, lunch, and dinner; wine tours: $15–$35 per person.
Class Frequency: Classes are offered in the winter and spring months (January–April), twice per month for the cooking program and once a month for the wine seminar.

Class Length: Package cooking class is from 12:30 to 5:30 p.m. on Saturday.

Class Type: Demonstration/hands-on.

Class Size: Twelve to fourteen students maximum.

Lodging: Of the eleven guest accommodations available at the chateau, one is an executive apartment with a kitchen, dining room, living room, and two bedrooms. Eight are suites with sitting rooms, and two are standard hotel rooms. Each one, of course, has modern amenities and a private bath, and access to the chateau's great room. Although the chateau doesn't serve meals other than breakfast, on special occasions it has food events. There are restaurants nearby that the staff can recommend.

For more information contact: Chateau Chantal, 15900 Rue de Vin, Old Mission Peninsula, Traverse City, MI 49686; (231) 223-4110; www.chateauchantal.com.

Maple Sweet and Sour Red Onion Jam

Copyright © 2007 by Nancy Krcek Allen

This condiment matches well with meats and grilled food. You can also toss a little onto your favorite pasta or steamed vegetables.

Ingredients
- Caramelized onions (see recipe)
- 4 tablespoons maple syrup, more to taste, up to $1/2$ cup
- $1/2$ cup sherry wine vinegar
- 1 cup red wine

1. Heat the onions and the maple syrup in a heavy high-sided skillet or soup pot over medium heat. Stir well to mix. Cover the pot and lower the heat. Simmer the onions on low heat for several minutes, stirring occasionally. Add the vinegar and wine, and leave uncovered.
2. Raise the heat to medium and cook for about 5 minutes. Taste it, and add more maple syrup as needed to balance the vinegar. Cook until a thick marmalade forms.

Makes 8 servings.

Fonds du Cuisine Cooking School
Walloon Lake Village, Michigan

A decent meal can often be prepared by simply following a good recipe, but that same meal will undergo a spectacular transformation if technique is introduced. Techniques like deglazing or emulsifying, when done correctly, mixed with the right ingredients, have been known to bring about extraordinary results in the kitchen and set the professionals apart from the amateurs. For aspiring cooks who need professional guidance, the Fonds du Cuisine at the historic Walloon Lake Inn, like so many recreational cooking schools around the country, is placing the emphasis on teaching techniques rather than recipes.

ABOUT THE CHEF

For twenty-five years, David Beier, the sole teacher at Fonds du Cuisine, has been offering cooking classes that focus on techniques. Most of what he knows about cooking he learned the old-fashioned way—at home alone with his pots and pans. During those early formative years, his mentor was copies of gourmet publications.

In college, he used his home-learned knowledge to earn extra money in restaurants to pay off college expenses. His first serious restaurant job was in Portland, Oregon, where he was hired by a Swiss and a German to work in the kitchen of their restaurant. With them he experienced a whole new view of cooking. Their meticulous attention to detail made him suddenly aware of what good cooking really was. (This was the era before schools like the Culinary Institute of America were popular, and many chefs didn't have today's cooking sensibilities.) Determined to master cooking on the highest possible level, Beier only took jobs with establishments that could help him refine his skills.

Most of what he prefers to prepare at the Walloon Lake Inn has been influenced by his preferential love for the foods of France and Italy.

The Walloon Lake Inn is home to the Fonds du Cuisine Cooking School.
PHOTO COURTESY OF JOE DAVID

Unlike some of the new wave chefs, he avoids fusing global flavors and prefers instead to develop a genuine ethnic taste, which he enhances by using the best ingredients available generally (and not just locally) to build his meal.

His many years of teaching have taught him that most students want great results in the kitchen—without spending a lot of time cooking. One way he tries to assist them achieve their goal is to encourage them to over-prepare and freeze leftovers. Teaching techniques and practical lessons like how to prepare foods in advance, the art of cooking foods last minute, and estimating the cooking time for meals have proven valuable to many of his students. Many walk away from his class a little more skilled and knowledgeable, and certainly more gifted at preparing what he calls everyday cooking: food that is tasty and uncomplicated to prepare.

ABOUT THE CLASSES

Everything from knife skills to learning about the chemistry of mixing foods are woven into Beier's lesson. To unravel the mysteries behind

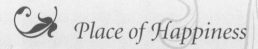

Place of Happiness

In the sleepy burg of Ellsworth, only a short distance south of Walloon Lake, there is a beautiful and elegant yet unpretentious restaurant with a lakefront view. The name of it is Tapawingo, a Chippewa Indian word that means "Place of Happiness."

Over the years this country house has received considerable attention. Writers representing some of America's most trendy gourmet publications have come, eaten, and made public pronouncements. Kelly Alexander at Saveur magazine sums up exactly what so many have said, that Tapawingo "is without doubt the finest restaurant in the area and one of the best in the whole Midwest."

The reason for its success: The flavors are familiar yet sophisticated, prominent but not disturbing. Each meal begins with a lively muse intended to brighten the palate and set the mood for what will follow and ends with a satisfyingly sweet dessert. The result is four courses of complementary foods that glide over the taste buds, teasing them pleasantly with contrasting flavors. Unlike the provincial French cuisine served at the nearby Rowe Inn, this restaurant experiments with Southeast Asian flavors, mixed adventurously with traditional and familiar recipes.

For years, during the winter months, Chef-owner Harlan "Pete" Peterson had offered classes for students to learn to cook the Tapawingo way.

good cooking, regardless of ethnic origin, certain basic cooking procedures need to be understood. Once understood, they can be applied to a variety of ethnic foods. (For example, sautéing in a wok and in a skillet are very similar. Both require high heat and little fat, and lots of room for the food to slide around in, and both achieve browning to preserve food juices.) His teaching routine is designed to enable students to grasp such similarities in technique and at the same time to receive the hands-on experience needed to apply this technique to a specific recipe.

Unfortunately, as of this writing, the future of Tapawingo's cooking program is uncertain. But if you are interested in learning more about it, maybe even visiting the restaurant, you should call. You won't be disappointed. This little area of Michigan is noted for some gourmet surprises.

The aforementioned Rowe Inn, also in Ellsworth, is where Chef Peterson got his early training. Both restaurants run about $50 per meal per person. A welcoming inn within walking distance of the two restaurants is the House on the Hill, a well-maintained fifty-three-acre farm property that has been converted into a charming bed-and-breakfast. The main house has four rooms, and the carriage house has three with a semiprivate deck that faces a gurgling creek. A three-course gourmet breakfast is served family style to all guests around a large breakfast table. In the early evening, guests enjoy wine and an informal social hour with the host and hostess in the main house.

For more information contact:

Tapawingo, 9502 Lake Street, Ellsworth, MI 49729; (231) 588-7971; www.tapawingo.net.

The Rowe Inn, 6303 East Jordan Road, Ellsworth, MI 49729; (231) 588-7351; www.roweinn.com.

House on the Hill, 9661 Lake Street, Ellsworth, MI 49729; (231) 588-6304; www.thehouseonthehill.com.

Osso Bucco

Compliments of Fonds du Cuisine

Most people have heard the adage that a stew is better when heated the second time. This dish is no exception. As a result, it is not a problem to make it one day and serve it two to four days later. Risotto is a classic accompaniment, and a suitable wine is a Côte du Rhône or Beaujolais. To prepare the recipe, you will need a two-inch-thick veal shank (osso bucco in Italian) per person. They freeze well, so you should consider buying extra if the butcher has some. Also, it is best to use a heavy-bottomed, four-quart braising pan with a lid.

Braising is a slow, moist-cooking method that breaks down the elements that make meat tough. It is often used to prepare stew meats, veal breast, lamb shanks, and pot roasts. The differences in handling these various types of meat lie primarily with the kind of seasoning used (for example, rosemary with lamb and lemon thyme with veal).

Ingredients
- 6 two-inch-thick veal shanks
- Salt and pepper
- 2 tablespoons olive oil (high quality unnecessary)
- 1 large yellow onion, peeled and chopped
- 4 carrots, chopped
- 3 stalks celery, chopped
- 4 cloves garlic
- 6 sprigs thyme
- Zest of $1/2$ lemon
- 1 cup dry white wine
- 3 cups chicken stock
- 1 cup canned plum tomatoes

1. Season the veal shanks with salt and pepper. Heat a braising pan and add olive oil; brown the shanks. When they are brown, remove them from the pan and set aside. Add the onion, carrots, and celery and brown them.
2. Return the shanks to the pan, add the remainder of the ingredients, and cover. Place in a preheated 350°F oven for about 2 hours. When the shanks are tender, remove them from the pan. Remove the vegetables and liquids, puree them, and strain to use as a sauce.

Serves 6.

Each one of his classes begins with the explanation of a technique, like poaching an artichoke, for example. This is then followed by a demonstration. Afterward, under Beier's supervision, students perform the techniques as they prepare a three-course meal (including bread, appetizer, entree, vegetable, starch, and dessert).

Classes run about four hours. How quickly or slowly they progress depends on the questions and ability of the students. Since the classes are limited to six people, each student receives a share of the chef's attention. After the food is prepared, students enjoy what they have cooked. Classes are held from September through May, excluding holidays.

Class Costs: Two-day program is $260 per person, including lodging ($160 per person without lodging; four-day program is $440 per person, including lodging ($260 per person without lodging).

Class Frequency: About nine two-day and nine four-day classes, September through May.

Class Length: About four hours of class with lunch, from approximately 8:30 a.m. to 12:30 p.m.

Class Type: Hands-on; some demonstration.

Class Size: Six students maximum.

Lodging: Lodging and classes are offered at the Walloon Lake Inn, a one-hundred-year-old country bed-and-breakfast. This quaint historic property, modernized just enough to provide sufficient comfort, has that unembellished look of times gone by. Facing Walloon Lake, the inn offers an uninterrupted view of the water. Each of the five rooms is small and practical, with a simple, country personality. They are all basic, clean, and comfortable, with period furniture. Ernest Hemingway, who used to fish in the area, might have once referred to it as "a clean, well-lighted place."

Amenities: Private bath, continental breakfast, boat docks, and access to bikes, a canoe, a kayak, and other customary water sports. Dining is offered seven days a week from 6:00 p.m. on, outside or in the main dining room (about $50 for a three-course meal).

For more information contact : Walloon Lake Inn, P.O. Box 459, Walloon Lake Village, MI 49796; (231) 535-2999; www.walloonlakeinn.com.

WISCONSIN

⤫

Savory Spoon Cooking School
Ellison Bay, Wisconsin

*D*oor County may not be as pristine as it was when the Europeans discovered it a few hundred years ago, but to many summer vacationers
who return loyally each year, it is a spectacular, underdeveloped paradise
with miles of natural beauty. Located in Wisconsin's Upper Peninsula, the
county is wedged between Green Bay and Lake Michigan and stretches from
below Sturgeon Bay to Washington Island.

Like most multiethnic areas, Door County has its share of traditions.
For tourists, perhaps one of the most talked about eating experiences is the
boil-over, a cookout passed on to modern diners by the early Scandinavian
settlers. For many first-timers this unique dining experience is anything but
elegant and savory, and, in fact, urbanites may find it primitive—but that
is part of its appeal to tourists.

The featured food for the boil-over is whitefish steak cuts, which are placed
into baskets before being submerged into a huge pot of boiling water containing sweet onions and potatoes. Before the baskets are removed from the pot,
kerosene is tossed on the fire, which explodes into a huge flame. This causes the
water in the pot to boil over, dousing the flames and washing away the fish oils
floating on the surface of the water. The baskets of fish are then removed from
the pot, and the food is served with plenty of butter and coleslaw. The feast
ends with a slice of the traditional Door County cherry pie.

Cooking school students who wish to contrast this with a more traditional and appetizing dining experience should head to the Savory Spoon
Cooking School near the tip of the peninsula in Ellison Bay. Classes are held
in a historic schoolhouse that has been converted into a handsome state-
of-the-art kitchen especially designed for teaching small groups of students.

Chef Janice Thomas, founder of the cooking school, prepares a pie.
PHOTO COURTESY OF THE SAVORY SPOON COOKING SCHOOL

Janice Thomas, who founded the school in 2004, shares the teaching spot-light with local food celebrities.

ABOUT THE INSTRUCTOR

The school is very young, but Thomas brings to it over twenty years of experience in the food industry, fourteen of them spent running a cater-ing company in Tucson, Arizona. During those years, when she wasn't helping her husband manage their four restaurants, she would cater events like the LPA and LPGA Golf Tournaments or christen new kitch-ens by holding cooking classes in them to demonstrate the appliances. She also took a four-week cooking class at Le Cordon Bleu in regional French cooking and, whenever time permitted, private classes with respected chefs in France, Mexico, and Ireland.

PHILOSOPHY

Her teaching goal is to connect students with food. She wants them to fall in love with cooking and create a recipe book that they can share with their families. She worries that, if the fast-food trends continue, Americans may never outgrow their fast-food dependency and will lose out on the joy of enjoying and creating flavorful slow foods.

ABOUT THE CLASSES

The class begins with a forty- to forty-five-minute demonstration/lecture on how to purchase products, slice foods, and more. For quick, efficient cooking, all ingredients are laid out for each student to use, measured exactly, identified, and covered with plastic wrap. The students are given five recipes that they prepare in groups. The recipes will require a mix of skills and steps, from the simple to the complex. Students will learn to use locally grown ingredients to create tasty and familiar foods like tacos, burritos, and enchiladas, and less-familiar foods like Asian Pâté with Grand Marnier on Wonton Crisps.

Each class has a unique focus, and students who want to make a long weekend of it can attend three or four distinctive evening classes. One might include Asian bistro flavors, another barbecue sauces, and another French countryside cooking. Students who prefer a shorter class can take a Sweet Saturday Morning class, which lasts one-and-a-half hours. In this class students make confections of all sorts to take home, from toffee to truffles.

Class Costs: $45 to $65 per person.
Class Frequency: Thursday, Friday, and Saturday nights, June through October.
Class Length: Three to three-and-a-half hours (6:00 to 9:30 p.m.).
Class Type: Demonstration/hands-on.
Class Size: Fourteen to sixteen students.
Lodging: The school does not provide accommodations, but the following lodgings are nearby:
Woodenheart Inn, 11086 Highway 42, Sister Bay, WI 54234; (920) 854-9097; www.woodenheart.com. This is a log home constructed to be a bed-and-breakfast in 1992. It offers full amenities, including wireless Internet access.

Spiced Rubbed Pork Tenderloin

Compliments of the Savory Spoon Cooking School

Ingredients
- 2 teaspoons ground cumin
- 2 teaspoons ground coriander
- 1 teaspoon fresh ground black pepper
- 1 teaspoon ancho chile powder
- 1 large shallot, minced
- 2 tablespoons olive oil
- 2 teaspoons adobo sauce
- 1 teaspoon salt
- 2 garlic cloves, minced
- 3$^1/_2$ pounds pork tenderloin, trimmed and cut crosswise into 8 equal parts
- 12 dried corn husks
- 4 ounces goat cheese
- $^1/_4$ cup chopped dried Door County cherries

1. In a small dry skillet over high heat, stir cumin and coriander until aromatic, about 1–2 minutes. In a small bowl, mix the cumin, coriander, pepper, chile powder, shallot, olive oil, adobo sauce, salt, and garlic until a paste forms. Rub all sides of the tenderloin with the paste; cover and chill overnight.
2. Choose corn husks that are wide and clean, and soak them in warm water for 1 hour. Drain and pat dry. Tear four of the corn husks lengthwise into strips $^1/_2$ or $^3/_4$ inch wide, and tie the strips together to create corn husk ribbons.
3. Place one pork tenderloin serving in the center of each remaining corn husk. Place one slice of goat cheese and 1 tablespoon of the cherries on top of the tenderloin. Wrap the corn husks around the pork and tie the center and the ends of each with corn husk ribbons, enclosing pork completely. Place pork bundles on a baking sheet.
4. Preheat oven to 350°F. Bake pork bundles uncovered until instant-read thermometer inserted into the thickest part of each registers 150°F, 20–25 minutes, depending on thickness of pork.
5. Place pork bundles on plates and remove the corn husk ribbon from one end of each, folding the corn husk back slightly to expose some of the meat. Spoon the Cherry Avocado Salsa alongside (recipe follows).

Serves 8.

Juniper Inn (Fish Creek), N9423 Maple Grove Road, Fish Creek, WI 54212; (800) 218-6960; www.juniperinn.com. This comfortable and attractive property is near Peninsula Park and two distinctive villages, Fish Creek and Ephraim. It has the usual basic appointments, including private bath, fireplace, and private deck. Hillside Inn, 9980 Water Street, Ephraim, WI 54211; (866) 673-8456; www.visit ephraim.com. This is small, elegant, nineteenth-century inn in picturesque Ephraim has been carefully restored in recent years to preserve its historic heritage.

Activities: Flanked by cherry and apple orchards, this relatively narrow area of the Upper Peninsula (about 75 miles long) is a mix of contrasting images—the remote and developed, the barren and lush—all within easy reach of each other. As a result, there is something for everyone, including five state parks, campgrounds, boat launches, hiking trails, sandy beaches, and a picturesque collection of communities like Fish Creek (which has the historic Alexander Noble House), Sister Bay (with its Old Anderson House museum), Egg Harbor (and its Cupola House), Crossroads (a nineteenth-century village), and much more.

For more information contact: The Savory Spoon Cooking School, 12042 Highway 42, Ellison Bay, WI 54210; (920) 854-6600; www.savoryspoon.com.

Cherry Avocado Salsa

Compliments of the Savory Spoon Cooking School

Ingredients

- 1 yellow pepper
- 12 ounces tart cherries, chopped into quarters
- $1/4$ cup sugar
- 2 tablespoons maple syrup
- $1/4$ cup fresh orange juice
- 1 jalapeño, seeded and chopped
- 1 tablespoon orange zest
- 2 ripe avocadoes, halved, pitted, peeled, and diced (always buy an extra one for backup)
- $1/4$ cup chopped fresh cilantro (leaves only, no stems)

1. Char pepper over gas flame until blackened on all sides. Place charred pepper in a plastic bag to sweat for 15 minutes. Peel, seed, and chop pepper. Set aside.
2. Combine cherries, sugar, maple syrup, and orange juice in a bowl. Add pepper, orange zest, avocadoes, and cilantro.

Makes 3 cups.

Destination Kohler
Kohler, Wisconsin

Eating is a universal pleasure that not only satisfies hunger, but also calms the soul. When people enjoy good food, their differences often disappear. A conviviality surfaces, brought about by the focus on the wonderful scent, taste, and look of exquisitely prepared cuisine. In the right setting, like the beautifully maintained, AAA Five Diamond resort hotel the American Club, one of several dining venues at Destination Kohler, the experience has been known to be memorable.

Food lovers who visit Destination Kohler can take advantage of the village's nine restaurants and three special cooking programs. This complete, full-service resort has everything needed to turn a short getaway into an extraordinary culinary event.

ABOUT THE CHEF

The man responsible for reviewing the menus at Destination Kohler is Chef Ulrich Koberstein, a graduate of Le Cordon Bleu (London) who received his work experience at Chez Nico (London) and the Ritz-Carlton Hotel (Boston) before coming to Kohler. Chef Koberstein's interest in food began at home at an early age. His mother, who was an excellent cook, spoiled him with foods like roast goose, veal schnitzel, and steak tartare. Today at Destination Kohler he personally oversees twelve Kohler chefs and sets high standards that reflect those of the resort restaurants that were so important to him growing up.

PHILOSOPHY

The culinary goal at Destination Kohler is to keep food flavors pure and intense—the main flavor should be dominant and not be confused by incompatible flavors. To achieve this, Chef Koberstein only uses ingredients that complement and enhance the quality of the main ingredient.

All the recipes used during classes have been selected to be guidelines, a reference point. According to Chef Koberstein, "A recipe is not a bible. There are variances that should always be considered: the thickness of the meat, seasonality of the produce, and the personal tastes of the cook. When planning a meal, many things must be taken into consideration to achieve success."

ABOUT THE CLASSES

Students choosing to sample A Taste of Kohler (a series of classes with a specific food focus, held six times a year) will learn the Destination Kohler approach to cooking during their two-night stay at the historic American Club. Each Taste of Kohler series takes students on a new journey—to Spain, Italy, France, or the local vineyards—and includes demonstrations, wine tastings and pairings, and cuisine samplings. The program begins with a wine and cheese reception at the Kohler Design Center and ends with students making a perfect sweet to enjoy before leaving.

Also offered are classes held in the Demonstration Kitchen at the Shops at Woodlake Kohler each Saturday at 11:00 a.m. and 2:00 p.m. between January and April. These classes are informal and allow students to interact with the Kohler chefs during the preparation and tastings of the food and wine. Demonstrations focus on some very specific aspects of cooking, like creating a romantic dinner for two, preparing food for a tailgate party, and spa cuisine.

Scheduled once a year, during the last weekend in October, is the Kohler Food and Wine Experience. Although this impressive event is less spectacular than the Food & Wine Magazine Classic in Aspen, Colorado (see sidebar on page 177), it is considered the Midwest's premier culinary event and draws its share of food-industry headliners. Cosponsored by *Food & Wine* magazine, the weekend is an extravagant mix of wine tastings, cooking demonstrations, wine and spirit seminars, product promotions, and more. A package program for couples includes accommodations at the historic American Club hotel and tickets to select special events. There is also a Feast of Talent dinner, which includes a five-course meal prepared by a selection of celebrity chefs.

Class Costs: Saturday demonstrations run $25 per person and $40 for two. A Taste of Kohler is priced as a package at $600. During the Kohler Food and Wine Experience, a two-night package for two can run from $800 to $1,400, depending on accommodations. Individually, seminars run from $20 to $40 each. Complimentary activities are planned throughout the weekend. The Feast of Talent dinner costs about $150 per person.

Class Frequency: Saturday demonstration classes are held between January and April; six Taste of Kohler packages are offered throughout the year on Monday through Wednesday; the Kohler Food and Wine Experience is held in October.

Class Length: One hour for the Saturday demonstration classes; class hours vary for the Taste of Kohler packages.

Class Type: Mostly interactive demonstration classes.

Class Size: The Demonstration Kitchen holds forty students; six to twenty students participate in the Taste of Kohler packages.

Lodging: Built in 1918 to house the immigrant factory workers in the Kohler company plant, the American Club has since been renovated and turned into a hotel. The Village of Kohler also offers a second hotel, the Inn on Woodlake, which sits attractively on the border of Wood Lake. Both first-class hotels offer excellent facilities. The primary differences between the two are the level of services and amenities. The American Club is a full-service resort hotel, while the Inn on Woodlake is a limited-service facility with spacious rooms and, of course, elegant bathroom facilities.

Activities: The beautifully planned community of the Village of Kohler, only an hour north of Milwaukee, offers championship golf courses, state-of-the-art health and exercise facilities, excellent restaurants, specialty shops, a private manmade lake, botanical gardens, and more. Many of its stylish and tasteful Kohler products, representing the latest trends in kitchens and bathrooms, are still created on the property and are on display, not only in the hotels and the Kohler Waters Spa, but in the impressive Kohler Design Center showroom.

For more information contact: Destination Kohler; (920) 457-8000; www.destination kohler.com.

Salmon Cakes with Poached Eggs and Crab Hollandaise

Compliments of The Kitchens of Kohler at Destination Kohler

This recipe achieves great flavor using simple ingredients. There isn't anything complicated about the flavors in this dish, which come mostly from the salmon and the crab, enhanced by the lemon juice. Chef Koberstein recommends that you use the freshest fish available, farm-fresh eggs, and keep the breading to a minimum.

Crab Hollandaise

Ingredients
- 3 egg yolks
- 9 ounces melted butter
- 1 teaspoon lemon juice
- 1 teaspoon white wine vinegar
- Pinch of cayenne pepper
- Tabasco sauce to taste
- 1 tablespoon warm water

In a large mixing bowl, whisk the egg yolks over a bain-marie (double boiler) until the yolks thicken to the consistency of whipped cream. Gradually add the melted butter, whisking continuously, until all of the butter has been incorporated. Add the lemon juice, white wine vinegar, cayenne pepper, and Tabasco sauce. Add a little warm water if the sauce is too thick.

Salmon Cakes

Ingredients
- 1 pound cooked and flaked salmon
- 1 egg
- 1 tablespoon whole grain mustard
- 2 tablespoons mayonnaise
- 3 tablespoons diced red peppers
- 3 tablespoons diced yellow peppers
- 1 tablespoon chopped chives
- 1 tablespoon fresh squeezed lemon juice
- $^2/_3$ cup bread crumbs

- White wine vinegar
- Salt and pepper to taste
- Butter for frying

1. Place the first ten ingredients into a large mixing bowl and mix well. Season with salt and pepper. Divide the mixture into eight equal portions. By hand, mold the salmon into balls, and then flatten out into cakes.
2. In a large pan over medium heat, sauté the salmon cakes in butter for 2 minutes on each side or until golden brown. Place on a paper towel and keep warm.

Poached Eggs

Ingredients
- 8 eggs
- White wine vinegar

In a large shallow pan, bring water to a simmer. Add vinegar. (For every 4 cups of water, add 1 tablespoon of vinegar.) Crack four of the eggs gently into the simmering water. (Do not add too many eggs at a time, as this will drop the temperature of the water.) Poach the eggs for 3–5 minutes, depending on how firm you want them to be. Remove eggs from the water and place on a paper towel; keep warm. Repeat this with the remaining eggs.

Assembly

Ingredients
- 4 ounces fresh crabmeat
- Sprigs of fresh herbs, chopped, for garnish

To assemble, place a little salad onto a plate with two salmon cakes. Place a poached egg on top of each salmon cake and pour hollandaise sauce over the top. Garnish with crabmeat and herbs.

Serves 4.

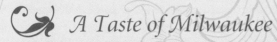

A Taste of Milwaukee

Wisconsin is a state that takes its cheese very seriously. Visitors should be prepared to experience some remarkable cheeses. The choices are not only increasing, but cheesemakers are turning out some tasty artisan varieties. Wondrous things, for example, are being done to Cheddar—by creating a cave aged to an organic and raw milk variety.

For a sampling of what the state offers, you should visit the Milwaukee Public Market in the Historic Third Ward, only a few blocks from downtown. The selection of gourmet foods isn't huge, but the quality is high.

On the second level of the market, there is a cooking school, Madame Kuony's Kitchen, with state-of-the-art equipment and a diverse cooking program suited for public and private demonstration classes. The school was founded by Madame Liane Kuony's culinary students in honor of her unwavering high standards and pioneering commitment to organic and genetically unaltered foods. A remarkable woman with unshakable French roots, she brought to Wisconsin a culinary quality unmatched for its time.

Classes begin at $29 and rise, depending on the program (demonstration, hands-on, private, or corporate classes) and are offered most weeks throughout the year. The one-and-a-half-hour weekday classes begin at

Jill Prescott's Ecole de Cuisine
Sheboygan, Wisconsin

Noteworthy success in the kitchen is never achieved by adding a secret ingredient to a meal or by demonstrating a technique that will give dramatic flair to the presentation. Instead, it can only occur after years of studying and reproducing subtle and even mysterious flavors learned from time-honored cooking traditions passed on from generation to generation.

5:30 p.m., and the weekend classes begin at 1:30 p.m. Not all the classes include ingredients that are organic or genetically unaltered. Some lessons include cooking with beer, native Indian cooking, and eating healthy.

For more information, contact the Milwaukee Public Market, 400 North Water Street, Milwaukee, WI 53202; (414) 336-1111; www.Milwaukee publicmarket.org.

The Third Ward is also a pleasant place to eat and shop. The area was originally settled by the Irish, later by the Italians. During the fires of 1892, it was demolished and rebuilt soon afterward. Today the buildings that were once factories and warehouses are galleries, restaurants, boutiques, specialty stores, condominiums and offices.

While visiting Milwaukee, you should tour the Pabst Mansion (2000 West Wisconsin Avenue, next to Marquette University, 414-931-0808), the breweries (Miller, 414-931-2337; Lakefront, 414-372-8800; and Sprecher, 414-964-2739), and especially the Milwaukee Art Museum, a futuristic building created by the internationally renowned architect Santiago Calatrava.

Two excellent turn-of-the-century hotels in Milwaukee are the Pfister (424 East Wisconsin Avenue, 414-273-8222, downtown, expensive from $260 up) and the art-deco Ambassador (2308 West Wisconsin Avenue, 414-342-8400, near Marquette University, from $199 up). Both are elegant and memorable historic properties with full hotel services.

For Chef Jill Prescott, it's even simpler than that: It means cooking the French way.

ABOUT THE CHEF

Students who take one of Chef Prescott's cooking classes will discover the subtle mysteries of fine cooking, taught to her by some of France's premier chefs and culinary artisans. What sets her apart from other French chefs is that she is very principled and never deviates from the rules.

Chef Jill Prescott demonstrates her whipping technique.
PHOTO COURTESY OF JILL PRESCOTT'S ECOLE DE CUISINE

Buried within her food is a history of French culinary art.

Like so many talented cooks, Jill Prescott avoids using what she calls "swill"—prepared foods loaded with chemicals to enhance flavor or preserve quality. Instead, each meal begins from scratch, sometimes from a basic stock (see recipe) with layers of carefully added flavors. Whether discussing the importance of stock or the superiority of Orléans vinegar over domestic vinegars, she always offers her students sensible cooking advice to help make them successful in the kitchen.

A chatty, warm woman, she has accumulated a significant amount of knowledge abroad working with professionals (in bakeries and restaurants) and studying at France's leading schools (at La Varenne, l'École Lenôtre, and l'École Ritz-Escoffier). During her many study-work trips abroad, she learned by doing—making vinegars, harvesting sea salt, foraging for truffles, and much more—which has made her wiser and more adept at fine cooking. Along the way, she befriended Julia Child, who encouraged her, and Simone Beck, to whom she pledged her uncompromising dedication to perpetuating the French traditions of preparing food.

Her reward for her hard work has included some noteworthy recognition. For several seasons she had her own successful PBS show (*Jill Prescott's Ecole de Cuisine*), and some of her students have included Hollywood stars.

PHILOSOPHY

Her goal is to provide recreational cooks with total immersion into some aspect of French cooking. A purist, she encourages perfection—whether preparing tomato soup or cassoulet, a pâté de foie gras, or steak au poivre. By being true to the French traditions, she hopes to pass on to her students a respect for France's high standard of culinary excellence.

ABOUT THE CLASSES

One-day, two-day, three-day, and five-day classes are available throughout the year for home cooks serious about learning how to prepare time-tested recipes.

Her premier five-day Classic French Cuisine is a total immersion program that introduces students to professional skills. All types of recipes are taught, from basic stocks to bread. At the end of each class, students enjoy a five-course meal that they prepared, suitably paired with wine. Another five-day program is French Patisseries and Classic Desserts, designed to teach students how to successfully create French classics and all-American desserts.

The two- and three-day programs include classes in French bistro cooking, as well as artisanal breads, dinner rolls, and cinnamon buns; also offered is a class in Italian trattoria food, which features such popular regional foods as pastas, focaccia, osso bucco, and some irresistible desserts.

One-day classes may include an introduction to French and Italian cuisine, a chef's choice class, food and wine pairing, French stocks and sauces, truffles, a Thanksgiving dinner, and more. These classes are offered on consecutive days, so students may take as few or as many as they wish.

Also offered are special classes for children between the ages of seven to thirteen, who will learn to make a full-course meal from scratch. Team-building classes are also available for corporations. Other types of classes, customized to your needs, can be arranged upon request.

Class Costs: Five-day classes: $1,275 per person; three-day classes: $575 per person; two-day classes: $425 to $475 per person; one-day class: $125 to $225 per person.

Class Frequency: Held throughout the year.

Class Length: Workshops run one to three hours; an average class like the one-, two-, three-, and five-day classes averages five hours a day, which include a daily lecture, hands-on cooking, and a full meal with wine.

Crème de Soupe d'Asperge
(Cream of Asparagus Soup)

Compliments of Jill Prescott's Ecole de Cuisine

Crème de Soupe d'Asperge is an elegant soup enhanced with fresh herbs and swirls of cream. To create the swirls on the surface of the beautiful green soup, squeeze a bottle filled with 1/3 cup of heavy cream over it. Serve the soup with a few sprigs of fresh tarragon or Italian parsley.

Crème de Soupe d'Asperge
(Cream of Asparagus Soup)
PHOTO COURTESY OF STEVE ELIASEN PHOTOGRAPHS

Ingredients
- 6 tablespoons unsalted butter
- 1 large shallot, chopped
- 2 medium leeks, cleaned and chopped (use primarily the white and a little of the light green portion)
- 1 pound asparagus, washed, ends trimmed 1/2 inch (slice diagonally)
- 6 cups chicken stock (more if soup is too thick), see recipe on p. 226
- 1 medium Idaho potato, peeled and thinly sliced
- 1 teaspoon finely ground sea salt

Class Type: Hands-on, demonstration, lecture.

Class Size: Two to ten students per class; corporate classes may include up to 150 students. Private classes are offered upon request.

Lodging: Blue Harbor, 725 Blue Harbor Drive, Sheboygan, WI 53081; (920) 452-2900; www.blueharborresort.com. A waterfront resort hotel facing Lake Michigan, Blue Harbor is popular with families. Amenities include an indoor water park, outdoor swimming pool, element spa, fitness center, and activity room for children and adults. Kid suites have pleasant nautical themes, and adult suites are standard modern rooms with refrigerators, microwaves, and wet bars (without the liquor).

For more information contact: Jill Prescott, (707) 260-4002; www.jillprescott.com. She is considering moving to Asheville, North Carolina, so check her Web site for updates.

- 10 sprigs fresh Italian parsley (leaves only; discard stems)
- 6 basil leaves
- 8 stems tarragon (leaves only; discard stems)
- 6–8 grinds freshly ground nutmeg (or a small pinch)
- Freshly ground white pepper
- $2/3$ cup cream
- Additional cream in a squirt bottle for decorating the soup
- Additional parsley or tarragon leaves for garnish

1. Melt butter in a Dutch oven over medium heat. Sweat the shallots and leeks in the butter until they begin to soften, not allowing them to brown. Add asparagus and sauté for 3 minutes, stirring constantly.
2. Add chicken stock, potato, and salt. Bring to a boil, then reduce heat to a simmer. Simmer for 15–20 minutes or until the asparagus is soft. Do not let the asparagus overcook as the color pales. Blend in fresh herbs and pepper. Cool the soup to lukewarm, and then transfer to a blender; puree until smooth. Before serving, add the cream and rewarm. Garnish with swirls of cream and fresh herbs.

Serves 6.

Fond de Volaille (Chicken Stock)

Compliments of Jill Prescott's Ecole de Cuisine

Without stock, there would be no French cuisine. Stock, or fond de cuisine (the foundation of cooking), is one of the most essential elements for adding flavor to sauces, soups, braises, and stews. Never use canned or powdered stock.

When preparing the stock, begin from scratch; if possible, make double batches and freeze it. Once the stock comes to a boil, immediately reduce the heat to a simmer for 5–6 hours. Do not allow the stock to simmer more than 6 hours, or it will taste fatty; don't allow it to boil for any length of time, or it will become greasy. The stock should have a light, clean chicken and herb flavor.

During preparation it is important to remove any gray scum with a fine meshed skimmer or spoon. Such impurities impart a bitter flavor to the stock. Prepared stock must be used or frozen within one day. Use only fresh herbs, as dried ones make the stock taste musty. Never add salt.

If your butcher does not have chicken bones, two cut up whole chickens are fine. You may want to freeze bones from time to time and use them later, when you have enough, to make a stock.

Ingredients
- 6 pounds chicken bones (wing tips, necks, backs, and other bones)
- 1 whole chicken, $2^1/_2$ to 3 pounds, cut up (a larger stewing chicken is best)
- 2 medium onions, peeled and quartered
- 6 carrots, peeled and cut into four pieces
- 4 leeks, cleaned and tied

- 6 stalks celery with leaves
- 4 cloves garlic, peeled
- 1 bouquet garni (6 sprigs of fresh parsley, 4 sprigs fresh thyme, 12 black tellicherry peppercorns, and 3 Turkish bay leaves tied in between 2 leek leaves)

1. Rinse the bones and the chicken well under cold running water. Place the bones, chicken, onions, carrots, leeks, celery, garlic, and bouquet garni into a stainless-steel-lined 16- to 20-quart stock pot and cover everything with 2 inches of cold water. Over a high heat, bring to a boil. Immediately adjust the heat to low and simmer, uncovered, for about 6 hours, skimming when necessary. Do not allow the stock to boil.
2. Using a fine mesh strainer or a chinois, strain the stock into another large container. Discard the bones, herbs, and chicken remains. Cool to room temperature quickly by placing the pot into a sink filled with cold water and ice. Change the water occasionally if necessary.
3. Once cool, refrigerate overnight. Do not cover the stock during the cooling process. After 8–10 hours, a layer of fat will rise to the top of the stock. Remove the hardened fat layer and discard. Use within one day, or store in the freezer in 4-cup batches.

Variation: You may substitute turkey bones for the chicken bones. In addition, the recipe may be halved, eliminating the cut up chicken meat and utilizing only the turkey carcass.

Makes approximately 8–10 quarts.

The Washington Hotel Culinary School
Washington Island, Wisconsin

*W*ashington Island is a peaceful, underdeveloped island separated *from Wisconsin's Upper Peninsula by a treacherous strait, once dubbed "Death's Door" by the French. According to legend, hundreds of ships attempting to pass through the strait were pulled apart by violent cur-*

Chef-proprietor Leah Caplan prepares her thin-crusted pizza.

PHOTO COURTESY OF THE WASHINGTON HOTEL CULINARY SCHOOL

rents and storms, and left to rest at the bottom of the water. Crossing the strait today is far from treacherous (at least in season); a ferry moves cars and people regularly from shore to shore without incident.

Visitors to the northern tip of Wisconsin's Door County have an unexpected surprise awaiting them after crossing the strait: a bucolic and historic fishing and agricultural community, committed exclusively to the sustainable food movement. At the center of this movement is the the Washington Hotel Restaurant and Culinary School, run with typical Midwest graciousness by chef-proprietor Leah Caplan.

 *A Chef with a Mission*

*W*hen Chef Leah Caplan moved to Washington Island in 2002, it lacked commercial farming. To avoid having it become another tourist site, covered with resorts and private homes, she joined forces with the locals to create an island paradise that could sustain itself. Because of her efforts—and the efforts of local farmers and residents—the economic position of the island has changed. One of her most significant contributions, which began years before she moved to the island, is her creation of and involvement with the Board of Home Grown Wisconsin, a cooperative that distributes local organic products to food markets in Madison, Milwaukee, and Chicago.

Today, noteworthy quantities of wheat and other rotational crops are grown on the island each year, and numerous regional foods, such as breads, ales, spirits, and spreads, along with the crops' output, are being sold in major markets. For students, this is a spectacular place to learn about the sustainable food industry, from farmers who produce food without herbicides and pesticides—and without commercialism! The community's goal is to grow healthy products—not in quantity, but in quality—that will always be considered special because they are grown on Washington Island.

ABOUT THE CHEF

An honor graduate of the Culinary Institute of America, Chef Caplan is a local authority on the sustainable food movement. Before becoming the chef-proprietor of the hotel, she worked for ten years as a restaurant chef and three years as a corporate chef in new products and concepts for Kraft Foods. It was while working with Kraft that she learned about the chemistry of food. Her project at Kraft was to develop DiGiorno pizza, which required her to learn how ingredients reacted together—how the

Island Wheat Crepes

Compliments of the Washington Hotel Culinary School

Warning: When preparing this recipe, be alert to the possibility that the alcohol in the liquor may burst into flame upon contact with the heat. To reduce this danger, remove the sauce from the heat before adding the liquor. Pour any alcohol that will be used for the crepes into a measuring container first, and then pour the alcohol into the pan. Never pour from the bottle. There is a possibility that a spark might cause the bottle to explode in your hand.

In case of fire in the pan, have a metal lid available to smother it. Remember, the higher the alcohol content, the higher the flame. The good news is that alcohol burns off quickly.

Crepes

Ingredients
- 2 teaspoons sugar
- $1/2$ teaspoon salt
- 1 cup bread flour
- $1/2$ cup whole wheat flour (ideally, Stone Ground Island Whole Wheat Flour)
- $1^1/2$ cups milk
- 3 eggs
- 2 tablespoons oil

1. In a bowl, mix the sugar, salt, and flours together. Set aside.
2. In a blender, combine the milk, eggs, and oil. Add flour mixture and blend well.

starch in pizza crust, for example, responded to the water in the crust and the heat in the oven. Once she grasped this basic science of food preparation, she was ready to apply this knowledge to her own cooking in an original and resourceful way.

Her interest in the subtleties of food preparation began early, during her formative years, while traveling abroad with her father. It was then that she acquainted herself with some important concepts about food preparation that remain with her and significantly influence her

3. Let the batter rest for at least 1 hour or up to overnight. Thin it, if necessary, with milk. The batter should have the consistency of heavy cream.
4. In a crepe pan or a nonstick pan, cook each crepe 80 percent on the first side. Flip and slide out.

Yield: 12 8- to 10-inch crepes (4–6 servings).

Cherry Sauce

Ingredients
- 2$^1/_2$ cups tart cherries
- 3 tablespoons honey
- $^1/_2$ vanilla bean
- $^1/_4$ teaspoon dried or fresh lavender buds
- $^1/_4$ cup vodka (ideally, Death's Door Vodka)
- 1 tablespoon butter

1. Heat the cherries, honey, vanilla, and lavender, simmering to thicken the liquid. Remove the vanilla bean, scrape the seeds into the sauce, and then return the vanilla bean to the pot. Remove from heat.
2. Carefully add the vodka. (It breaks into high flame if left on the fire.) Swirl in the butter.
3. To serve with crepes, fold each crepe into quarters, and spoon the sauce over or around it. Top with ice cream.

cooking style. The most important was taught in Japan, where she was introduced to the art of balancing food harmoniously in quantity and quality with aesthetic simplicity. A crowning example of this influence is evident today in her thin-crusted, smoked whitefish pizza with a sour cream base. In this pizza, all parts are blended seamlessly to create a judicious balance of key ingredients, appetizingly presented.

PHILOSOPHY

Her purpose has always been to stay in contact with organic and sustainable food producers. By knowing the origins of her food, she is able to create healthier meals while helping to revive the agricultural economy of the island at the same time.

ABOUT THE CLASSES

The year-round teaching program is devised to encourage students to buy, grow, and eat local and sustainable foods and to master sensible techniques that will make it easier to prepare and preserve the food. Types of classes that have been offered include the science, secrets, and nuances of baking in a brick oven; how the cacao bean is grown and processed; and the art of making handmade pasta from the whole wheat grown on the island.

In the summer, classes are held in a nearby all-purpose building that houses a portable stove. In the winter, private classes are held in the hotel's kitchen. The program includes talks about local foods from artisans. During the class, students are taught to create elegant, restrained meals that look the way meals ought to—attractive without being artificially decorated. At the end of each class, students receive original recipes to use at home.

Class Costs: $35 to $150 per person; special getaway packages that include lodging are from $300 to $1,000 per person.

Class Frequency: Weekly in the summer; private classes available in the winter.

Class Length: Two to three hours.

Class Type: Demonstration/hands-on with food samplings; talks by local growers and food artisans.

Class Size: Ten to twenty students per class.

Lodging: The restored hotel is neither pretentious nor luxurious; instead, it is a pleasant getaway spot that is both comfortable and attractive in its rural simplicity. Overnight guests at this century-old property on Lake Michigan will sleep on soft sheets made from organic cotton, walk on naturally dyed rugs, and eat locally grown products. The sleeping quarters have the usual basic essentials and a shared bath.

Amenities: Steam shower, dining room.

For more information contact: The Washington Hotel Restaurant and Culinary School, 354 Range Line Road, Washington Island, WI 54246; (920) 847-2169; www .thewashingtonhotel.com.

WEST

A HOG team-building event. PHOTO COURTESY OF HANDS ON GOURMET®

CALIFORNIA

St. Regis Monarch Beach
Dana Point, California

*W*hat distinguishes the St. Regis Monarch Beach from so many other fine resort hotels is its spectacular presence on the Southern California coast. Built with polished stone and European marble, this Tuscan-like revival palazzo with its multilevel gushing fountains sits at the ocean's edge, proudly exposing itself to the refreshing Pacific breezes.

Awarded five stars by Mobil Travel Guide and listed among the top ten hotels in the world by the Robb Report, the St. Regis has made it to the top, where it has remained for some time, not just because of its memorable setting, but also because of its flawless European-style service and food, which has been known to equal, even surpass, the grandness of the property.

Responsible for overseeing all food preparation is Executive Chef Frédéric Castan. His impeccable training in well-respected kitchens throughout America provides him with the background to bring to the St. Regis the refinement of culinary flavors that discriminating resort guests expect. Each meal at the St. Regis has his signature imprint of quality and artistry—which makes it not only a joy to view, but, when laced with his simple and sophisticated flavors, a pleasure to eat.

ABOUT THE CHEF
Chef Castan was born in Avignon, France, and received his early training in Marseille at the École Supérieure Hôtelière de Marseille. His most influential mentor during his formative years was France's renowned Pierre Hiély of Hiély Lucullus in Avignon. Working closely with this very strict and passionate chef, Chef Castan learned a commitment to detail.

This, coupled with his affinity for artistic shapes and colors, which developed early in his career, helped him become an award-winning talent. (In 2005, he won France's most prestigious award, the Maître Cuisinier de France.) In the past thirty years, he has worked as executive chef in Ritz-Carlton Laguna Niguel and Pasadena, Bighorn Golf Club in Palm Desert, Sofitel Water Tower in Chicago, and Westin South Coast Plaza in Costa Mesa, where he has had the opportunity to polish his culinary skills to almost shameless perfection.

PHILOSOPHY

He believes each meal must be an artistic creation of visual and taste perfection, and to help achieve this, he insists on using the best products and the freshest ingredients available, including his favorites: fresh herbs from Provence (thyme, basil, rosemary, lavender, sarriette), garlic, extra virgin olive oil, and balsamic vinegar.

ABOUT THE CLASSES

St. Regis offers anywhere from eight to twelve culinary experiences yearly; all of them, except two, are suited for adults. Each one has a theme, which changes yearly, and all are overseen by Chef Castan.

The classes all vary slightly in focus and approach. For example, the Aficionado Wine Dinner Series allows guests to watch the chef prepare wonderful foods and interact with him while sipping wine or champagne that has been carefully chosen to complement the meal.

Other classes include a Springtime Spa Cooking class, in which the freshest available ingredients are matched to create a light meal (like slow-poached Alaskan halibut with heirloom tomato salsa; see recipe); a grilling class, in which such favorites as Malaysian chicken satay or steak bavette are prepared over an open fire (and washed down with a selection of microbrews); a Wines of Italy class, in which a fine Italian wine is paired with an elegant meal, such as breast of squab Piemontaisa; and a Cooking with the Chefs Series, in which respected chefs from the St.

St. Regis Monarch Beach Slow-Poached Halibut

Courtesy of Executive Chef Frédéric Castan, St. Regis Monarch Beach

Chef Castan recommends purchasing the freshest fish available. Avoid using frozen or thawed fish, which will produce water during the cooking. He also recommends that you infuse the extra virgin olive oil with herbs (thyme, basil, rosemary, or even garlic) at a low temperature to give the oil more flavor. Finally, cook the fish very slowly, but leave it slightly undercooked. After the fish is cooked, you can strain the oil and save it for future use.

Slow-Poached Halibut

PHOTO COURTESY OF ST. REGIS MONARCH BEACH

Chef Castan also recommends you serve the halibut with a fume blanc, pinot grigio, or a dry sauvignon blanc. If it is a pleasant spring or summer day, you may accompany the fish with a baby organic greens salad and heirloom tomatoes in a balsamic and extra virgin olive oil vinaigrette; however, if it is a cold winter day, he suggests a light Provencal Pistou soup made from a base of chicken or mixed, organic vegetable broth, served with slices of toasted baguette with Parmesan cheese.

Black Olive Oil Ingredients
- 1 cup cured and pitted Provence black olives
- 2 cups extra virgin olive oil

Slow-Poached Halibut Ingredients
- 1 quart extra virgin olive oil infused with 1 bunch thyme, 2 crushed garlic cloves, and 2 bay leaves
- 2 pounds halibut steak
- Salt and pepper to taste
- 2 ounces microgreens (small versions of salad greens with big flavor)

Red Quinoa Ingredients
- 3 cups water

- 8 ounces red quinoa (a cereal grain from Peru)
- $1/2$ zucchini, diced into $1/4$-inch cubes
- 2 ounces extra virgin olive oil, divided
- 1 teaspoon chopped garlic
- $1/2$ cup green peas
- $1/2$ cup fava beans
- 2 ounces sun-dried tomatoes
- Salt and pepper to taste

Red Heirloom Tomato Salsa Ingredients
- 1 large heirloom tomato, chopped small
- 2 green onions, chopped small
- Juice from one lemon
- 2 tablespoons extra virgin olive oil
- 2 tablespoons capers
- 1 tablespoon chopped basil
- Salt and pepper to taste

1. To prepare the black olive oil, oven-dry the olives in a 160°F oven for 2–3 hours. In a blender, combine the olives with the olive oil for 2–3 minutes. Allow this mixture to infuse for one day. Black olive oil can be stored for several days and used when needed.
2. To prepare the halibut, bring the extra virgin olive oil to 160°F in a saucepot. Season the fish with salt and pepper, and very slowly poach it for 12 minutes.
3. In the meantime, start preparation for the quinoa: In a stainless steel pot, bring the water to a boil and add the quinoa. While it is cooking, sauté the zucchini and 1 ounce of the olive oil in a separate skillet. Add garlic and remaining vegetables, and season with salt and pepper. When the quinoa is cooked, add to it the vegetables and remaining olive oil.
3. For the salsa, mix the first six ingredients in a bowl. Season with salt and pepper, and refrigerate for 1 hour.
4. To plate, place a portion of quinoa on the center of each plate and top with a halibut steak. Top the fish with a large spoonful of salsa. Drizzle black olive oil around the dish, and finish by placing a small portion of microgreens on top of the fish.

Serves 4.

Regis Monarch Beach share their skills and special dishes with students. Sometimes the classes are hands-on, depending on the chef and the menu, but usually they are demonstration classes.

A children's program, offered during the summer for ages five to twelve, is especially popular because it is designed to allow children to apply their ingenuity to creating their own meal. The simple-to-prepare menu is conceived to appeal to their tastes and skill level. One such class is the Pancake Academy, which encourages children to make their own pancakes (buttermilk, whole wheat, and buckwheat) and top them with an assortment of their favorite treats, from chocolate chips and fresh fruits to Snickers and marshmallows. Participants receive a St. Regis Pancake Academy apron and diploma. During holidays, children may also attend the resort's annual Gingerbread House Academy program, where kids (and parents) join together to prepare an elaborate gingerbread house topped with candy and frosting.

Class Costs: Adult classes and/or wine dinners range from $50 to $125 per student; Pancake Academy, $50 per student. Lodging is not included.

Class Frequency: Six dinner classes per year. Check the Web site for dates.

Class Length: Adult classes are scheduled from 5:00 to 7:00 p.m.; Pancake Academy classes usually run from 1:00 to 3:00 p.m.

Class Type: Primarily demonstration; some hands-on.

Class Size: Adult classes: as few as six and as many as fifteen students; wine dinners: up to one hundred; Pancake Academy classes: minimum of ten and maximum of forty.

Lodging: Each guest room is spacious, with a clean, contemporary elegance— from the plantation shutters and the marble bathrooms to the custom-designed furniture in warm earth-tone colors. All rooms have a private balcony overlooking the well-maintained grounds or the Pacific Ocean.

Amenities: Pratesi Italian linens, luxurious goose-down comforters, Lissedell Irish terry towels and Laboratoire Remède bath products. Rooms and suites all have fresh flowers and plants, and high-tech touches from Internet to flat-screen televisions.

Activities: Surfing, spa activities, hard-surface lighted tennis courts, eighteen-hole golf course, and a nature trail. A short distance away in Dana Point there is the Ocean Institute, with hands-on marine education, and just a few miles north in Laguna Beach there are art galleries; interesting, one-of-a-kind shops; and the Laguna Art Museum, with its huge collection of historical California art. A pleasant day trip to Catalina Island can be arranged for guests who want to enjoy its water activities, shopping, and fine dining.

Shoppers won't be bored. About thirty minutes away by car is Fashion Island in Newport Beach (with designer stores like Neiman Marcus, Bloomingdales, and more) and South Coast Plaza in Costa Mesa (with its impressive selection of high-end shops, like New York Fifth Avenue or Rome Via Condotti).

For more information contact: St. Regis Monarch Beach, 1 Monarch Beach Resort, Dana Point, CA 92629; (949) 234-3200; www.stregismb.com.

Relish Culinary Adventures
Healdsburg, California

*T*he nineteenth-century town of Healdsburg has dressed itself up smartly with interesting boutiques, gourmet restaurants, wine shops, and more, and it has taken on a new look, providing a very urban tone to what was once a Sonoma County farm town.

For foodies this isn't just an area to learn about wine. It is also an area to learn about good food—the healthy, organic, seasonal, right-from-the-garden fresh variety. About 70 miles from San Francisco, this quaint community is quickly becoming a fun destination, with historic properties, wineries, farms, and a variety of outdoor activities nearby for visitors to enjoy.

One of the attractions is Relish Culinary Adventures. When it first opened its doors in 2003, it became known as the "roving" culinary program that conducted its demonstration classes in restaurants, wineries, private homes, orchards, and art galleries. Today that is changing. Although it still uses a variety of interesting venues for many of its demonstration classes, its hands-on classes are being offered almost exclusively at its new permanent address at 14 Matheson Street, just off the town plaza. Totally designed

A "roving" outdoor wine/dinner demonstration class.
PHOTO COURTESY OF RELISH CULINARY LLC

with sustainable and green products, the new location is laid out to provide scheduled hands-on classes for up to twenty students and demonstration classes for up to thirty-six students.

ABOUT THE CHEFS

Instructors are chosen from a group of freelancers, professionally trained chefs, farmers, and food suppliers, living in the Sonoma County area. It isn't uncommon for local star chefs like John Ash, Charlie Palmer, and Mark Stark to be among them.

PHILOSOPHY

The goal of the school is to introduce students to a one-of-a-kind learning experience featuring the county's many physical wonders and its bountiful food and wine sources.

ABOUT THE CLASSES

Each class has a particular focus. For example, students may visit a peach orchard and sample the fruit, and afterward in a cooking class learn all the wonderful things that can be done with it in the kitchen. They may visit olive orchards, forage for wild mushrooms, learn about creative ways of decorating cakes, and much more.

Besides its choices of one-day classes for adults and children, it also offers a two-day, three-night package at the charming boutique Hotel Healdsburg. Included in this package may be a visit to local farms, where you will involve yourself in the production process of one of its local products, which afterward will become an important part of a four-course gourmet cooking workshop. The second day may include a visit to an award-winning winery for a tour and tasting, followed by a lesson on how to blend your own wine to take home. The entire two-day, three-night package, which ends with a six-course dinner at Charlie Palmer's Dry Creek Kitchen, is designed to provide you with knowledge about the Sonoma County food and wine scene.

Class Costs: Most single classes run from $75 to $125; two-day, three-night all-inclusive package is $1,300 per person double occupancy, $1,800 for a single.
Class Frequency: Classes are offered throughout the year.
Class Length: Demonstration classes run about three hours; hands-on classes about three-and-a-half hours.
Class Type: Demonstration and hands-on, plus wine education and kids' cooking classes.
Class Size: Maximum for demonstration class, thirty-six; twenty for hands-on class.
Lodging: Hotel Healdsburg, 25 Matheson Street, Healdsburg, CA 95448; (707) 431-2800; www.hotelhealdsburg.com. This luxury hotel is located on the edge of Healdsburg plaza, across the street from Relish Culinary Adventures. It provides a tranquil setting, including full hotel services and such nice extras as a spa, swimming pool, and country gardens. Its restaurant serves noteworthy cuisine with fresh, seasonal ingredients. The guest rooms are modernly designed, comfortable, and unpretentious.
For more information contact: Relish Culinary School, 14 Matheson Street, Healdsburg, CA 95448; (707) 431-9999; www.relishculinary.com.

COPIA
Napa, California

A visit to Napa begins at COPIA. Within one building, you will be able to sample a broad variety of wines from the valley, pair food and wine, learn the history of foods, have either a hands-on or demonstration cooking class, and much more. By offering a large choice of activities, COPIA is able to provide a complete wine, food, and arts experience.

This nonprofit discovery center, created with seed money from Robert Mondavi and support from the wine and food community, attempts to unveil the secrets of both wine and food. It will take you on a journey of food around the world, where you will learn what wines to enjoy with what foods and even how Grandma used to cook her meals. If you want to sample up to forty different wines (half or full glass), you can visit the ten wine stations. Each station holds four bottles and features a specific drinking experience. For example, you can compare chardonnays that are aged in different containers, taste or sniff wines that have faults, and test your ability at identifying different varietals.

ABOUT THE CHEF

The world's top chefs, cookbook authors, farmers, and artisanal food producers come to COPIA to share their passion for food. Each day, the culinary arts come deliciously to life with cooking demonstrations, hands-on workshops, exhibits, and plenty of opportunities to taste.

PHILOSOPHY

The general purpose of the exhibitions and classes is to increase awareness of wine culture and the pleasure of food and wine pairing, and to encourage better and healthier eating habits, with an emphasis on fresh, local foods prepared simply.

Students learn about pairing complementary wines with a meal.
PHOTO COURTESY OF FAITH ECHTERMEYER

ABOUT THE CLASSES

COPIA offers both public and private demonstration/hands-on programs, which may include team-building and even children's classes. Special programs are regularly scheduled; examples include a program celebrating Julia Child and featuring her cookbook recipes; a program with a Dr. Seuss theme, in which clever and healthy foods suited to growing children are prepared; or a program with a summer harvest theme, in which students create a meal from foods selected from the garden. Although COPIA makes no attempt to be a culinary school, it does include just enough basic cooking-skills information (like the proper way to use knives, sauté, and more) to get you acquainted with cooking.

Each Friday from 1:00 to 2:15 p.m., COPIA offers its signature Taste of COPIA lunch series, which includes a cooking demonstration, wine pairing discussion, and garden talk with COPIA's experts. Visitors will expand their culinary horizons while enjoying a tasty three-course meal served with three complementary wines.

In addition, there is a wide range of award-winning dining options. Named for culinary legend Julia Child, Julia's Kitchen has been touted by the *New York Times* and ranked among the top three restaurants in the Napa Valley by *Wine Spectator*. For lighter fare, the Bistro at COPIA offers an assortment of delectable small plates. The bistro's pleasant setting features Julia Child's famous copper cookware, a portrait by Rise Delmar Ochsner, and various awards and memorabilia.

Class Costs: General admission: free; demonstration class: $10 to $100; private class and corporate classes vary (call for a quote).
Class Frequency: Demonstration classes are offered daily.
Class Length: Approximately thirty minutes to two hours.
Class Type: Demonstration/hands-on.
Class Size: Minimum two students, maximum seventy per class.
For more information contact: COPIA, 500 First Street, Napa, CA 94559; (888) 512-6742; www.copia.org.

Hugh Carpenter's Camp Napa Culinary
Napa, California

*T*he most romantic way to see Napa is in a hot-air balloon, drifting aimlessly like a slow-moving cloud. It is then that you can appreciate how truly beautiful the area is, with its perfect rows of orchards and vineyards, its baronial mansions, and its quaint communities all laid out like an exquisite tapestry, resting over a hilly terrain that seems to stretch to eternity.

In this magic world, one can temporarily put aside the madness of nine to five and forget, and one of the best ways to do so—what many valley visitors are doing—is to attend a cooking program, ideally at one of the local wineries, where you will be able to eat and drink merrily.

Hugh Carpenter (center rear) oversees a class. PHOTO COURTESY OF CAMP NAPA CULINARY

One such cooking program is Hugh Carpenter's Camp Napa Culinary, which for almost two decades has been intimately associated with the Cakebread Cellars, a respected family-operated winery that prides itself in encouraging the healthy marriage of wine and food. Headquartered on the family's sixty-acre estate, Hugh's culinary camp offers five six-day cooking programs July through October, the peak growing season.

His program, which is prepared with the independent traveler in mind, allows participants enough free time to discover the valley on their own and enough program structure to learn some important cooking skills. Included in the structured cooking program are visits to some very private homes and wineries selected to provide students with a fuller Napa Valley experience.

ABOUT THE CHEF

Hugh started cooking without formal culinary training. In the seventies, after leaving Dartmouth College and the University of Michigan graduate school, where he majored in Chinese culture, he opened his own catering service preparing Chinese dinners. This love for Chinese cuisine grew, and he began to share it with others by offering cooking classes and working in restaurants in Los Angeles. As California's ethnic population also grew, so did his interest in cuisine. What emerged was a unique style

 Tips from Chef Hugh Carpenter

To avoid a complicated menu, don't plan a meal for eight to ten people that can't be prepped and ready the night before. If it is going to be a dinner party, provide about three appetizers (served at room temperature or chilled). The entree should not include more than one dish that needs final preparation before serving. Conclude the meal with a salad/cheese course and a dessert.

of cooking and teaching in which he began to fuse the wonderful flavors of the world together to create his own unique taste.

While mastering his cooking skills, he was inspired by the writings of James Beard, and by Craig Claiborne and Virginia Lee's book *The Chinese Cookbook,* which introduced him to some very sophisticated and complex flavors. Hugh, who has been teaching for over thirty years, has also made his contribution to the cookbook market by publishing fifteen books.

PHILOSOPHY

As a teacher, Hugh wants to encourage home cooks to use foods that have layers of flavor and that are simple to prepare.

Most cooks, Hugh has learned over the years, don't want an intellectual approach to cooking. They simply want a tasty meal quickly with an exact recipe that will please the family. He believes that by introducing students to fifty to sixty easy-to-prepare recipes from his books, using labor-saving techniques, his students will want to re-create them in their kitchens. Many of the flavors that he uses—such as ginger, lemon, garlic, pomegranate, and more—are widely available and are natural building blocks for creating rich and delicious flavors. This saves time and eliminates the necessity of creating beef or chicken stock or reduction sauces.

ABOUT THE CLASSES

During the weeklong classes, students will experience an intense exposure to the Napa Valley wine and food culture, with eighteen noteworthy events scheduled during the six days. Each class is a little different; one will be on grilling, another on oven roasting, a third on appetizers with foods from all over the world. The fast, easy recipes that the students prepare are from Hugh's books, and each student will receive his hands-on guidance. Students are divided into groups, and each group prepares a different food project (appetizers, entrees, or desserts) that they bring to the table as part of a complete meal. The trick to putting together these

South of the Border Burgers

Originally published in *Fast Entrées* by Hugh Carpenter and Teri Sandison (Ten Speed Press, 2002). Reprinted with permission.

To create the perfect burger, Hugh strongly recommends using freshly ground beef with a medium fat content (22 percent). Frozen meat or meat with less fat will have a dry texture. When forming the burgers, avoid overpacking. To maintain juiciness, he doesn't recommend cooking beyond medium. Serve the hamburgers on the best available buns or on sliced and toasted sourdough bread.

Hugh recommends serving the burgers with a corn and arugula salad and deli-bought soup, and pairing it with a glass of zinfandel, beer, or ice tea.

Ingredients
- 2 pounds ground beef, 22 percent fat
- $1/4$ cup chopped cilantro sprigs
- 4 cloves garlic, minced
- 2 to 3 serrano chiles, minced, including seeds
- 1 cup shredded sharp cheddar cheese
- 1 teaspoon ground cumin
- $1/2$ teaspoon salt
- 4 hamburger buns
- Vine-ripe tomatoes, sliced
- Lettuce
- Homemade or store-bought salsa
- Homemade or store-bought guacamole

1. Advance preparation: Place the beef in a bowl and add the cilantro, garlic, chiles, cheese, cumin, and salt. Using your hands, mix thoroughly. Form the mixture into four equal-size balls, then flatten gently with your palm. (The patties can be covered and refrigerated for up to 8 hours before grilling.)
2. Last-minute cooking: Prepare a medium fire in a charcoal grill or preheat a gas grill to medium. When hot, brush the grill rack with oil and place the burgers on the rack. Grill, turning once, for about 3 minutes on each side for medium-rare or to desired doneness. Alternatively, cook the hamburgers in a cast-iron skillet over medium heat, or broil them 4 inches from the heating element. While the hamburgers are cooking, toast the buns. Place the burgers on the buns and serve immediately, accompanied by sliced tomatoes, lettuce, salsa, and guacamole.

Serves 4.

meals is to understand how to create a menu, and Hugh demystifies this by identifying the important parts of a meal and how they are brought together to make a wonderful dinner.

There is nothing static about this program. The trips to area wineries and farms are planned to expand practical knowledge about food and wine. Since this program is designed for the independent traveler, nothing is done by motor coach; students arrange hotel rooms and transportation to suit their tastes and budget. It is all devised to provide a solid program for six days with enough free time to move independently about the area.

Class Costs: $2,100 per person, which includes instruction, recipes, apron, and multicourse lunches with wine pairings. It does not include lodging.

Class Frequency: Five six-day cooking programs July through October.

Class Length: Around three hours a day, for five of the six days.

Class Type: Demonstration/hands-on.

Class Size: Twelve to sixteen students per class.

Lodging: The following two properties are among the many that Hugh recommends to his students. For a complete list contact him directly.

Auberge du Soleil, 180 Rutherford Hill Road, Rutherford, CA 94573; (707) 963-1211; www.aubergedusoleil.com. This respected Relais & Châteaux property overlooks Napa Valley and has contemporary art and Mediterranean-style decor. It's the embodiment of absolute luxury. Each of its suites has Italian linens, custom-made bath amenities, terraces, fresh fruit daily, and more.

Rancho Caymus Inn, 1140 Rutherford Road, Rutherford, CA 94573; (707) 963-1777; www.ranchocaymus.com. This Spanish hacienda has the timeless look of an old-world property. Handsomely maintained, each of its rooms is named after early Napa Valley pioneers like Black Bart and Lillie Langtry. Rooms have spacious walnut beds, handmade furniture, one-hundred-year-old oak beam ceilings, handmade Indian rugs, and more.

For more information contact: Hugh Carpenter, Camp Napa Culinary, 3960 Hagen Road, Napa, CA 94558; (888) 999-HUGH (4844); www.hughcarpenter.com.

Peju Province Winery
Rutherford, Napa Valley, California

A cooking technique that has been gaining popularity in America is sous vide (French for "under vacuum"), in which vacuum-packed foods are poached in plastic bags at even temperatures below simmering. While it requires expensive equipment to maintain a safe low temperature for long periods of time, the benefits are that it locks in the juices and the flavors of the ingredients, and breaks down stubborn meat or vegetable fibers. The result is a truer taste, enhanced significantly by whatever seasoning may have been added.

Unfortunately, if care isn't taken, cooking at low temperatures can result in possible bacterial contamination. To date no problems have occurred, and the technique has been used in France since the 1970s, but many eye it with trepidation. Nevertheless, it is gaining in popularity and being employed in some of the most chic kitchens, like the French Laundry in the Napa Valley, where it has been offered since the 1990s. Although only restaurants can afford the equipment, and it requires skilled staff, some in the business expect the technique to make the leap into America's kitchen in the near future. In the meantime, if you want to learn firsthand from professionals what this new cooking technique is like, you may want to visit Peju Province Winery.

This family-owned and operated boutique winery, located in the Napa Valley, has been producing award-winning wines made from organically grown fruits since 1982, and they have created a wine country dining experience for visitors by offering cooking classes that feature some of their prized wines. Hosting the cooking demonstrations; interactive, hands-on cooking classes; and food-and-wine pairings is Executive Chef Marianne Cushing.

ABOUT THE CHEF
Before joining Peju in 2007, Chef Marianne worked at the Café Marquesa in Key West, Florida, under the guidance of Executive Chef Susan

Ferry. She also worked as a contract chef for A La Belle Catering firm in northern Virginia, and for a short period she cooked at the Blair House in Washington, D.C. She received her Associate of Culinary Arts Degree from Stratford University in northern Virginia and her level I and level II Certified Wine Professional certificates from the Culinary Institute of America (Greystone campus).

Wine and Food Tips from Chef Marianne Cushing

When pairing wine with food, there are some important rules to keep in mind:

- *The more acidity in the wine, the better it is for cutting oily, fatty, salty, or mildly spicy/salty flavors. For example, you should pair wines like sauvignon blanc or cool-climate chardonnays with salads that are tossed with vinaigrette, butter and cream-based sauces, deep-fried foods, or oily fish.*
- *Sweet wines make a good contrast to salt and reduce the edge of tart or spicy foods (like some Asian foods). When serving a sweet wine with a dessert, the wine should be sweeter than the dessert.*
- *Too much salt in the food will cause the wine to seem more alcoholic or hot. When the wine has excess tannin, you should avoid serving a salty dish. On the other hand, if the wine has a good bit of acidity or sweetness, it should go well together with salty dishes like fried calamari.*
- *Tannins are usually associated with a bitter taste in the mouth, found in some bold red wines. These wines are best served with foods that have been grilled or blackened, or foods that are rich in protein and fat. Exception: Tannic wines do not usually go very well with strong, oily fish.*
- *The more alcohol a wine has, the more full-bodied the wine seems. You should match the body of the wine and the food so that one doesn't overpower the other.*

Peju Napoleon

Compliments of Chef Marianne Cushing,
Peju Province Winery

*This napoleon is made up of thin
layers of hazelnut cream, vanilla
cream, and ganache, and it should
be served cold with some fruit. Ideally, it would be served with Peju
Zinfandel Port.*

Peju Napoleon

PHOTO COURTESY OF PEJU PROVINCE WINERY

Rectangle Layers

Ingredients
- 6 egg whites
- 1 teaspoon baking powder
- 2 cups sugar
- 2 teaspoons vanilla
- Approximately 60 crushed butter crackers (like Ritz)
- 1¹/₂ cups ground pecans

1. Lightly grease a half sheet pan and place parchment on the bottom. Preheat oven to 350°F.
2. Beat the egg whites with baking powder until stiff. Fold in sugar, vanilla, crackers, and pecans. Evenly spread this mixture on the half sheet pan and bake for 25–30 minutes. Cool completely.
3. Cut into 20 (2 x 4-inch) rectangles and set aside until assembly.

Fillings

Vanilla Cream

Ingredients
- ¹/₂ cup heavy cream, chilled
- 2 tablespoons unsalted butter, softened
- 2 tablespoons confectioners' sugar
- 1 teaspoon vanilla extract

In a mixing bowl, whip the cream until soft peaks form. In another mixing bowl, beat the butter until it is fluffy. Add the sugar and vanilla, and beat until smooth. Fold the whipped cream into the butter mixture.

Hazelnut Cream

Ingredients
- $\frac{1}{2}$ cup heavy cream, chilled
- 2 tablespoons unsalted butter, softened
- 2 tablespoons confectioners' sugar
- $\frac{1}{4}$ cup unsweetened hazelnut paste, room temperature

In a mixing bowl, whip the cream until soft peaks form. In another mixing bowl, beat the butter until it is fluffy. Add the sugar and hazelnut paste, and beat until smooth. Fold the whipped cream into the butter mixture.

Ganache

Ingredients
- 6 ounces bittersweet or semisweet chocolate, chopped
- $\frac{1}{2}$ cup heavy cream

1. Place the chocolate in a mixing bowl; set aside.
2. In a saucepan, bring the cream almost to a boil, then pour it over the chocolate. Whisk until smooth. Cool to room temperature.
3. When the mixture is cool, place it in the bowl of a stand mixer fitted with a whisk attachment, and whisk until it is light and fluffy.

Assembly

Place one rectangle layer on a plate and spread the ganache over it. Top this with another rectangle layer, and spread the vanilla cream on it. Top this with a third rectangle layer, and spread with the hazelnut cream. Finally, put the fourth rectangle layer on top. Press the assembled napoleon slightly with a sheet pan to level it out. Sprinkle the top with either cocoa powder or powdered sugar. Refrigerate for at least 3 hours.

Makes 5 servings.

PHILOSOPHY

Chef Marianne's goal is to provide a unique culinary experience for students, something they will never experience elsewhere. This isn't a traditional cooking program where you just receive demonstrations and recipes—instead, you will learn about new techniques and how to use the best ingredients in the simplest way, broadening your knowledge of the culinary arts.

ABOUT THE CLASSES

Classes are one of a kind, custom designed, and adjusted to your personal needs. All classes begin with a tour of the estate and emphasize the winery's strengths, its cabernet sauvignon and cabernet franc. You will receive insider pointers on how to pair the various wines at Peju with appropriate foods.

Before each cooking class, you will harvest foods from the kitchen garden on the Peju property, which you will then turn into a tasty lunch. It isn't uncommon for the owners or the winemaker to join in the meal, and you may even meet the "yodelmeister," Alan Arnopole, who has been known to break into a perfect yodel while pouring the wine. Since the food is organically grown and enjoyed fresh in season, the best time to visit is when the harvest is at its peak, between July and November.

Three basic programs—food and wine pairing, hands-on cooking classes, and demonstration classes—are offered under the watchful eye of Chef Marianne:

Food and wine pairing: What wine goes with what food, how do certain ingredients chemically mix with wine, and does chardonnay pair with steak? In this class, such questions will be answered, and you will sample many foods and wines to learn what works best for your palate. Since this is a winery, students will have access to a large assortment of wines to taste, which is something most people can't easily duplicate at home.

Hands-on cooking classes: Participants in this class will be introduced to food-and-wine pairing and special cooking techniques (like *sous vide* or wood grilling using oak at high heat), and they will prepare a four- or five-course dinner.

Demonstration classes: During this lunch or dinner food experience, students will watch Chef Marianne present a wine-and-food class. It is intended to give students a close-up, Food Network–like experience.

Chef Marianne also offers team-building classes for companies who want to break down employee-employer barriers and strengthen corporate ties.

Class Costs: For all classes, $185 per person for a lunch class and $210 per person for a dinner class.

Class Frequency: Reservations are accepted throughout the year.

Class Length: Classes run about four hours.

Class Type: Hands-on/demonstration.

Class Size: In general, minimum of six students per class, maximum twenty; maximum of twelve for the demonstration classes and twenty-five for food and wine pairing classes.

Lodging: Meadowood Napa Valley, 900 Meadowood Lane, St. Helena, CA 94574; (800) 458-8080; www.meadowood.com. Located in a 250-acre valley, this magnificent hillside property echoes memories of gracious living of bygone days. All the essential activities are available: golf, croquet, tennis, swimming, health spa, cultural affairs, and more. The eighty-five cottages, suites, and lodges are private, modern, and comfortable.

The Beazley House, 1910 First Street, Napa, CA 94559; (800) 559-1649; www.beazley house.com. This historic 1902 inn is located within walking distance of downtown Napa and very near COPIA and the Napa River. Many of the rooms include private baths and garden views, whirlpool tubs, spa service, free wireless Internet, fireplaces, and more. They all have old-fashioned vintage furniture and the warm look of another time period.

For more information contact: Peju Province Winery, 8466 St. Helena Highway, P.O. Box 478, Rutherford, Napa Valley, CA 94573; (800) 446-7358; www.peju.com.

Napa Valley Cooking School
St. Helena, California

Napa Valley College offers an Enthusiast Program with a wide range of evening and weekend classes aimed at serious-minded amateurs or advanced cooks. The in-depth, one- to four-day series of classes are all taught by professional chefs.

ABOUT THE CHEF
Executive Chef Barbara Alexander came to the Napa Valley College after a year as chef instructor for the Culinary Institute of America at Greystone. A graduate of Canada's Dubrulle International Culinary and Hotel Institute, she has been a chef in fine-dining restaurants in London and Sydney, including Sydney's famed Paramount Restaurant (an international foodie paradise until its closing in 2000), for twenty-four years. While executive chef at the Paramount, she was responsible for launching the high-end Paramount Stores, which became one of Sydney's trendy gourmet food retailers.

PHILOSOPHY
Her program is educational and focus-driven, and it lifts learning to a higher level than most recreational schools attempt. These classes may not appeal to students looking for nothing more than just a way to pass an evening. "This is the place to come to learn better ways to think about food and develop a stronger interest in viewing food in a sustainable and ecofriendly way," Chef Barbara says.

ABOUT THE CLASSES
In each Enthusiast Class the purpose is to teach professional techniques mixed with some etiquette (such as how to carve meats and poultry, and

An instructor gives students a lesson in preparing light foods.
PHOTO COURTESY OF NAPA VALLEY COOKING SCHOOL

eat finger foods like quail). "So many of the little touches of refinement once taught at home," Chef Barbara says, "are tossed into the lesson to acquaint students with subtle eating techniques."

The class structure, regardless of the subject, is standard. It begins with a small lecture and demonstration; afterward, students are broken into teams to work in the kitchen. After the food is prepared, it is set on a buffet with some wine for everyone to enjoy. The class ends with an overview of what was taught. In private classes, students have the freedom to select the topic and choose the food.

A Sophisticated Palate

A renowned food and wine educator and a celebrated chef, John Ash believes a chef should think of himself as a stage manager, someone who props up his leading ingredient elegantly from behind the scenes without obscuring its natural and essential flavors. "The trick to good cooking is to keep it simple," he says. "A cook should never put the entire pantry into one meal, but instead prepare tasteful and exciting flavors using only essential ingredients."

The best way to do this is to use locally grown, seasonally fresh, and flavorful foods—what he calls "ethical cuisine." Although this isn't a new idea today, it certainly was in the seventies when it surfaced in California. At that time, most Americans covered the main course with heavy sauces and filled themselves with chemically altered prepared foods. This all began to change in the seventies, when Chef Ash and his West Coast friends bravely resisted the popular trend and became early pioneers for healthy eating.

In his writings and teachings over the years, he has repeatedly stated, "We must pay attention to our food. Where it is grown and how it is grown." This careful consideration to the origin of food is the very essence of what many popularly call (among other things) California Cuisine. For Chef Ash, though, this is only half of an unforgettable dining experience.

Chef Ash has repeatedly been identified as America's pioneer of wine country cooking since the publication in 1995 of his award-winning cookbook From the Earth to the Table: John Ash's Wine Country Cuisine, in which he states that serving fresh, seasonal food from a reliable food source isn't enough—you must also have the proper wine. When it is in proper balance with the food, it completes the dining experience and creates what he calls Wine Country Cuisine.

Pairing wine and food together isn't new either; it is, in fact, a very old European practice. Most foods go well with wine, as Julia Child so often proved. By cooking with the same wine that she served with the meal, she was able to bring balance to the food and elevate the dining experience to noteworthy heights.

During his journey to culinary glory, Chef Ash was favorably influenced by Julia Child, who remained a longtime friend, and by Mary Frances Kennedy Fisher, whose prolific writings on eating simply and well deeply shaped his thinking and became the building blocks for many of his ideas. Before meeting Mrs. Fisher, he had read everything she had written.

Although initially Chef Ash did not have any formal culinary training, he learned some of his first lessons in cooking from his grandmother. Brought up on a Colorado farm, he had to learn to cook and can foods for the long winters. Although he developed a skill at cooking, he never considered it as a career, and his first job out of school in the 1960s was in advertising in New York City. One of his clients, Del Monte foods, offered him a job on the West Coast, developing food products. When he left after six years, he took his savings and went abroad (London, Paris, and the northern Burgundy region of France), where he attended professional cooking schools for a year.

This experience abroad became the foundation for what soon followed. In the 1970s he worked in restaurants in San Francisco and fell hopelessly in love with Sonoma (which reminded him of France with its hilly terrain, orchards, vineyards, and farms). In 1980, he opened his restaurant John Ash & Company, which catapulted him to national fame.

Today Chef Ash and his associate Andy Wild work together in harmony at the Culinary Institute of America (CIA) at Greystone campus, offering food connoisseurs a cutting-edge food and wine program. The two- or four-day program (called the Sophisticated Palate) introduces students to vintners, farmers, chefs, restaurants, and others who share Chef Ash's views on food and wine. It is an excellent program for students who want to receive hands-on training and expand their culinary horizons by meeting with leaders in the industry.

Besides offering Sophisticated Palate classes and some special events, travel, and public cooking demonstration programs, the CIA at Greystone also offers a twenty-one-month associate's degree program in culinary arts. It features the same curriculum as the program in Hyde Park, New York.

For more information contact: CIA at Greystone, 2555 Main Street, St. Helena, CA; (707) 967-2328; www.ciachef.edu/california.

Grilled Asparagus
with Lemon Olive Oil and Pecorino

Compliments of Chef John Ash, from his book *From the Earth to the Table: John Ash's Wine Country Cuisine* (Dutton, 1995 and Chronicle Books, 2007)

One of the simplest and best ways to cook asparagus is to give it a light coating of olive oil and grill it, which brings out its sweetness. Chef Ash prefers grilling to steaming or boiling, because it also reduces the "vegetal" notes, and keeping the asparagus away from water minimizes "asparagus pee." For a delicious antipasti course, he recommends that you add some good olives, thinly sliced meats such as coppa or proscuitto, and maybe a sprinkling of some fried capers. Finally, to give it that California Wine Country lift, he recommends a glass of sauvignon blanc with it.

Ingredients
- 1 pound fresh asparagus, tough ends discarded
- 2 tablespoons extra virgin olive oil
- Sea salt (such as Maldon's)
- Freshly ground black pepper
- 3 tablespoons or so lemon-infused extra virgin olive oil
- $^1/_2$ cup shaved Pecorino or Parmigiano cheese (shaved thinly with a vegetable peeler)

1. Brush the asparagus with the olive oil and season generously with salt and pepper.
2. Over hot coals or a gas grill preheated to medium-high, grill the asparagus until it takes on a bit of color. Roll and turn so that it's cooked on all sides.
3. Place on a plate; drizzle with lemon olive oil and scatter cheese over it. Add more salt and pepper if desired. Serve warm or at room temperature.

Serves 4.

The four-day home chef series unveils the many secrets of a professional chef, including developing knife skills, preparing vegetables properly, creating basic stocks and soups, and preparing fish and meat. Besides the usual share of Italian and French cooking lessons, they offer specialized classes (for example, different ways to prepare duck, and European cakes and tarts, like the mille-feuille, Princess Cake, or the famous

Sacher-Torte). There has even been a class about preparing foods like the specialized vendors at the "Hawker Centers" in Singapore serve, such as *murtabek* (an Indian flat bread stuffed with lamb or chicken), *nasi udang* (rice with shrimp sambal), or the famous Singapore Chili Crab.

Class Costs: Each class, with rare exception, runs about $75, including the series. Private classes run $750 per day, regardless of the number of students.
Class Frequency: Depends on the class, but classes are held either on weeknights (6:00 to 9:30 p.m.) or on weekends (10:30 a.m. to 2:00 p.m.).
Class Length: About three-and-a-half to four hours.
Class Type: Mostly hands-on, with some demonstration.
Class Size: Minimum of ten students, maximum twenty per class.
For more information contact: Napa Valley Cooking School, 1088 College Avenue, St. Helena, CA 94574; (707) 967-2930 (twenty-four-hour voice mail); www.napavalley.edu.

Hands On Gourmet (HOG)
San Francisco, California

HOG is a Bay Area mobile cooking program that specializes in interactive cooking classes for private and corporate groups. Because of its mobility, it can be whereever you want it for as long as you want it. Although it primarily services Northern California, it has traveled as far as Colorado.

The program runs about three hours and will accommodate almost any size crowd and any budget, from the modest to the corporate. Each event is customized to meet the particular needs of the customer, regardless of the number of participants. To keep large classes intimate and manageable, they are broken into small groups of about ten people, each with their own professional chef.

The food prepared is usually identified as fine cuisine and may be anything you prefer, from ethnic to fusion foods. Examples may include

Members of a corporate team-building class. PHOTO COURTESY OF HANDS ON GOURMET®

chopped niçoise salad with albacore tuna, manicotti with sauce Bolognese, tekka maki *sushi with green onions and* togarashi, *and more. Twice a year, Executive Chef Stephen Gibbs prepares a master menu from which you may select your recipes. These recipes may then be used to create a special menu exactly to your taste.*

HOG was founded in 2004 by three partners who love food and who love to bring people together with food: Molly Fuller, president; Stephen Gibbs, executive chef; and Anne McCarten-Gibbs. Working with them is a crew of about thirty professional chefs who supervise the teaching and cooking.

ABOUT THE CHEF

Executive Chef Stephen received his culinary training at the California Culinary Academy and worked in such well-respected restaurants as Wolfgang Puck's Postrio, Roland Passot's La Folie, and Jeremiah Tower's Stars.

PHILOSOPHY

HOG strives to provide a fun event that will bring participants in intimate contact with food in an informative and relaxed way.

ABOUT THE CLASSES

Since each event has its own focus, HOG will prepare an exact menu and party plan that will work for your event. The menus are all custom designed and adjusted to your dietary needs, and no two events may offer the same meal. For each of these events, the customer does not have to make any preparations; everything that's needed is packed into a HOG mobile truck and delivered anytime, anywhere to your kitchen or auditorium.

Class Costs: $250 per person, including drinks.
Class Frequency: Twenty to thirty events are held each month.
Class Length: About three hours.
Class Type: Hands-on/demonstration.
Class Size: Minimum ten people; maximum three hundred.
For more information contact: Hands On Gourmet, 2325 Third Street, No. 330, San Francisco, CA 94107; (415) 553-8894; www.handsongourmet.com.

A Gourmand's Paradise

*E*ating well on budget in San Francisco has never been easier than it is today. Food lovers visiting the Golden Gate City may enjoy exceptionally tasty meals at reasonable prices—all under one roof, minutes from downtown at the San Francisco Ferry Building. This once well-kept San Francisco secret, which opened to the public in 2003, has become world famous.

The Main foodhall in the Ferry Building
PHOTO COURTESY OF THE FERRY BUILDING

Trendy local and globe-trotting gourmands in search of irresistible cheeses, breads, quiche, caviar, oysters, chocolates, organic foods, vegetarian dishes, wines, and much more are filling up their shopping bags whenever they are in the area.

Known locally as the old Ferry Building, this long-time San Francisco landmark with its 245-foot clock tower is one of the lucky buildings in the city to have withstood the 1906 and 1989 earthquakes. Although the Ferry Building is still a transportation point for shuttling passengers across the Bay, it is no longer thought of as such; instead, it is earning a reputation as one of the best food markets anywhere.

Although the shops and food marts in the Ferry Building are open daily from 10 a.m. to 6 p.m., it is on Saturdays and Tuesdays that the market truly springs to life. Farmers selling everything from flowers to vegetables surround the building. Shoppers who may have forgotten the taste of a ripe tomato or melon will discover the pleasure once again after one bite into the magic fruit or vegetable available there. By cutting out the middleman and bringing seasonal products to the market, sellers are reducing their product cost and increasing their profits.

The best day to visit is on Saturday morning around 8 a.m. It is then that countless stalls, selling everything from mushrooms to walnuts are filled to capacity. Throughout the week, during regular business hours, permanent shops are open. Those serving food have counters or tables for comfortable dining. Here are some of the noteworthy businesses inside:

The Acme Bread Company is a legendary Bay Area bakery, which began business about twenty-five years ago in Berkeley where it still maintains its original location. A full selection of artisan breads are baked fresh in a hearth oven throughout the day at the Ferry Building location. Acme Bread is made with only organic flour, and the company works closely with farmers who supply the grains for its flour.

The Cowgirl Creamery's Artisan Cheese Shop offers a full range of cheeses, from France, England, Italy, Spain and more, representing leading names like Jean d'Alos, Neals Yard's English Farmhouse cheese and more, including the award-winning cheeses of proprietors Sue Conley and Peggy Smith.

Tsar Nicoulai Caviar is a small Parisian-style caviar café and retail shop which sells a variety of domestic and imported caviar. The menu, which changes daily, includes such shamelessly delicious treats as blini, sturgeon sausage, and whipped potato waffles with smoothed sturgeon and vodka caviar sauce.

Hog Island Oyster Company is a twenty-five-seat oyster bar, cafe, and retail outlet that offers an assortment of raw oysters on the half-shell, traditional oyster stew, steamed clams, and clam chowder. The shellfish is refined using a technique from France that sorts shellfish by hand and places them into a state-of-the-art tank where the seawater is purified by an ultraviolet sterilizer.

Mushroom lovers will appreciate the selection of wild and organically grown mushrooms at Far West Fungi. The choice changes seasonally. For those interested in unraveling the mysteries of mycology, there is an extensive collection of books on mushrooms—from growing to identifying them

For more information, contact: Ferry Building Marketplace, One Ferry Building, San Francisco, California 94111; (415) 693-0996; www.ferry buildingmarketplace.com.

Joanne Weir's Cooking School
San Francisco, California

*W*hen the legendary Chez Panisse restaurant opened in Berkeley in
1971, it unveiled a unique approach to cooking that was eventually
referred to as California Cuisine. The star chef responsible for this culinary
event was Alice Waters and her loyal group of idealistic friends.

What immediately set Chez Panisse apart from other restaurants
of that period was Chef Waters's unwavering commitment to providing
extraordinary meals made only with fresh, seasonal ingredients organically grown and purchased from trusted producers and farmers dedicated
to sustainable agriculture. Maintaining loyal relationships with these suppliers over the years enabled her to regularly deliver memorable meals
that were simply and tastefully prepared. As a result, she was able to place
Chez Panisse on the world culinary map, and it won many sought-after
awards.

Today the concern for healthier food, as defined by Chez Panisse, has
spread across the country and is being adopted by many health-conscious
Americans—thanks to Waters's many dedicated chefs, including Joanne
Weir, who are industriously spreading the word.

ABOUT THE CHEF

Chef Joanne Weir is known to millions of PBS viewers from her popular
TV series, *Weir Cooking in the Wine Country*, *Weir Cooking in the City*,
and her latest, *Joanne Weir's Cooking Class*. During the years that she
has been on television with these programs, she has been convincing her
audience that the best foods are the freshest, seasonally selected and purchased directly from local farmers.

Chef Weir is the fourth generation of women in her family to dedi-
cate her life to cooking professionally. To prepare for her career, she
studied with award-winning instructor and author Madeleine Kamman

Chef Joanne Weir works one-on-one with a student. PHOTO COURTESY OF JOANNE WEIR

in New England and France for one year, where she developed a fondness for classic Mediterranean cuisine. In 1985 she was awarded a Master Chef Diploma, and for five years, from 1986 to 1991, she worked alongside Alice Waters at Chez Panisse in Berkeley.

In recent years, Chef Weir has traveled the world, sharing her extensive knowledge of food (particularly Mediterranean and American regional cuisine) in over twenty countries. As a teacher, author, and television personality at the top of her field, she is continuously in demand for her classes. A James Beard Award Winner and winner of the Julia Child Award for Teaching Excellence, she has written fifteen books. Her two favorites are *From Tapas to Meze: Small Plates from the Mediterranean* and *Weir Cooking in the City: More than 125 Recipes and Inspiring Ideas for Relaxed Entertainment,* because the recipes are easy to prepare and the results are impressive.

PHILOSOPHY

Chef Weir's educational goal is to keep cooking simple and pleasurable while providing students with essential information and techniques that will be useful. In this way she hopes to encourage them to return to the kitchen and use their newly acquired skills to prepare healthier foods. By designing lessons that are technique- and information-driven, she strives to make it easier for students to transfer what they have learned in one class to many different recipes. (For example, creating a simple puff pastry that can be adapted to other recipes.)

ABOUT THE CLASSES

Whether she is teaching students to make creamy Spring Vegetable Risotto or to beat egg whites correctly for a light Spicy Corn Soufflé, Chef Weir is always striving to demystify cooking by replacing labor with pleasure. Her knowledge of food and her approachable style make her an effective instructor.

She offers weeklong cooking programs taught from her home in San Francisco (which is also the set for her latest TV show), and each has a special theme, such as "Weir Having a Party," "Italian Favorites," or "Summer Grilling," and they may feature foods from Spain, Morocco, France, or Italy (with each class focusing on a different region of the country). Since she is committed to seasonal foods paired with suitable wines, she often will invite winemakers or wine store managers and food artisans to class to discuss some aspect of wine and food.

Roasted Game Hens with Toasted Bread Crumb Salsa

Compliments of Joanne Weir, Joanne Weir's Cooking School

Chef Weir loves roasted game hens and serves them year-round. She is constantly searching for ways to give them a special seasonal flavor by combining them with fresh vegetables. In the spring, for example, she will use artichokes, but in the summer she particularly favors this recipe. In colder months, she might switch to bacon and caramelized butternut squash. Regardless of the season, she always serves the hens with roasted potatoes and finishes with one of her favorite desserts, such as a fresh seasonal fruit crisp or a light lemon sorbet. This recipe pairs well with an unoaked chardonnay or pinot noir from the Santa Lucia Highlands or the Russian River.

Ingredients
- 6 1- to 1½-pound Cornish game hens, halved
- 7 tablespoons extra virgin olive oil
- Salt and freshly ground black pepper
- 2 tablespoons white wine vinegar
- 1 tablespoon chopped capers
- 2 anchovy fillets, soaked in cold water 2 minutes, patted dry, and chopped
- 1 clove garlic, minced
- ½ teaspoon chopped fresh thyme
- ½ teaspoon chopped fresh rosemary
- ¼ cup chopped fresh parsley
- 1 tablespoon lemon zest
- 1 green onion, white and green parts, thinly sliced
- 1 cup coarse toasted bread crumbs

1. Preheat the oven to 450°F. Arrange the game hen halves in a single layer, skin side up, on a baking sheet. Brush the skin with 1 tablespoon of the olive oil and sprinkle with salt and pepper. Roast the game hens for 30 to 35 minutes.
2. While the game hens are roasting, whisk the vinegar and remaining olive oil together in a bowl. Add the next 8 ingredients and toss together. Season with salt and pepper.
3. Check to see if the game hens are done with an instant-read thermometer inserted into the thickest part of the thigh. It should register 170°F. Place the game hens on a platter, top with the bread crumb mixture, and serve immediately.

Serves 6.

Each year Chef Weir conducts several culinary classes abroad, to France, Italy, and Spain. For six days participants enjoy hands-on cooking classes, preparing such local recipes as bouillabaisse with aioli or paella with chicken. Students stay in a historic estate or villa and meet with local celebrities.

Class Costs: $2,000 for the weeklong San Francisco program (includes instruction, recipes, apron, and a multicourse lunch with wine pairings); $4,300 for the culinary classes abroad (includes instruction and lodging, but not airfare).

Class Frequency: Weeklong San Francisco programs are offered three times a year.

Class Length: Six hours per day (10:00 a.m. to 4:00 p.m.), Monday through Friday, for the weeklong San Francisco program.

Class Type: Demonstration/hands-on.

Class Size: Eight to ten students per class for the San Francisco program; maximum of fifteen for the classes held abroad.

Lodging: Joanne Weir's Cooking School doesn't offer accommodations, but she has worked out special preferred rates with the Joie de Vivre Hospitality Group for students who attend her program. Two hotel properties that offer discounted rates to students are:

Laurel Inn, 444 Presidio Avenue, San Francisco, CA 94115; (415) 567-8467; www.jdvhospitality.com/hotels/hotel/8. It is ideally located in the quiet, respectable Pacific Heights area. The rooms are modern, clean, and elegant. Each has a welcoming splash of color and is designed to have the warmth of a studio apartment. Hotel Drisco, 2901 Pacific Avenue, San Francisco, CA 94115; (415) 346-2880; www.jdvhospitality.com/hotels/hotel/6. Wedged between some of Pacific Heights's magnificent mansions, the 1903 world-class hotel is within easy walking distance of Joanne Weir's Cooking School. Its traditional, elegant style suits the neighborhood.

For more information contact: Joanne Weir, 2107 Pine Street, San Francisco, CA 94115; (415) 262-0260; www.joanneweir.com.

Tante Marie's Cooking School
San Francisco, California

*M*any young adults who have grown up with frozen dinners and microwaved warm-ups have never learned to cook from scratch or even entertain with style. In order to assist these people, Tante Marie has stepped in by offering programs like the Art of the Cocktail Party, How to Cook with Ease, and A Dinner Party for Friends.

Her recreational culinary programs aren't designed to be super-sophisticated classes in developing depth of flavor or creating complicated dinners. "Recreational cooks aren't that serious about food. All they want is to have an enjoyable experience," Tante Marie's founder, Mary Risley, says. "Learning how to create a nice flavor with a good taste balance is often enough for them." She introduces such cooks to elementary skills like mirepoix and how to use wine and bouquet garni to give life to a meal.

ABOUT THE CHEFS

Many of Mary's teachers are graduates of her Six-Month Culinary Program, which she offers to serious-minded chefs. Some of her teachers are also well-respected names like Malcolm Jessop, a Westminster Culinary School graduate who has worked in many prestigious restaurants, including London's Grosvenor House; Bruce Aidells, founder of Aidells Sausage Company; and Alice Medrich, founder of Cocolat, a respected chocolate store. For ethnic-food classes, she prefers to hire only established instructors who are native to the country where the food is dominant and who maintain a strong cultural tie to the cuisine.

PHILOSOPHY

Beyond just offering students the basic fundamentals, the staff at Tante Marie want to build students' confidence in the kitchen and free them from precise food measuring. "If you need to add pepper, it needn't be exactly the amount the recipe requires. It could be instead what you perceive is the right amount," Mary says. "Or if your recipe calls for Grand Marnier and you have only brandy, you should learn to feel perfectly comfortable just using brandy."

ABOUT THE CLASSES

Mary has had a full-time cooking school since 1979, one of the first such schools in the States. Over the years, her recreational cooking program has turned out its share of successful home cooks.

ZAP

For nearly two decades, San Francisco has hosted the Zinfandel Advocates & Producers (ZAP) Festival. Scheduled annually in January, the four-day festival has become the most talked-about wine event in the city, attracting a broad group of wine drinkers with a common interest in zinfandel.

To appeal to this broad group, a mix of wine-related activities is scheduled. For example, for the erudite, a distinguished panel of wine connoisseurs may examine the magic and mystery of one-hundred-year-old bottles of zin—and deconstruct it by components to make it easier to appreciate as a whole. Such panels may be made up of respected leaders from universities, research centers, and even newspapers.

Food lovers, on the other hand, may enjoy a less-intellectual event, such as a food-and-wine-pairing evening. Attendees will sample some perfectly matched wines and foods and chat one-on-one with the zinfandel producers and respected area chefs responsible for the event.

For an elegant evening at a five-star hotel, wine lovers may meet with winemakers and enjoy a dinner tasting and reception followed by an auction. Special bottles of zinfandel and unusual zinfandel-themed entertain-

Like many West Coast schools, Tante Marie uses seasonal, local, and fresh ingredients. Unlike other schools, though, Mary avoids offering classes in fusion cuisine. Ethnic foods are generally prepared with the pure culinary flavors of the country they represent.

Nevertheless, Mary is a businesswoman. Since food fashions change, she continuously keeps up with the latest trends by reviewing popular

Visitors at a ZAP Festival wine tasting study the clarity of a wine. PHOTO COURTESY OF ZAP

ment packages are sold at premium prices. The four-day event ends with a walk-around tasting in which between two hundred and three hundred zinfandel wineries generously pour wine for as many as nine thousand visitors. The building used for the wine tasting invariably becomes a lively village of zinfandel enthusiasts who alternate their tasting experience with stops at the bread-and-cheese stations.

For more information about the next ZAP Festival, contact: (530) 274-4900; www.zinfandel.com.

magazines and books, adjusting her program to provide contemporary appeal.

Besides an assortment of one-day classes, she offers three-day classes, one-week classes, and a six-day evening series. These classes may focus on just California cuisine, French cuisine, a series of basic cooking lessons, and more, and they introduce home chefs to everything from one-pot meals to vegetarian foods.

In each class, she encourages her staff to go a step further than teach information that can't be found in cookbooks. Instead, she wants them to include material like how to bone chicken breasts and how to tell if

 Turning Back the Clock to Yesteryear

Napa Valley Wine Train

Roll back the clock and enjoy a gourmet lunch or dinner on the Napa Valley Wine Train. For three hours you will enjoy a scenic train ride from Napa to St. Helena and back on faithfully restored vintage cars. Select cars have brass fixtures, Honduran mahogany paneling, etched glass partitions, 360-degree swivel armchairs, and velvet and brocade fabrics. All the appointments are as fine as those on the Andalusian or the Venice-Simplon Orient Express. The gourmet meal, served with damask linens and silver flatware, costs $89 (for the three-course lunch) to $149 (for a five-course special-events dinner). Dinner could be roasted beef tenderloin with fennel gratin and vegetable sauté or a fresh-catch seafood dinner. Lunch might be pan-seared salmon encrusted with Parmesan potato in orange beurre blanc and garnished with a trio of caviar or a fennel flan with grilled vegetables and morel mushrooms. Special programs like a murder mystery, concert series, and a family fun night are also available. The train ride is scheduled daily, for both luncheons and dinners.

the meat is cooked. Students attending a Tante Marie class receive many recipes, some techniques, some local culture, and a touch of history.

Class Costs: A series of classes may run $375 to $630; a one-day class may run from $50 (two-hour class) to $185 (five-hour class).
Class Frequency: Classes are held seven days a week, day and night.
Class Length: Classes run about two to five hours, depending on the specific class.
Class Type: Hands-on; some demonstration.
Class Size: Minimum of six students, maximum fourteen.
For more information contact: Tante Marie's Cooking School, 271 Francisco Street, San Francisco, CA 94133; (415) 788-6699; www.tantemarie.com.

For more information contact: Napa Valley Wine Train, Inc., 1275 McKinstry Street, Napa, CA 94559; (800) 427-4124; www.winetrain.com.

Flying Horse Wine Tours, Sonoma Valley

Enjoy an old-fashioned carriage ride along winery lanes to four boutique wineries in Sonoma County's beautiful Alexander Valley. The wineries, which are only a short distance from historic Healdsburg, are small, private properties that produce respectable artisan wines with their own signature varietals. For four hours (12:30 to 4:30 p.m.) you will spend a relaxing afternoon sipping wines at the wineries and enjoying a leisurely picnic under a shaded tree. The price per person is $125, with a minimum of two and a maximum of ten persons per carriage.

For more information contact: Flying Horse Carriage Company, 321 South Main Street, #14, Sebastopol, CA 95472; (707) 849-8989; www.flying horse.org.

Ramekins
Sonoma, California

*R*amekins, a culinary events center in Sonoma, has been a destination stop since 1998 for cookbook authors on tour. Every year hundreds of chefs share their skills and imaginative teaching styles with students eager to learn restaurant-quality cooking skills from prominent chefs.

To list all the programs available, Ramekins must produce three catalogs yearly, each containing from 110 to 118 scheduled classes. Many feature local and national celebrity chefs who have established a reputation for their theatrical demonstration or intimate hands-on classes. Some of these classes are instant sellouts, and rarely are any two classes alike in content and presentation.

Chef Pilar Sanchez extols the virtues of ginger. PHOTO COURTESY OF CECE HUGO

ABOUT THE CHEFS

Many respected cooks, such as Jacques Pépin, Bruce Aidells, and Pilar Sanchez, and several of those featured in this book, such as John Ash, Hugh Carpenter, and Joanne Weir, are among the many who have taught classes at Ramekins.

PHILOSOPHY

Sonoma County, like most of the Northern California area, has a strong interest in sustainable food and local wines. As a result, one of Ramekins's goals is to feature these local products and teach students how to bring them together in harmony.

Another goal is to break cooks of their dependency on recipes and encourage them to rely more on their taste. Lisa Lavagetto, manager of Ramekins, believes recipes should be used only as a general guide; your taste buds and personal preferences should determine the exact ingredients and portions.

"It is important to keep in mind that food changes in flavor the longer it lives," she said. "Too much of one ingredient might be perfect during the cooking stage, but totally overwhelming after being refrigerated for a while." For this reason she believes it is important that one cooks with an easy hand, adjusting the flavor slowly and saving the final touch for just before serving.

ABOUT THE CLASSES

Ramekins's choices of classes vary, and each one may appeal to a different audience. Some, though, are extremely popular and sell out quickly, especially true when a prominent chef and winery are brought together to match wines and food, course by course, in one smooth wine-food demonstration. Another popular class is the chef's table, in which a well-known chef cooks and dines with about eleven students.

Sometimes they may have a really popular local headliner like Narsai David. For celebrities with his pull, they usually turn the class into a

Tips from Lisa Lavagetto

*L*isa Lavagetto strongly believes that young cooks need only a few good kitchen tools: an eight- or ten-inch chef knife, an immersion blender, a peeler, a zester, and a Vita-Mix blender. She rarely uses food processors, except for preparing dough. "If you learn to use these basic tools to their maximum," she says, "you will probably not need much more."

culinary event with 125 to 150 guests. To accommodate such numbers, the class is set up as a demonstration. As the chef displays her skills, the kitchen crew prepares the food to be served to the attendees. Classes like this are all carefully coordinated so that the demonstration-dining experience is smoothly joined together in logical order from start to finish.

Ramekins rarely provides a series of classes; most have a single focus. But someone who wants a full weekend of cooking can easily take about four different classes in three days. Although they all may have different themes, they all provide important cooking hints and skills that will always be useful in the kitchen. Examples may include: how to maintain and use knives; how to get the maximum usage from minimum equipment; how to braise or sauté, and more.

Class Costs: Classes may cost as little as $45 or as much as $195.
Class Frequency: Classes are offered daily.
Class Length: Classes run three hours.
Class Type: Hands-on/demonstration.
Class Size: Minimum varies from instructor to instructor (approximately ten); maximum twenty people per class for hands-on; minimum twenty, maximum thirty-six for standard demonstration classes; larger classes for special event/ celebrity chefs in the Great Room.
Lodging: Ramekins offers visitors six comfortable, contemporary suites, each with whimsical touches. The building is decorated with food-related art, including a staircase, which features the asparagus.
For more information contact: Ramekins, 450 West Spain Street, Sonoma, CA 95476; (707) 933-0450; www.ramekins.com.

INDEX OF RECIPES

General Index

ABOUT THE AUTHOR

Joe David has been traveling the globe in search of the perfect meal for decades. To support his food habit, he has taught school; worked in public relations, marketing, and magazine advertising; authored countless articles (many on food and international cooking schools) and four books; and reported five radio stories for NPR's *The Best of our Knowledge.* He has been a guest on numerous radio and TV shows and is a longtime member of the National Press Club in Washington. Recent articles he has written include an interview with Jacques Pépin and a piece on the Ritz Escoffier Cooking School in Paris.